THE POLITICS OF HOPE AND
LABOUR'S CHALLENGE

Britain
Needs
Change

EDITED BY
GERRY HASSAN AND SIMON BARROW

\Bb\
Biteback Publishing

First published in Great Britain in 2024 by
Biteback Publishing Ltd, London
Selection and editorial apparatus copyright © Gerry Hassan and Simon Barrow 2024
Copyright in the individual essays resides with the named authors.

Gerry Hassan and Simon Barrow have asserted their rights under the Copyright, Designs
and Patents Act 1988 to be identified as the editors of this work.

ISBN 978-1-78590-934-4

10 9 8 7 6 5 4 3 2 1

A CIP catalogue record for this book is available from the British Library.

Set in Adobe Caslon Pro

Printed and bound in Great Britain by
CPI Group (UK) Ltd, Croydon CR0 4YY

FSC
www.fsc.org
MIX
Paper | Supporting
responsible forestry
FSC® C171272

Contents

Foreword

Baroness Helena Kennedy of the Shaws KC

No one should need reminding of just how hellish fourteen years of Conservative rule have been. It all comes rushing back as you read this collection of writings by some of our finest political commentators. Every single British institution is on its knees – the NHS, schools, universities, the court system, prisons, local authorities, social services, police, the military – driven into the ground by deliberate austerity policies, ineptitude, economic incompetence and a swaggering disregard for truthful engagement with the public. As well as destroying our economy and our welfare state, our global reputation has been trashed and our relationships with other nations have been seriously undermined. And in my own field of law, I see the Rule of Law being trampled underfoot if it does not suit the Cabinet.

The big lie was not invented by Donald Trump. His claim that Joe Biden had corruptly stolen the US presidential election of 2020 was born of his malignant narcissism. Here in the United Kingdom, the big lies of recent times started with the repeated mantra by the coalition government of 2010 that it was Labour that had caused the economic crisis of 2008, when it was in fact a global catastrophe caused by deregulated banking and disgraceful American mortgage practices, with knock-on effects internationally. Huge debt was created bailing out the banks, but the cost was born by the ordinary British public.

Lies feed on other lies, and the shameless lies told by Nigel Farage, Boris Johnson and their ilk in the run-up to the European referendum were monumental and deceived many people into believing Europe and bloody foreigners were the cause of our national woes. But if lying is a way of life in some parts of our politics, it should have come as no surprise that it was the lies of a serving Prime Minister over the COVID-19 'Partygate' scandal that led to his undoing. The sheer weirdness of Liz Truss and her self-delusion just added to public disgust at Boris Johnson's behaviour.

The relief in the days after the July 2024 general election was not expressed in a festival spirit. It was all too glum for that. A friend said she felt like an abused spouse who had just got rid of a violent husband. But there was a sense of returning to honesty, a re-establishment of integrity and probity. Adults were back in charge. But, as the election guru and pollster John Curtice's chapter shows, this landslide victory, of Labour winning by a majority of 174 seats, requires a deeper analysis. The pundit question was, 'Did Labour win, or did the Conservative Party lose?'

Labour's share of the vote was worryingly low, at a little under 34 per cent, and the Reform Party captured more of the electorate than they deserved. Farage's 'sour English nationalism', to quote Fintan O'Toole, 'tapped into the hopelessness many ordinary people feel'. Labour in its election campaign had been forced to tread with great caution, seeking to reconnect with working-class voters it had alienated but anxious not to overpromise and to look fiscally imprudent. In 2006, I chaired The Power Inquiry, a cross-party investigation into a decline in voter turnout and the disillusionment felt by communities about the whole political system. All the augurs were there. The people felt powerless and felt their future looked bleak.

Reading the essays in this book confirmed for me the need to acknowledge that neoliberal globalisation – an economic model pursued by New Labour as well as the Conservatives – has brought huge gains for those at the top but stagnant wages and often job losses for working people. We have even seen the de-professionalising of the professions because public service medicine and lawyering were being seriously defunded.

The winners under neoliberal economics used their windfall to buy influence in high places, affecting legislation and policy. Deregulation became the name of the game. We now have inequalities of income and wealth not seen since the Great Depression of the 1920s. Workers receive a smaller and smaller share of the profits they produced. The recent violent demonstrations against immigrants and asylum seekers, incited by a surge of online hatred from the far right, is our own version of populist nationalism, echoing events in Europe and the USA. Newcomers are blamed for our housing crisis, for low wages, for pressure on schools, for crime. Labour in government has a huge task (and a money squeeze), so honest messaging from ministers does not raise the spirits. What is missing is a governing vision about the common good, showing to the public that Labour's purpose is to create a fairer society by checking corporate power, from water companies to banks and tech companies, to regulate markets in the interests of all, so that everyone flourishes. If tax has to be raised, why is income tax higher than tax on stocks and share dividends? Why not a tax on financial transactions? Why not pass legislation that requires companies to have employees given seats on the board? This is especially important, as we need more engagement by workers in dealing with the ways modernity will affect employment, e.g. artificial intelligence and ending the use of fossil fuels. And if we could borrow to the hilt to save the banks when there was a crisis, why not to save our economy by borrowing to resource new enterprises, new manufacturing and the creation of new jobs?

The chapters in this book are full of ideas that our new Labour government might adopt or adapt. The authors argue for progressive responses to the challenges of our times. There has to be an overarching Labour ambition, a big picture that is about fairness, opportunities and dignity in decent, well-paid work. This book is a vital contribution to that debate, buzzing with energy, observations, analysis and an awareness of the huge challenges we face as a society and globally.

Baroness Helena Kennedy of the Shaws
2024

Acknowledgements

This book examines the changing political landscape of contemporary Britain. It does so particularly within the context of the challenges and opportunities faced by a newly elected Labour government and the choices and debates flowing from this. Ultimately it seeks to explore the hope of making the nations of these islands better, fairer, more egalitarian, decent and humane for all who live here, as well as in relation to how the UK acts in the world.

In planning and commissioning this volume, our aim has been to examine the political terrain in an ecumenical, generous and non-tribal way. The overall perspective is broadly centre-left, arising from long and deep involvement in key debates on the left and within progressive opinion (in the UK and internationally), many of which are reflected here.

This book is the fifth that we, as a partnership, have undertaken in recent years. The previous four all related to the changing political debate in Scotland. Like this book, they were committed to exploring and pushing against the boundaries of official politics, questioning shibboleths and dogmas. We are driven by the need to nurture creative, forward-looking ideas and extend their role in political debate.

This book is undertaken in association with Compass, the advocacy and campaigning group that, over the past twenty years, has made a serious and important contribution to political thought both within and well beyond the Labour Party, talking to and engaging with those in other parties (and none) in a spirit of genuine openness.

Compass has always advocated for, and championed, a different kind of politics, one that is more progressive but also more human and spirited. One that is connected to real life and lived experience, reflecting the diversity of the modern UK – something that too much current political argument sees as a problem, or even a threat. Compass has always embodied a politics of co-operation, collaboration and pluralism, challenging those economic and social orthodoxies that have cast a shadow over Britain in recent years and that have so conspicuously failed.

We would like to thank a host of people for their time and support on this project. First, the wide-ranging, impressive contributors who gave of their expertise and insights and who were a pleasure to work with. Second, another cast of people freely offered their views and opinions, reading draft chapters, checking facts and replying to queries and questions from us. These included Pauline Bryan, Lisa Clark, Craig Dalzell, Stephen Davies, Stephen Fielding, Alan Finlayson, Jonathan Freedland, Tom Hurcombe, Michael Keating, Karen King, Simon Lee, Ruth Lister, Helen McCarthy, Iain McLean, Henry McLeish, James Meadway, Robbie Mochrie, Dave Moxham, Henry Potts, Bill Ramsay, Richard Rose, Jordan, Shona and Oshin Tchilingirian, Hilary Wainwright, Lesley Wall, Stuart Ward, Karl Williams and Richard Wyn Jones. This is not an exhaustive list, and we apologise to anyone we have mistakenly omitted.

Third, we owe an enormous amount to the professionalism and encouragement of Olivia Beattie and the team at Biteback Publishing. They have been pillars of support, calmness and helpful advice. Olivia in particular has a diligent and meticulous attention to detail, way beyond the call of duty. This book is the better for her and everyone at Biteback's contribution, for which we are enormously grateful.

Finally, as in every book project that we have undertaken, we have been ably assisted by the encouragement, patience and intellectual support of our partners, Rosie Ilett and Carla J. Roth, for which we are most thankful and which we never take for granted.

We hope readers find this book as enjoyable, stimulating and thought-provoking as we did in assembling it at this time of immense change, disruption and flux – not just in the UK but globally. We have done this work with the express aim of pushing against the constraints of small-c conservatism and of the outdated ideological assumptions that characterise too much of politics in the UK. These factors have not only restrained the Labour Party but have inflicted self-harm and pain on millions of people in the forms of Cameron–Osborne austerity and a hard Brexit, to take but two glaring examples.

This is a book about the state of Britain; the new Labour government; why things must change and how; who will resist radical change, and different possible futures for the UK and its nations. Politics should ultimately be about positive ideas engaging with the real world of decision and action. We hope this book is a constructive contribution to that ongoing process.

Gerry Hassan
gerry@gerryhassan.com

Simon Barrow
simonbarrowuk@gmail.com

August 2024

Labour's Paradoxical Victory: The End of an Era and the Beginning of a New One?

Gerry Hassan and Simon Barrow

'When I was a child, I was taught to "know my place", "do as I was told" and not answer back. And that seemed alright, because we believed that the vicar, the teacher, the policeman and the government could be trusted to look after us ... All went reasonably well, until another ruling class emerged based on obscene inequality of wealth and education ... For me, the lack of respect for this group is typified by Jacob Rees-Moggs's comments about the people who died in Grenfell Tower. He said to an interviewer, "I think if either of us were in a fire, whatever the Fire Brigade said, we would leave the building. It just seems a common-sense thing to do."'
SHEILA HANCOCK (2024)

'Could things have turned out differently? Looking back on the free market counterrevolution of the last half century, it is hard to avoid a sense of historical fatalism ... This sense of inevitability has become so engrained on both left and right that it comes as a shock to realise that the neoliberal resolution to the capitalist crisis of the 1970s was by no means self-evident to those we now consider the victors.'
MELINDA COOPER (2024)

Setting the Scene

The July 2024 election produced a historic result. Labour's victory under Keir Starmer was only the fourth time the party has won an overall majority from opposition; 1945, 1964 and 1997 being the other three. It is only the eighth time the party has won an overall majority in its entire 124-year history – the others were 1950, 1966, 2001 and 2005.

Labour won the lowest share of the vote of a majority government since records began (33.7 per cent); the Conservatives won their lowest vote ever (23.7 per cent); the combined Labour–Tory vote of 57.4 per cent was the lowest since the two became the dominant parties in 1922. Add to this the re-emergence of the Lib Dems as 'the third force' in the Commons, with the largest Liberal group since 1923. There was the emphatic defeat of the SNP, falling back from their post-2014 Westminster bulge, the bridgeheads of Farage's Reform UK and Greens, alongside the success of a host of independents.

The above is the conventional account, but beneath it is the atrophying of UK democracy and the failure of politics and government. One obvious disjuncture in British democracy is the long-term decline in electoral turnout: 59.7 per cent in the UK in 2024: the second lowest since 1945, only excelled by Tony Blair's second victory of 2001 on a 59.4 per cent turnout. The 2024 figure flatters the level of turnout measuring share of registered voters.

Up to 8 million voters are now missing from the electoral register according to the Electoral Commission – disproportionately younger, poorer and from BAME communities (Simpson, 2023). This has been affected by deliberate Tory changes to voter registration, such as the switch from household to individual registration; appropriately, the new government have announced plans to act on this with automatic voter registration.

Understanding Starmer's Labour

Against this backdrop, how can Starmer's Labour address the multiple challenges facing the UK? As the dust of the election campaign recedes into the rear-view mirror, this is what this book set out to explore, alongside larger questions about politics as a hopeful (rather than purely technocratic) project and the wider context of what is by any measure a significant change of guard at Westminster. Four distinct interpretations of the Starmer Labour project can currently be identified:

The 'revolution betrayed' viewpoint, associated with the Momentum left. This stresses that Starmer is the betrayer of Corbynism, that he was elected upon a left-wing platform of ten promises he subsequently jettisoned. Hence nothing Starmer says can be trusted. Labour, in this take, are not much more than 'red Tories', with little difference between the two.

The Tory/Daily Mail/Telegraph view. Labour have not really changed. They are still 'tax-and-spend Labour'. All the changes that Starmer has made are merely for electoral expediency and to suit 'flip-flop Starmer'. He will revert to 'Labour type' when in office. This is the time-honoured Tory charge against the party: that, underneath, it is the 'same old Labour', which the Tories, if they successfully define, find easy to defeat.

Centrist commentary. This portrays Labour as facing many of the same issues it did in 1997, only now they are more entrenched. Hence, Starmerism is Blairism revisited and reheated, seen in the return of Tony Blair and Peter Mandelson as advisers. The Starmer Labour government will face the same choices as Blair and Brown did concerning growth, taxes and public services, just in much less advantageous circumstances.

A more nuanced left take. Labour governments do not happen that often in the UK, and with all its limitations this is a historic opportunity that has to be seized. That does not mean ignoring the shortcomings in Starmer's Labour; its weak popular mandate and uphill battle intellectually, domestically and internationally; or the hollowed-out nature of what passes today for social democracy.

This book locates itself broadly in this final perspective while encouraging pluralism and diversity and also asking some much larger questions about the nature of politics and the global challenges it faces.

Labour came to office facing a set of hugely challenging crises and challenges. Some of these are of recent origin and the cumulative effect of fourteen years of Tory governments; others are the product of longer timeframes and consequences. These include a crisis of the UK political system, British state and government. These interlocking institutions have increasingly failed to adapt and respond to the challenges of a divided, unequal, fractious society, characterised by immense wealth, poverty and hardship, sitting side-by-side.

This introduction examines the political and intellectual background of post-1945 Britain that has contributed to the present. It attempts to avoid the simplistic dichotomy of posing the entire era into two periods – 1945–79 and post-1979 – acknowledges different periods in each and overlap between them. It explores the wider context within which Labour, party politics and debates develop, and from this, it assesses the constraints and opportunities for a more radical politics while recognising the nature of the UK economy, capitalism and global factors.

Labour has to address this on a popular vote of 33.7 per cent – amounting to 9,708,716 – which is less than their 10,269,051 in 2019 and 12,877,918 in 2017. The story is even more marked: Labour's high watermark was 13,948,883 in 1951 – the registered electorate has grown by 14 million from then to now (and would be much bigger if all electors were registered).

In the context of a 59.7 per cent UK turnout, Labour won a mere 20.1 per cent of the registered electorate. This is half the share Labour gained at the high point of its appeal in 1951 when it won 40.3 per cent – polling more votes than the Tories but losing office because the vagaries of the electoral system gave Churchill and the Tories a small parliamentary majority. As an aside, in the three contests of Labour versus Tories in the Attlee–Churchill era, Labour won the popular vote in all (1945, 1950 and 1951). Churchill, the greatest hero of Toryism, PM for nine years, never won the popular vote. Labour's inability to tell its own story makes this a relatively unknown fact.

Labour's 2024 victory, a 'loveless landslide' according to the *Daily Mail*, saw the party win the same level of support as a share of the electorate as it did in 1983 (20.0 per cent): its worst electoral performance since it became a national party in the 1920s. The story underlying this as shown in Table 1 is that Labour's electoral decline from its 1951 peak is more marked as a share of the electorate than voters driven by the fall in turnout. The Conservatives have seen their support fall massively as well; it has declined over the same period from 48.0 per cent of voters in 1951 to 23.7 per cent in 2014; and 39.6 per cent of the electorate in 1951 to 14.2 per cent in 2024 (see Table 1 on Labour support).

Table 1: Peak Labour and Labour's Seven Elections Which Took Them into Government

Election	Lab % of Vote	Lab Vote	Lab Lead over Tories	Lab % of Electorate
1923	30.7	4,439,780	−7.3	20.9
1929	37.1	8,370,417	−1.0	29.0
1945	48.0	11,967,746	+8.4	36.0
1951	48.8	13,948,883	+0.8	40.3
1964	44.1	12,205,808	+0.7	34.0
1974 Feb	37.2	11,645,616	−0.7	29.3
1997	43.2	13,518,167	+12.5	30.8
2024	33.7	9,708,716	+10.0	20.1

Source: Colin Rallings and Michael Thrasher, British Electoral Facts 1832–2012 *(2012), Cracknell et al. (2024).*

Over forty-five years ago, Labour's electoral prospects were the subject of heated debate – 'The Forward March of Labour Halted?' began an Eric Hobsbawm lecture reprinted in *Marxism Today*. He noted the inexorable decline of Labour's support and class politics (Hobsbawm, 1978). This led to charges and counter-charges, most infamously Tony Benn claiming that Labour's emphatic defeat in 1983 had been a victory for socialism because it was 'the first time since 1945 a political party with an openly socialist policy had received the support of eight and a half million votes' (Benn, 1983).

Labour's 1997 victory saw the party win an unprecedented three elections in a row – but some of the long-term fundamentals remained unchanged. After 1997, Labour's support continued slowly downward until the brief Corbynista wave of 2017, which came and went. The wider landscape has been the decline of Labour and Tories, the rise of multi-party politics since the 1970s and the decline of party identification and loyalty, alongside a more volatile electorate and the denationalisation of UK politics.

Understanding the Past to Change the Future:
Labour and Post-War Britain

The Labour Party has to engage in the electoral and ideological realm, in the latter challenging the existing economic and political narratives that have defined the UK. Any Labour strategy in these areas has to understand where the party is coming from, its traditions, values and ethos (Drucker, 1979). Firstly, there is the enduring belief in a powerful political central state, parliamentary sovereignty and centralisation. A second factor has been and still is Labour's weakness and inability to speak beyond the party's constituencies and communities to non-Labour supporters.

Finally, there is Labour's long-standing tradition of conservatism. The party has historically looked to conserve the collectivist gains it made and to defend public services and institutions against Tory attacks. Historian David Edgerton, author of *The Rise and Fall of the British Nation* (2018), argues that Starmer's Labour has now formed a new consensus with the Tories, breaking with the party's own values and past:

> It [Labour] believes in the sagacity of private capital and thinks it will unleash growth through financial orthodoxy and deregulation – exactly the policy not only of the past fourteen years, but the past forty. Labour very obviously no longer believes in the programmes of 1945, 1964 or 1974. Like New Labour, it believes in the power of capitalism, whether entrepreneurs or financiers. Labour no longer believes as it once did that it had a more truthful account of the country than the Tories: it believes and tells Tory stories about the nature of public spending or foreign policy.
> (Edgerton, 2024)

The conventional take of post-war Britain splits it into two distinct periods – 1945–79 and post-1979 – one under the theme 'the post-war consensus'; the other, the age of neoliberalism. This simplification obscures all sorts of nuance and change that went on in each period, as well as continuities over the piece.

The first era is now presented by left and liberal accounts as a 'golden age' of British society and capitalism, and by the right as the inexorable rise of government intervention, regulation and public spending (Hutton, 1995; Williams and Colvile, 2024). Labour's social democratic tendency at the time saw the achievements of 1945 as creating a 'post-capitalist society' with Tony Crosland writing in 1952, 'It is now quite clear that capitalism has not the strength to resist the process of metamorphosis into a qualitatively different kind of society' (1952, p. 38).

At the same time in Britain in the 1950s, a small part of the ideological right objected to the over-reach of government and rise of collectivism. This was marked by the set-up of the IEA in 1955, then a right-wing outrider swimming against the intellectual tide championing free markets; by Enoch Powell's economic thinking in the 1960s pre-'rivers of blood' speech; and expanded in the ferment of the 1970s, with the establishment of the Centre for Policy Studies in 1974 by Keith Joseph and Margaret Thatcher (Crockett, 1994). The latter think tank was described by current head Robert Colvile in the 1970s as 'at the start … it is this guerrilla unit, this gang of outriders … testing the waters but also pushing at frontiers' (Moore and Colvile, 2024, p. 20).

In the 1960s and 1970s, a major stand in this counter-charge was the claim of the UK being shaped by 'a rachet effect', whereby government intervention produced policy failure leading to greater intervention (Greenleaf, 1983). Joseph laid out how this contributed to an inexorable leftward shift:

> Now since the left-wing always takes the status quo as its point of departure, it follows that the more the middle ground moved to the left, the further the left pitched their own demands, so the middle ground would shift yet once more. First, the Labour Party and unions would go more left under pressure from their extremes. Then the Conservatives in turn would edge along towards them to remain on the mystical middle. (Joseph, 1976, p. 21)

The idea that 'the middle ground' was a quicksand leading to socialism and 'the common ground' something different where public opinion could be found gained traction on the right after the Tory defeat in 1974. It developed a critique on the overload of government, ungovernability of Britain and the need to curb the state and trade union power (Bosanquet, 1983). This shifting debate cannot be seen as a solely British story, taking place in the aftermath of the collapse of the Bretton Woods international financial order, the floating of the dollar and other currencies, 1973 and 1979 OPEC oil price shocks, and New Right ideas being implemented in Chile and Argentina under military dictatorship (Klein, 2007).

All this can be seen as a conventional story, but the ideological shift did not just begin with Thatcher in 1979. Rather, in the midst of hyper-inflation and economic problems the Labour government under Jim Callaghan was forced to accept IMF public spending cuts in 1976. In this context, Callaghan told the Labour conference in his first address as Prime Minister, 'We used to think that you could spend your way out of a recession,' embracing right-wing monetarism prioritising controlling inflation over unemployment (Labour Party, 1976, p. 188). Three years later, facing electoral defeat to Thatcher he noted the changing political mood: 'You know there are times, perhaps once every thirty years, when there is a sea-change in politics' (Hennessy, 2000, p. 379).

A dominant thread of interpreting post-war Britain poses 1979 as the hinge year and the two periods either side as distinct. The year 1979 was one of change with the election of Thatcher, but the process of change began earlier. The 45-year era should not be seen as one homogeneous period characterised by the rise of neoliberalism, which can be defined as 'the intensification of the influence and dominance of capital' and 'a project to strengthen, restore, or in some cases, constitute anew the power of economic elites' in the words of one analysis (Thompson, 2005, p. 17; see Harvey, 2005; Monbiot and Hutchison, 2024).

Rather, the post-1979 era can be divided into three distinctive periods with a degree of overlap and common features. First, there was the period of ascendant Thatcherism, which saw the reconfiguration of the state through attempts to reduce public spending social programmes, to remake the government's economic role, prioritise inflation over unemployment and push back trade union power. Second, the era that began under the John Major administration and reached its zenith under Tony Blair and New Labour. This saw the advancement of an administrative and technocratic order via hands-off and intermediate agencies that diluted accountability and transparency and aided the emergence of a new class of bureaucracy.

Third, is the period that began under Gordon Brown and the 2008 banking crash, which revealed the underlying weaknesses of the UK economic model and saw an even more pronounced shift to an insider class of power across politics, society and economics, which could be characterised in Colin Crouch's words as 'post-democracy' (2004).

The culmination of these trends has reinforced the idea that politics and government is in cahoots with the rich, powerful and those who can buy access. It has seen the rise of a way of doing government that reduces the democratic sphere and the arena that can be discussed and changed. This has contributed to the hollowing out of public institutions, spaces and cultures, a process which had the ultimate effect of reducing politics to being a spectator sport and spectacle where the public are not active participants.

This is then multiplied in the UK by the lack of citizenship rights and fundamental law, which reinforce the disempowerment inherent in this situation. Think the Post Office scandal, Windrush, Grenfell Tower, the contaminated blood transfusion outrage – any number of examples in which the powerlessness of people in the face of system abuse and contempt is laid bare.

This account is often seen as synonymous with a left-wing take, but there is common intellectual ground across the political spectrum about the empty nature of what passes for political discourse and public space and how this assists a new political dispensation of power. Here is Stephen Davies, head of education at the right-wing Institute of Economic Affairs (IEA), describing post-Thatcherite Britain:

A central feature of this is that all of the major British traditions, and particularly the Labour, Conservative, and Liberal ones, have been supplanted by a kind of technocratic anti-politics that replaces actual debate and the clash and reconciliation of interests with supposedly neutral 'problem solving'. This comes with social democratic, conservative, and liberal flavours, but the common reality is a procedure and rule-driven approach to governance and policy in which all kinds of decisions and debates are taken out of the realm of public debate.
(Davies, 2024)

Related to this is the framing of this debate in the UK. The mainstream UK media in the form of the print press and broadcast media do not cover politics in an ideological vacuum. The print press has always been defined by the right-wing and have shifted further right under the influence of Brexit – the *Mail*, *Express* and *Telegraph* in particular. Broadcast media operates with regulatory restrictions but has been influenced by this context and with the BBC being browbeaten by successive governments.

The BBC sits in an ideological space representing a particular vision of Britain: liberal, London-centric, condescending of much of the country; this version is now contested from right-wing and left-wing critics underlining that the BBC's version of Britain is increasingly challenged (Mills, 2016). Related to this the pioneering work of the Glasgow University Media Group (GUMG) in the 1970s showed the biases of the BBC and ITV on a host of news and current affairs issues, such as how they covered strikes and trade union issues, often seen through the perspectives of employers and business; and similarly, the rightward shift of UK politics from the 1980s saw broadcast media follow and legitimise it, contributing to a framing of the political debate (GUMG, 1976; 1980).

Britain and the World beyond Neoliberalism?

The evolution of UK politics and its trajectory from the 1970s needs to be fully understood. There was no homogeneous era pre- or post-1979: no singular 'post-war consensus' in the former and era of neoliberalism in the latter. Such overarching and widely used terms are bandied about and become framing devices within political discourse.

Rather, post-1979 Britain has gone through three distinct phases – Thatcherism, the New Labour administrative and technocratic state and the emergence of a post-democratic class and political system, all contributing to government and statecraft becoming increasingly captured by a worldview at odds with looking after the welfare and well-being of the population.

Such has been the right's ascendancy for much of this period that not only have the centre-left operated on their terrain, but the post-1979 world has been defined mostly by the right. Hence, Thatcher describing the economy as a 'household', saying, 'You cannot spend more than you have,' whose influence is still seen in 2024 with Labour Chancellor Rachel Reeves talking of the Tories 'having maxed out on the credit card' and there being no money left (Chakrabortty, 2024).

Yet it is salutary to understand the political landscape from multiple perspectives, and to many on the right, 1997 offers a breakpoint as well where Labour successes have become entrenched. Karl Williams, deputy director of the right-wing Centre for Policy Studies, puts it:

The broader discontinuities symbolised by 1997 are much more important in shaping thinking on the right, especially among right-wingers in their 20s and early 30s. New Labour instituted a constitutional, legal and cultural revolution – the Human Rights Act, devolution, the creation of a Supreme Court, the Equality Act 2010, the massive expansion in the welfare state and so on. These are all things Cameron and his successors failed to repeal, undo or reform, and which have and continue to cause

enormous problems for the country and any conservative agenda for
government. An apt analogy would be the failure of Churchill/Eden/
Macmillan/Heath to roll back much of the 1945–51 settlement.
(Williams, 2024)

The term 'neoliberalism' does not do justice to everything since the
1970s. For starters, it is not used much outside of left-wing and academic circles. More importantly, it attempts to offer a sweeping description
of four and a half decades, ignoring significant political and economic
shifts in this era in the UK and globally, from the fall of the Berlin Wall
to the 2008 banking crash. Will Hutton describes the post-1979 world
in terms of a taxonomy of '1979 to 2008 – the era of market supremacy,
and 2008 to the present – the era of contestation' (2024).

This has not just been a British story, but one seen across the developed capitalist world as the forces of the New Right attempted to
reconfigure the state and row back social public spending, then followed by an era of 'progressive globalisation' and accommodation, and
subsequently – since the 2008 bankers' crash – a systematic failure of
politics and economics aiding the continued concentration of power
and wealth.

A significant element of Labour, including much of the leadership,
embodies the values of post-democracy, believing in an insider class
elite politics that works by and for those who already have access,
power and wealth. The political philosopher and writer John Gray has
accurately described this in the aftermath of the election, saying that
Starmer represents 'a world without politics – for a legal bureaucratic
and managerial mind' reducing politics to 'rational administration' and
rile by experts, technocrats, non-elected bodies, judges and judicial
review – which is the progressive version of post-democracy (2024).

Peter Geoghegan, writing in the *London Review of Books*, analysed
the role and funding of the advocacy and quasi-lobbying group Labour

Together ('a protean think tank') and how in the 2024 election the big money flowed in one direction: to Labour and away from the Tories, with the potential consequence that the party may row back on reform of 'cleaning up British politics' which is in 'Labour's long-term interests' (2024).

What Chance for Labour Resetting the Agenda?

A Labour government whose main mantra is competence, service and stability would be a welcome break after the descent and moral abyss of Tory rule. But it would not be enough on any level. Nor is the current Labour offer in the words of James Meadway:

> We're already breaking out of 'the post-1979 partial settlement', although not in ways anyone on the left is likely to enjoy. This absolutely does not mean we are also getting a return to pre-1979 levels of social protection and state social spending. Labour is likely to be the exemplar here: plenty of talk of 'securonomics' as a driver for growth, plans for industrial strategy and trade strategy, but no real increase in social expenditures. What seems likely is a hardening of the insider–outsider mechanisms neoliberalism had already introduced – of an expanded means-testing and harder divisions introduced into the labour market between favoured 'insiders' and disfavoured 'outsiders'.
> (Meadway, 2024)

Politics has to engage with several different dimensions and players at the same time which address timescales; the importance of the short term, medium term and longer term, and which engage with immediate issues, set out reforms, has a long-term direction and recognises the importance of ideas (Crick, 1984).

The short-term agenda is obvious – addressing the failures of fourteen years of Tory rule; the medium term is to start healing the divisions, bruises and inequities of 'broken Britain'; and the longer-term is to set a direction in terms of the kind of country we aspire to be and the importance of ideas and ideology, finally turning a page on failed free market dogmas but also the closed political order that is post-democracy.

This may sound like a Herculean task and setting up the new Labour administration to fail. But that is not so. Politics is about multi-tasking, and this multi-tiered politics is not just about parties, politicians and Westminster. Instead, it is about the widest version of political community, agency and actors imaginable, one that on an idealistic level can reach out and include every single one of us.

A politics of different dimensions and timescales has happened before. In the 1970s, Thatcherism gained ascendancy aided by right-wing think tanks such as the IEA and Centre for Policy Studies, by a shift in the intellectual climate against collectivism and Keynesianism and broader changes in the global capitalist system undermining the post-war managed system. Similarly, the Attlee government of 1945 drew on a host of detailed wartime plans, such as the Beveridge reports on the welfare state and full employment, the influence of Keynes and Keynesianism on recognising the role of government in the economy, and the establishment of a new international order of co-operation in the West.

Today we have not created the foundations for a new consensus in the UK or internationally. But we do know the free-market revolution has failed; that since the 2008 banking crisis living standards in the UK and West have stagnated; and that post-democratic politics anywhere are part of the problem, not a solution.

What can a politics that addresses these challenges look like? And what chances are there of it beginning to emerge in the UK? It has to start from understanding the interlinked nature of the crises and challenges the UK faces: that the dysfunctional, broken political system with its concentration of power, centralisation and lack of democracy has been critical in aiding economic and social policies that have not nurtured the public sphere and services and have not had the capacity and confidence to embark on reforming and modernising Britain.

We should be clear that part of the terrain needed to tackle what is wrong in Britain has been in part explored by previous Labour and Tory governments. The Macmillan, Wilson and Heath administrations all embarked on programmes defined by modernisation, only to be defeated by the ancient state, the cult of amateurishness at the centre and powerful vested interests – from the City to the Treasury and trade unions.

A Vision for a Different Kind of Britain and Future

Missing from Labour's recent agenda is an informed critique of what is wrong with present-day Britain, beyond the superficial and the immediate, usually concentrating on fourteen years of Tory rule, incompetence and division. Previous Labour governments came to office with a rising tide and ferment of intellectual energy and ideas that the party had a relationship with: this is true of 1945, 1964 and 1997.

The conditions are fertile to start laying out this terrain. First, the British system of government is broken. It is undemocratic, centralist and at its core has embraced overload and micro-managing the UK economy and society. Second, the Treasury is a major part of this problem. This used to be pivotal to the Labour case and Wilson in the 1960s but became forgotten in the New Labour era. This terrain cannot be left to the radical right. The Treasury is not a department of economic growth but of managing public spending, and it needs radical transformation.

Third, the structure of power across the UK is not sustainable. It is a half-finished revolution with devolution to Scotland, Wales and Northern Ireland, and with city government for London. This has been added to by an ad-hoc system of regional mayors, none with popular mandates via referendums, all hailed by the Tories as innovation, but in reality the latest Westminster wheeze. A more democratic system is needed, and it must be entrenched and backed by referendums, with the English status quo seen as unsustainable.

Fourth, the art of politics has become reduced to the public being passive spectators with no real active involvement. Party politics has little living connection into civil society, which does not bode well; the fraud of Farage's Reform UK, a private company masquerading as a political party, is a potential harbinger for the future.

Fifth, connecting all of the above, UK politics have become defined by the emergence of post-democracy: an insider class connecting government, corporate business, elites and lobbyists, defined by access, privilege and monies and inherently open to corruption. It is a closed system with more in common with pre-democracy, when government saw its business as acting in the interests of the monied and propertied classes.

Sixth, for all the talk of reform, the core dynamics of British capitalism have remained unchanged through successive governments and eras. It is remarkably short-termist, speculative and driven by shareholder value, rather than any longer-term and wider interests. Britain's productivity problem and the gap between innovation and ideas and successful products and firms is due to the historic failure to invest and nurture research and development (Hutton, 1995). Moreover, the overbearing influence of finance capitalism has hurt the economy, with the City of London 'crowding out' investment and support in the real economy: in the way the right in the 1970s used to make such claims about trade union power (Bacon and Eltis, 1976). The Thatcher revolution for all its boosterist rhetoric about an 'economic miracle' addressed none of these fundamentals about the structural weaknesses of British capitalism.

Seventh, is Britain's geopolitical place in the world, where it positions itself, the values and relationships it embodies, and who and what it identifies with. Britain post-Brexit is a diminished entity on the world stage and internationally. The UK has weaker relationships with its two main post-war pillars – the EU and US – and neither of these can be easily put back. But the UK has to decide how it acts, builds alliances and what it wants to be.

If this is the broad challenge, then the political case for change has to be made, intellectual ground prepared and specific policies devised for the short, medium and longer term. The success or not will not just be down to the actions of Keir Starmer and the Labour government but the wider political community and public sphere. In an age of discontent and disinformation, alongside cynicism and falling trust, it is a monumental task: a once in a generation task to rebuild and remake Britain and break out not just of the legacy of fourteen Tory years but the broken political system, fossilised institutions and lingering hold of discredited, outdated dogmas that have wreaked damage on the UK and its people (Toynbee and Walker, 2024).

Who aspires to speak for Britain matters and has consequences. For too long this has been the Tories and the right, with Labour apologetic even in office. Yet, if we examine the nature of public opinion and the fallacy of 'the centre ground', we can see most voters do not tidily sit in the middle but lean left-wing on economic issues, public spending and public ownership and right-wing on law and order and immigration.

This takes us back to Keith Joseph's 'common ground', cited earlier, which he described thus: 'The middle ground consensus is only the middle ground between politicians. It is an ephemeral political compromise. It has no link with achieving the aspirations of the people' (Joseph, 1976, p. 25). This take was used to undermine the post-war welfare statism and Keynesian economics and holds relevance in today's Britain, where public opinion supports railway nationalisation (76 per cent), GB Energy (75 per cent), imposing VAT on private school fees (60 per cent), alongside being hard on law and order and immigration. This is the potential terrain of Starmer's Labour and common ground (Smith, 2024; Conner, 2024).

That will require a political project as ambitious and far-reaching as undertaken at previous hinge points in the UK's history. In the case of 1945 and 1979, the tide had already turned on the previous order by the time a general election ushered in a new administration with a new set of ideas. In 2024, we already have one set of conditions met: the bankruptcy and discrediting of the ideas of the right, which have been so dominant for so long. The second part of the equation is mapping out a prospectus for the future, credible policy ideas and a picture of what the future could look like have yet to be made.

John Kay observed of debates on the nature of business, the economy and capitalism that 'business has evolved but the language that is widely used to describe business has not' (Kay, 2024). The same is true of the language of politics, its left-wing version and social change. The inconvenient truth is that the forces of reaction have been better at describing the world after neoliberalism, invoking divisive framing terms such as 'culture wars', 'cancel culture', 'the war on woke' and 'virtue signalling' as well as having a right-wing print press and well-funded platforms to promote these tropes. The forces of the left and progressive opinion over the same period have conspicuously failed to offer a convincing set of descriptions and names beyond speaking to itself about neoliberalism.

All around there are dismissive takes from sections of the left of Starmer and Labour, as Robert Saunders notes, peddling 'stories of doom' (2024). This includes right-wing framing as 'same old Labour' and centrist commentary that sees present day events through the lenses of Blair and New Labour. A more nuanced reading of present-day Labour, the centre-left, and the challenges the UK faces, is more accurate and constructive, acknowledging that this is a story still being written.

This book offers a contribution to that debate: one engaged and involved in the battle of ideas in a way that is nuanced and drawing from that fourth strand. We are at the end of one era and the beginning of the next. The future is being created in the actions of the present.

The pluralist range of perspectives in this volume reflect that this is a moment in flux. The positive potential of Labour in office, understood in a particular way, is emphasised by Will Hutton. A more critical analysis is offered by Jeremy Gilbert; a more historical take from Tom Egerton and Anthony Seldon, and a more qualified sense of possibility from Neal Lawson and the editors. Similarly, how Labour understands (or not) the economy, political economy and British capitalism will have a critical bearing on the direction and chance of success of the government. Mariana Mazzucato and Ann Pettifor make the case that Labour have to break with the past, with economic orthodoxy and the Treasury mindset, while Adam Tooze and Aditya Chakrabortty highlight the alternative economic ideas of 1980s UK municipal socialism as one potential source of inspiration.

In the first months of the Labour government, tensions and limitations are already self-evident. There are at least two distinctive voices to Labour in office. The first, from Keir Starmer and Rachel Reeves, is driven by the need for reassurance, fiscal rectitude and the politics of Treasury spreadsheets. This reflects their desire to not scare former Tory voters who switched to Labour, the right-wing media and the City, but it also embodies Starmer and Reeves's respective backgrounds – as Director of Public Prosecutions and a Bank of England economist. Focused on putting government back together, competence and efficiency, at its core this is administrative and technocratic, lacking soul or an obvious popular and galvanising story. The core aim has also been undermined by widespread reports of infighting, the removal of former senior civil servant Sue Gray as the PM's Chief of Staff and grubby public arguments about the receipts of gifts and large corporate donations.

Sitting alongside this is the centre-left pressure from a host of ministers. These include Ed Miliband's plans for a publicly owned energy company (albeit with limited assets); Louise Haigh renationalising railways and regulating local buses in England; and Angela Rayner restoring some rights at work stripped away by the previous Conservative government. This more progressive agenda has been overshadowed by Starmer and Reeves, combined with a clearly missing proactive No. 10 Downing Street communications strategy and political antenna.

The dominance of the Treasury, with its micromanagement and financial short-termism, is a predicament seen before under Labour governments. It mitigates against long-term investment and support for public services and can lead to major political own goals, such as scrapping the winter fuel allowance for many pensioners. Labour under Wilson in the 1960s attempted to bypass the Treasury and failed. Gordon Brown addressed this by building the Treasury into a centre of alternative power to Blair's No. 10.

Combine this with the current absence of a coherent economic policy and narrative about how 'broken Britain' will be put back together, or how to tackle vested interests and the long-term problems of British capitalism, and this for now does feel an ominous mix made for failure and disappointment. But these are early days, and the UK needs more than a Labour government fixated on balancing the books and spreadsheet politics. It requires an idea, not just sketching out the journey of the next few years but a vision of the ultimate destination and shape of a future Britain.

The stakes are high. This Labour government could succeed in resetting the political agenda, making the UK a better place to live, and begin to embark on fundamental reform. Or it could muddle through making the UK a more civilised country but not addressing any of the big issues. More seriously, it could fail and the forces of virulent reaction and populism on the right rise up, claim they are speaking for the dispossessed and pretend that they are the voice of those ignored for too long. No one should say as we start on this new journey that politics do not matter or that we do not face fundamental choices about who we are and want to be.

Section I

Past Times Revisited

1

After the 2024 Election: Parliamentary Strength, Electoral Weakness

John Curtice

The principal challenge facing the new Labour government would appear to be obvious. How can it turn around a flatlining economy and ailing public services against a backdrop of severe fiscal constraint? Still, difficult though that task may be, at least it can comfort itself with the thought that it will be doing so on the back of a landslide election victory. That surely means that, initially at least, voters will be inclined to give a fair wind to its efforts to tackle the country's difficulties.

Except that it was not a landslide victory – at least in terms of votes. As Table 1 shows, while support for the outgoing Conservatives collapsed by twenty points since 2019, leaving the party with its lowest share ever, Labour's vote increased by less than two points. At a little under 35 per cent, the party's share of the vote in Great Britain was the lowest ever enjoyed by a majority government, let alone one with a parliamentary majority as large as 174. Its vote was not only well short of the 41 per cent Jeremy Corbyn secured in 2017, but it was also a pale shadow of the 44 per cent vote that underpinned Tony Blair's landslide victory in 1997. Indeed, the party's support in 2024 was lower than at any election between 1935 and 1979.

Table 1: The Result

	% Vote (GB)	Change in % vote since 2019	Seats (UK)	Change in Seats since 2019*
Labour	34.7	+1.7	412	+211
Conservative	24.4	−10.4	121	−151
Reform UK	14.7	+12.6	5	+5
Liberal Democrat	12.5	+0.7	72	+64
Green	7.0	+4.1	4	+3
Scottish National Party	2.5	−1.5	9	−39
Plaid Cymru	0.7	+0.2	4	+2
Independent	1.9	+1.1	6	+6
Other	1.7	+1.3	17	−1
Turnout	59.8	−7.7		

* Change in seats is as compared with estimated outcome of the 2019 election on the new parliamentary boundaries introduced in 2024 (Rallings and Thrasher, 2024).

Source: Calculated from BBC website.

Labour's leadership tries to argue its electoral success in the election is the product of the change that Keir Starmer brought to his party. However, in truth, voters seem to have rejected the Conservatives much more than they embraced Labour. As a result, the party's parliamentary strength obscures the fact that its success is built on rather weak electoral foundations and, despite Keir Starmer's changes, a pattern of support that in many respects looks remarkably unchanged since 2019. Consequently, the political challenge of maintaining public support for the government as it tackles the difficult legacy it has inherited from the Conservatives looks not inconsiderable too.

Conservative Calamity

Three developments were central to the outcome of the 2024 election. They are all ones that concerned the Conservatives, not Labour. The first is 'Partygate'. Until the first stories suggesting the COVID-19 lockdown regulations had been interpreted in Downing Street in a uniquely liberal fashion appeared in the media in early December 2021, the Conservatives had never been consistently behind Labour in the polls. In particular, the government's success twelve months earlier in securing an early roll-out of a COVID-19 vaccine boosted its support, as reflected in its success in May 2021 in winning the Hartlepool by-election. At that point, Labour and Starmer appeared to be on the ropes. However, following the first Partygate stories, Conservative support fell on average by five points in four weeks. By the end of January 2022, Labour, on 40 per cent, were five points up on the party's standing at the end of October, enough to put them as much as eight points ahead of the Conservatives.

The second key event was the adverse market reaction to the Liz Truss 'fiscal event' of September 2022. As with all previous governments that presided over a market crisis – from Harold Wilson in 1967 to John Major in 1992 and Gordon Brown in 2008–9 – the drama on the financial markets severely undermined the government's reputation for economic competence. Whereas six months earlier, Ipsos had reported that the Conservatives were six points ahead of Labour on 'managing the economy', following the 'fiscal event' they were as much as thirteen points behind. In similar vein to what happened in the wake of Partygate, support for the Conservatives fell precipitately – by six points – during Ms Truss's short tenure in Downing Street. By the time it came to an end, Labour, on 50 per cent, were briefly as much as twenty-five points ahead of the Conservatives.

In short, the political and economic turmoil that accompanied the regimes of Boris Johnson and Liz Truss were the decisive political events that turned the electoral tide during the 2019–24 parliament. True, voters noticed Labour's move to the centre. Shortly after the 2019 election, YouGov reported that 46 per cent reckoned Labour were 'extreme', but by the time the Partygate scandal erupted that figure had more than halved to 22 per cent. That change may have helped Labour gain the confidence of Tory supporters who became disenchanted with the Johnson and Truss regimes. However, without the self-inflicted Tory turmoil of Partygate and the 'fiscal event', it is unlikely that Labour's electoral prospects would ever have been as bright as they proved to be.

Meanwhile, the third crucial development was the rise of Reform – at the expense, primarily, of the Conservatives. Support for the party began to edge up in the wake of the Liz Truss fiscal event, though only enough to put it at 5–6 per cent. However, the party's standing began to rise more markedly in the autumn of 2023, just as the government decided to make reducing both legal and 'illegal' immigration one of its policy priorities. Trouble was, that focus on immigration helped amplify what many of the Brexiteers who backed the Conservatives in 2019 regarded as one of the government's policy failures. According to polling conducted by Redfield & Wilton for 'The UK in a Changing Europe', by the time of the 2024 election, 42 per cent of those who voted Conservative in 2019 believed that immigration was higher as a result of Brexit, while just 15 per cent reckoned it was lower. In any event, by the time the election was called in May 2024, Reform had risen to 11–12 per cent. That proved enough to entice Nigel Farage into returning to the political fray, and, as Table 1 shows, by polling day the party had reached nearly 15 per cent under his leadership, even more than the 13 per cent UKIP registered in 2015.

It was Reform, not Labour, who in the end drew most support away from the Conservatives on polling day. On average, four post-election polls conducted by Lord Ashcroft, Ipsos, More in Common and YouGov suggest that almost twice as many (23 per cent of those who cast a ballot in 2024) 2019 Tory voters switched to Reform as swung to Labour (12 per cent), while even fewer (7 per cent) backed the Liberal Democrats. Moreover, in seats the Conservatives were trying to defend, support for Reform increased by twice as much (sixteen points) on that registered in 2019 by the Brexit Party as it did in constituencies held by Labour (eight points). This was not only because support for Brexit is higher in such seats but also because the Brexit Party did not contest Tory-held seats in 2019, and thus any support that Reform registered in those seats represented an increase on zero.

This pattern was fundamental to Labour's ability to secure a parliamentary landslide. Not only did support for Reform rise most in Conservative-held seats, but among these seats it tended to do so most of all in constituencies where the Conservatives had previously been strongest. Where the Conservatives won more than 60 per cent of the vote in 2019, Reform on average won 20 per cent. In contrast, in Tory-held constituencies where the party won less than 45 per cent in 2019, the average increase in Reform support was thirteen points. This pattern is important in explaining why support for the Conservatives fell on average by as much as thirty points in seats where the party was previously strongest, nine points above the fall in its support in more marginal constituencies it was defending. And it is the fact that support for the Conservatives fell more heavily in places where the party was previously strongest that is a key reason to why the party lost so many seats, both to Labour and the Liberal Democrats. To that extent, and uncomfortable though it might be for many Labour activists, the rise of Nigel Farage's Reform Party contributed significantly to their party's ability to secure a parliamentary landslide on so low a share of the vote.

Lack of Enthusiasm

Meanwhile, among those voters were not inclined to back Reform, many were seemingly indifferent to the choice between Labour and the Liberal Democrats. They tended to back whichever of these two parties was better placed locally to secure a Conservative defeat. In constituencies where Labour started off second to the Conservatives, support for the party increased on average by six points, while that for the Liberal Democrats slipped by two points. But in constituencies where the Liberal Democrats started off second to a Conservative incumbent, their vote increased on average by nine points while Labour's support did not advance at all. This pattern meant of course that Labour's support was more 'efficient' in translating votes into seats, but it was an indication of voters' antipathy towards the Conservatives rather than any particular enthusiasm for Labour.

Other indicators too, point in the same direction. Starmer's personal ratings were at best disappointing. Shortly before polling day, Ipsos reported that, while 33 per cent were satisfied with the job he was doing as Labour leader, as many as 51 per cent were dissatisfied – a net satisfaction rating of −18. In contrast, Tony Blair had a net rating of +22 in the weeks leading up to the 1997 election, while even David Cameron had a rather better rating, +3, shortly before his success in 2010. According to YouGov, while 38 per cent felt that Labour was ready to form the next government, rather more (43 per cent) took the opposite view. Meanwhile, Labour's emphasis on not raising the main rates of tax despite the government's fiscal difficulties was not necessarily in line with the public mood. For example, just before the election was called, Opinium found that 33 per cent reckoned the government should increase taxes and spend more on public services, while only 17 per cent took the opposite view. The state of the health service was mentioned as a concern by many more voters than was the level of taxation. In any event, voters seemed somewhat sceptical about Labour's stance on tax. More in Common reported in their post-election polling that as many as 52 per cent reckoned that, in practice, they will be paying more tax in five years' time.

There is also some evidence that Labour may have found it more difficult to get its supporters to the polls. True, such evidence has to be treated with circumspection, given that pollsters find it more difficult to persuade people who do not vote to participate in their surveys. But according to More in Common's polling, 23 per cent of those who voted Labour in 2019 did not cast a vote this time around, compared with 18 per cent of 2019 Conservative voters and 14 per cent of those who had previously backed the Liberal Democrats. Meanwhile, al-though younger voters – at recent elections one of Labour's core con-stituencies – are always less likely to vote than those who are older, according to Ipsos the gap was wider than in 2019. They report that just 37 per cent of 18–24-year-olds and 41 per cent of those aged 25–34 cast a ballot, compared with figures of 47 per cent and 55 per cent respectively in 2019. In contrast, at 73 per cent, turnout among those aged sixty-five and over was little different from 2019.

Lost Ground

Not that those youngest voters who did make it to the polls supported Labour to the same extent as they had done at other recent elections. One of the striking features of voting behaviour in the 2017 and 2019 elections was a widening of age differences in vote choice, such that age became the principal demographic dividing line between Labour and the Conservatives. Younger people predominantly supported Labour while older people backed the Conservatives (Chrisp and Pearce, 2021). However, as Table 2 (based on the post-election polls by Lord Ashcroft and Ipsos) shows, the age gap in Labour support narrowed compared with 2019. While the party gained some ground among older voters, it fell back among those aged thirty-five and especially among the under-25s (many of whom, of course, will have been voting for the first time). Much of the damage to Labour's standing among younger voters appears to have been inflicted by the Greens, whose support rose markedly among younger voters. (YouGov's post-election poll reported using different age categories, but nevertheless much the same pattern is discernible there too. Their poll puts Labour on 41 per cent among 18–24-year-olds, down fifteen points on 2019, with the Greens on 18 per cent, up fourteen points.)

Table 2: Vote by Age Group, 2024, and Change since 2019

		18–24	25–34	35–44	45–54	55–64	65+
		% (+/–19)	% (+/–19)	% (+/–19)	% (+/–19)	% (+/–19)	% (+/–19)
Con		10 (–10)	10 (–15)	15 (–18)	20 (–14)	27 (–19)	41 (–13)
Lab		41 (–19)	47 (–6)	42 (n/c)	37 (+7)	32 (+5)	24 (+6)
Lib Dem		13 (+3)	12 (+1)	13 (n/c)	13 (+1)	12 (n/c)	12 (+1)
Reform		8 (+7)	11 (+10)	14 (+11)	17 (+15)	18 (+15)	15 (+13)
Green		17 (+13)	13 (+10)	9 (+5)	7 (+4)	5 (+2)	3 (+2)

Source: Average of polls by Lord Ashcroft 2–4.7.24 and Ipsos 5–8.7.24. Comparison is with average of same two sources' equivalent polls in 2019.

Here, it seems, are signs that Labour's move to the ideological centre under Keir Starmer's leadership did not come without cost. More 2019 Labour voters (9 per cent) switched to the Greens than switched to any other party, including the Liberal Democrats (8 per cent) and Reform (3–4 per cent). For the most part, where the Greens advanced most, Labour suffered. In constituencies where the Green vote was up by less than two points compared with 2019, Labour's vote increased on average by nearly seven points. In contrast, where the Greens' support rose by more than eight points, Labour's support was down by nearly seven points. Meanwhile, according to More in Common, the Greens were most successful among those voters it labels as 'progressive activists', that is, the most left-wing and socially liberal section of British society. The Greens won as much as 20 per cent of the vote among this group, while Labour's own support fell on 2019 by as much as eighteen points (More in Common and UCL Policy Lab, 2024).

But this was far from the only sign of Labour losing ground among some of its core constituencies. The party's share of the vote fell on average by seven points in constituencies it was trying to defend. The party lost ground heavily above all in constituencies where relatively large parts of the population identify as Muslim. One of the most strongly promoted features of Keir Starmer's changes to the Labour Party had been to take action to eradicate antisemitism in his party. But some of his remarks defending Israel's right to defend itself in the wake of the attack by Hamas in October 2023 caused disquiet among the party's many supporters who identify as Muslim.

In seats where more than 20 per cent identify as Muslim, the party's vote fell on average by a staggering twenty-three points, while even in those constituencies where between 10 per cent and 20 per cent regard themselves as Muslim the party's support was down by seven points. As a result, the party lost four seats with large Muslim populations to independent candidates standing on a pro-Gaza platform, while ostracised former Labour leader Jeremy Corbyn, long known for his pro-Palestinian sympathies, also successfully defended his relatively diverse Islington North constituency as an independent. Meanwhile, Ipsos reported that support for Labour among ethnic minority voters as a whole was down by eighteen points on 2019, with only 39 per cent of those from an Asian background supporting the party.

Labour also lost ground in its stronghold in Wales, where support for the party was down by four points. This is, of course, a part of the UK where it has been the sole or principal party in the devolved government ever since its creation in 1999. That government's record for handling the health service has been heavily criticised, just has that of the UK government in England. With the SNP also losing ground heavily north of the border (see further below), voters appear to have swung against whoever was in power locally, irrespective of their partisan colour. It suggests that, in their current mood at least, voters may not be forgiving if Labour do not rise to the economic and fiscal challenge it now faces.

A Voter Base Little Changed

Meanwhile, not only did Labour's repositioning not come without costs, but Labour also made relatively little progress towards some of the key electoral objectives that its repositioning was supposed to achieve. Shocked by the loss in 2019 of its so-called 'Red Wall' seats, that is, traditionally Labour-voting, working-class constituencies that had been attracted to the Conservatives by their 'Get Brexit done' message at the 2019 election, the party accepted Brexit, ruled out any return to the EU single market and customs union, emphasised its patriotism, focused on economic inequality and moved away from a socially liberal position on some issues, most notably on the legal recognition of transgender people (Mattinson, 2020; Starmer, 2020). Such a strategy was regarded as essential if the party was going to have any chance of winning the 2024 election. Yet in the event, the party made only modest relative progress among Brexiteers, while its support among working-class voters remained no better than that among their middle-class counterparts.

Indeed, as Table 3 shows, if anything Labour's support rose most among middle-class 'AB' voters, while it fell back a little among working-class 'DE' voters. In any event, there was certainly little sign of Labour being particularly successful at restoring its strength among those in working-class occupations. As a result, the social profile of its vote was very different from that which propelled Tony Blair to his landslide victory in 1997. On that occasion, according to Ipsos, as many as 59 per cent of DE voters and 50 per cent of C2s voted Labour at that election, whereas only 31 per cent of ABs and 37 per cent of C1s did so. Indeed, as in 2019, Labour's strength is to be found above all among university graduates, 43 per cent of whom (according to Ipsos) voted Labour compared with 28 per cent of those without any qualifications.

Meanwhile, with the Conservatives' support falling heavily among all social grades, there was once again little sign of the class divide that once strongly structured the pattern of support for Britain's two largest parties. The only party whose support did vary substantially by social grade was Reform, which was around twice as popular among working-class voters as among middle-class ones. It was also nearly three times more popular among those with no qualifications (18 per cent) as it was among graduates (7 per cent).

Table 3: Vote Choice, 2024, and Change since 2019, by Social Grade

	AB	C1	C2	DE
	% (+/−19)	% (+/−19)	% (+/−19)	% (+/−19)
Conservative	26 (−17)	24 (−10)	24 (−14)	23 (−11)
Labour	36 (+5)	35 (+2)	32 (+1)	33 (−3)
Lib Dem	15 (n/c)	12 (+1)	10 (+1)	10 (+1)
Reform	10 (+9)	13 (+11)	22 (+19)	19 (+16)
Green	7 (+4)	8 (+5)	5 (+2)	6 (+3)

Source: Average of polls by Lord Ashcroft 2–4.7.24, Ipsos 5–8.7.24 and YouGov 5–8.7.24. Comparison is with average of same three sources' equivalent polls in 2019.

Labour's relative strength among younger voters and graduates is, of course, redolent of the pattern of support for Brexit (Curtice, 2017). Table 4 shows that despite the collapse of the pro-Leave coalition that propelled Boris Johnson to victory in 2019, Labour only made modest progress, an increase of four points, among those who had backed Leave in 2019. Leave voters who were disenchanted with the Conservatives mostly switched to Reform rather than Labour.

At the same time, those polls conducted during the campaign that asked voters how they would vote in a second EU referendum (rather than how they voted in 2016) suggest that as much as 73 per cent of Labour's vote came from those who would vote to join the EU, only modestly less than the equivalent figure of 82 per cent among Remain supporters who backed the party in 2019. In short, there is a significant gap between Labour's official stance on Brexit and the attitude of many of the party's supporters towards the EU, a gap that contains the potential at least to be a point of tension during the current parliament.

Table 4: Party Support by 2016 EU Referendum Vote

	Voted Remain		Voted Leave	
	% vote	Change in % vote since 2019	% vote	Change in % vote since 2019
Conservative	17	−3	37	−36
Labour	46	−3	19	+4
Liberal Democrat	17	−4	7	+4
Reform/Brexit	3	+3	29	+25
Green	8	+4	3	+2

Source: Average of polls by Lord Ashcroft 2–4.7.24, Ipsos 5–8.7.24 and YouGov 5–8.7.24. Comparison is with average of same three sources' equivalent polls in 2019.

Scottish Success for Labour

All that said, Labour did achieve one of its key electoral objectives – restoring its fortunes in Scotland. The party's share of the vote north of the border rose by as much as sixteen points, enough to put it ahead of the SNP by five points and to secure thirty-seven seats, only four fewer than it won in 2010 before its position north of the border collapsed in the wake of the 2014 independence referendum. However, the initial roots of the Scottish party's revival were much the same as in the rest of the UK – it was first evident in the wake of Partygate and then strengthened further in the wake of the Liz Truss fiscal event.

Even so, despite now standing at 30 per cent, eleven points up on 2019, Labour still trailed the SNP by thirteen points. However, it then profited from a decline in SNP support triggered by the party's leadership election in February and March 2023, following Nicola Sturgeon's decision to resign. Even though there was no sign of any decline in support for independence, with Ms Sturgeon's successor, Humza Yousaf, proving a much less popular and adept leader and with the SNP government struggling to turn public services around after the pandemic, by the summer of 2023 Labour were only two points behind the SNP in the polls.

Meanwhile, shortly before the election, Humza Yousaf abruptly ended a substantive agreement with the Greens and threw two Green ministers out of the devolved government. This made the SNP a minority administration again, and Yousaf found himself obliged to resign under political pressure. Voters north of the border reacted unfavourably to this political turmoil, just as they had done at a UK level with Partygate and Liz Truss's fiscal event, and Labour pulled ahead of the SNP. Between them, the difficulties facing the Conservative and SNP governments meant that Labour were able to argue that a vote for them was a way voters could express disapproval of them both. As a result, the party was able to secure the support of 22 per cent of those who voted SNP in 2019, including 20 per cent of those who were still in favour of independence, as well as 26 per cent of those who backed the Conservatives (a higher proportion than elsewhere). In short, here too the principal foundation of Labour's success was the perceived incompetence of their opponents.

Conclusion: A Fractured System

Voters went to the polls in 2024 unhappy about the way they had been governed. They wanted, above all, to see an end to Conservative rule across the UK, while in Scotland and Wales some were unhappy with their devolved government too. This was hardly surprising. Not only were many of them poorer than five years ago and dealing with worse public services, but they had come severely to doubt the integrity and competence of the outgoing Conservative administration.

However, voters were not particularly attracted by any of the alternatives, including Labour. Consequently, they cast their favours across the political spectrum, voting in whatever way they felt best expressed their dissatisfaction or for whoever seemed better able to defeat the Conservatives locally. As it happened, that produced an electoral geography that worked very much to Labour's advantage. But it has also produced a fractured party system that means voters have plenty of alternatives before them should they conclude that Labour have not met the policy challenge that now confronts them. Governing in this parliament could well prove even more of a test for Labour's leadership than was being in opposition in the last one.

2

There Is an Alternative: Labour, Social Democracy and Changing Britain

Will Hutton

Over the 124 years since its foundation, the Labour Party – established to champion workers' interests, equity, fellowship and the common good – has struggled with an ideological curse. Those broad aims, devised to include Methodists as much as Marxists and to create the widest possible movement, might be easily shared, but how were they to be achieved?

Were they a minimum, a lowest common denominator whose realisation would wax or wane with circumstance and conjuncture, or were they a launching pad for the final goal – the transformation of capitalism into some quasi- or wholly socialist society? With these questions never settled, the party has lurched between socialist idealism and pragmatic reformism in the name of electability and respectability. The potential for bitter internal strife collapsing into schism has been ever present – and on occasion has been realised.

Therefore, we can see a pattern over the party's history: from Ramsay MacDonald's compact with the Tories in 1931 to leading a national government that so split the party, or to the breakaway Social Democratic Party in 1981. This can explain the paroxysms of the Socialist

League in the 1930s, the Bevanites in the 1950s, the Bennites in the early 1980s and the Corbynites in the late 2010s (Cruddas, 2024). Also the unsuccessful compromises of Harold Wilson and Jim Callaghan in trying to keep alive the post-war settlement between 1964–79 and ultimately the failure of New Labour to strike out in a distinctive and lasting progressive direction. Only Clement Attlee managed to govern both transformatively and practically to deliver those quadruple goals – but the settlement he conferred upon the UK could not survive the disruptive, stagflationary 1970s.

Keir Starmer's Labour

Can Keir Starmer put all these demons and failures behind him? Can the curse be finally laid to rest, a new ideology forged and a prolonged era of successful reformist Labour government be charted moving forward? Unlike Tony Blair, Starmer is unquestionably a Labour man, with working-class roots firmly anchored in that quartet of Labour values and aims. If he can deliver, he will. For all the difficulty of what he has inherited from the Tories, he has been bequeathed several major positives, along with the political space that his predecessors never possessed. If he can capitalise on these opportunities, he could be the author of national renewal.

First and foremost, British capitalism has its back against the wall – and it is obvious to all that a Tory party broken by the delusions of Brexit is intellectually and politically incapable of fixing it (Hutton, 2024). Rather, it is the author of the crisis. But it is incapable of the honesty necessary to recognise its failure. The 45-year arc from 1979 to today, in which the elixir of economic growth has been thought to be about reducing the state crowding in on a vibrant private sector (one that will self-organise itself to invest and innovate to optimal outcomes) – that has ended abruptly. Nobody who has lived reflective-ly through those decades can any longer support these self-evidently exploded propositions. Economies do not self-organise to best out-comes; markets oscillate wildly; firms deliver goods and services to society – there is a reciprocal interdependence that cannot be escaped.

A series of great catastrophes have been launched in pursuing the myth of the small state as the enabler of the vibrant market. Ideolog-ical monetarism and its hand-maiden, deindustrialisation, succeeded through reckless financial deregulation that triggered a twenty-year credit boom. This created Britain's singular financial and economic col-lapse in the 2007–8 financial crisis – more acute than any other country. The resulting economic and social scarring (and extraordinary inequal-ities) would be made more intense by austerity – driven by the same enthusiasm to shrink the state. Brexit, to escape the imagined shackles of a European super-state, followed – so unravelling the gains in GDP growth and competitiveness that EU membership had offered. All was then capped by the infamous Truss Budget, which brought the country so very near to a first-order intertwined financial and sterling crisis. Whatever else may be said, there cannot be more of the same.

Labour Pains and Opportunities

The turning point in post-war politics that unleashed these dis-asters was Harold Wilson's premiership and his inability to reform the post-war settlement (see Egerton and Seldon's chapter for more detail). Within days of becoming Prime Minister in 1964, he was told by Bank of England Governor, Lord Cromer, that he would have to abandon his ambitious plans to marry Keynesian economics, nation-al planning and a technological revolution to rejuvenate the British economy. Protecting the pound from devaluation, and thus City of London interests, took precedence – if necessary curbing the power of over-mighty trade unions who did not respect collectively struck wage contracts as legally binding, and so consistently won inflationary pay deals. Wilson resisted, but ultimately the pound was devalued, and planning and Keynesian demand management sidelined. Wilson even came to the view that too powerful trade unions were a problem. 'In Place of Strife', a white paper of 1969, proposed to make free collective agreements legally binding while reciprocally offering unions mandatory recognition rights.

This approach was opposed implacably by trade union leaders in the name of socialism, so consigning the proposals in 'In Place of Strife' into a meaningless commitment to make wage agreements 'solemn and binding'. The victory was joyously celebrated at the time as a triumph for both socialism and the Labour movement. Instead, it killed stone dead the prospects of social democratic reform for the post-war settlement. Success would have transformed the reflex anti-capitalist ethos and unjustifiable legal immunities of British trade unionism – and reconfigured social democratic Britain. One immediate consequence was Labour losing the 1970 general election. That defeat would set in train the events that led to the evisceration of liberal conservatism, the rise of Thatcherism, the accompanying torments of the British liberal left, the humbling of British trade unionism, and a series of great policy catastrophes.

But fifty-five years later, the slate has been wiped clean. Starmer faces no serious threat from the now-reduced trade union movement, who two generations on have learned some salutary lessons. Rather, he has the opportunity to reinvent them, offering an array of rights to alleviate workplace insecurities and a chance to create saner forms of collective bargaining agreements that will be enforceable within the law. Nor does he face a self-interested City of London or a self-confident British business sector determined to resist working with a distrusted, even dreaded, state – as Wilson and Blair both did.

Britain's stock market now ranks tenth in the world, populated by legacy companies and low-growth outfits. Over the past decade, it is reckoned that 2,300 high-growth companies that could have formed the backbone of a rejuvenated economy and stock market have been sold abroad. When chip-maker Arm was sold to the Japanese for $30 billion weeks after the Brexit vote, Prime Minister Theresa May, Chancellor Philip Hammond and Brexit Party leader Nigel Farage all hailed the purchase in Thatcherite terms, as proof positive that 'Britain was open for business'. Now it is trading in New York at a value of $170 billion, mourned as a brutal loss to the British economy and stock market. It would have been the UK's third-largest company. 'Being open for business' turns out to be a euphemism for conniving in our economy being stripped of its technological assets.

Instead of defying a Labour government to protect their freedoms, City and business leaders are rather looking to partner actively with it in order to stop the rot. Another generation of Tory mistakes would devastate Britain's economic standing, already reeling from a longer period of stagnant real wage and productivity growth than at any time since the Napoleonic Wars. There is widespread recognition that every sinew and policy lever must be pulled to raise chronically low levels of both private and public investment.

Britain's £3 trillion pool of potential risk capital, held in pension funds, cannot be allowed to stand aside from investment in the national economy: our fledgling high-tech companies of tomorrow must be supported, instead of sold abroad. The Treasury cannot any more be allowed to veto public investment, so that Britain continually trails our peers. There is no opposition to scaling up the British Business Bank and UK Infrastructure Bank. Business supports the creation of a National Wealth Fund. Insurance company Phoenix, along with investment bank Schroders, have set up a £10 billion private 'future growth fund', larger than the UK government's own £7.3 billion public wealth fund. Nine leading investment houses have pledged they will invest at least 5 per cent of their assets in private unlisted high-tech companies. Even ten years ago, this kind of proactivity towards investment would have been unthinkable. Today, with the London Stock Exchange establishing an emergency committee to explore better ways to increase investment and bring forward a flow of young companies, it is vital to rejuvenate the stock market. Starmer's government faces none of the business and financial opposition and scepticism that Wilson, Callaghan, Blair and Brown encountered. Rather the opposite.

Equally, it is obvious to all that the deformations and rank inequalities of British society can no longer be allowed to fester. The necessary if insufficient precondition for 'better' is more resources – some combination of growth-generating higher tax revenues and the judicious taxation of wealth, doubled as a share of GDP over the last forty years, will be vital. But here again, the protests that might be expected about higher taxes are muted. There is no gainsaying the need for more public resources, stronger public services and a determined effort to rebuild our infrastructure and decarbonise the economy.

A Social Democratic Moment?

Nor is there any immediate prospect of a Tory revival. The party is menaced on one side by the significant millions attracted to the neo-racist, anti-immigrant nihilism of Reform, and on the other by the flight of what used to be its natural supporters to the Liberal Democrats and moderate Labour. There is no strategy that will allow the party simultaneously to retake its old southern and county heartlands and the left-behind parts of Britain. Equally, British voters have learned the art of voting tactically in a First Past the Post system: Lib Dem MPs can look to Labour voters to support their re-election as their second choice. Labour MPs can expect the same in reverse, especially if both parties position themselves as reformist progressives.

Only Attlee, after his landslide victory in 1945, could look upon a political landscape as benign as this – however formidable the economic and social challenges.

Starmer also has one more piece of good fortune. He inherits a Labour Party constitution, refashioned by Tony Blair, that eschews commitments to socialise the commanding heights of the economy. Rather, the party talks a language of how acting together helps improve the chances of every individual and how collective endeavour can be coupled with individual aspiration. It matches the needs of the moment – of partnership, of iterative policy-making and of acting together to improve economy and society in all our interests. It is a far cry from Thatcherite individualism, shrinking the state and distrusting collective action as crowding out potential for the individual. In Starmer's worldview, collective action crowds in individual potential. His ideology has been made for him, and he embraces it. So does the vast majority of his party, prepared for the compromises of holding and exercising power.

The curtain has emphatically gone down on the market-oriented individualism and distrust of public initiative that characterised the decades since 1979. It may only be a relatively short time after Labour's 2024 election victory, but already the outlines of the new are emerging. It will be a Labour Party pursuing labour interest, equity, fellowship and the common good, leaving behind the ideological warfare of the last century. It will make mistakes – it must not be in too much thrall to the Treasury's anti-investment proclivities, for instance, nor listen too attentively to a stage army of self-seeking lobbyists pleading their special interests. But step-by-step, it can begin the long journey of remaking Britain. The curse is being lifted, I would argue, though the early stages of Starmer's government have undoubtedly been rocky in certain respects. It is now up to Labour to steady the ship and build the consensus necessary for change.

3

Learning from the Successes
and Failures of Post-War
Labour Governments

Tom Egerton with Anthony Seldon

When considering a new Labour government, it is easy to succumb to the hype of the present and the mythology of the past. Labour's history is, if anything, the most contested and complex of any British political party, embellished with personal brilliance and abject failure, dynamic crisis against periods of relative calm. While everyone may have their favourite leader or period, there are lessons to be learned from each of the post-war Labour governments and a study of their successes and failures is helpful in the pursuit of an achieving premiership for Keir Starmer and Labour.

The Attlee Premiership (1945–51)

Clement Attlee's premiership has become, in Hennessy's words, 'the lodestar for the efficient and successful conduct of peacetime Cabinet government' (2001, p. 150). Attlee's premiership certainly offers a wide-ranging list of successes. But its ability to reforge the structure of Britain, and the world, despite the country's terrible post-war state, remains underappreciated. Achieving governing success in times of domestic and international instability are the markers of great Prime Ministers and governing parties (Egerton, 2024). The Attlee era demonstrates that Labour's governing successes come from a healthy mixture of individual brilliance, strategic judgement and controlled creativity, while minimising factional fighting, inaction and hubris.

Attlee inherited a Britain that had just faced the largest external shock in its entire history: the Second World War. Britain had lost over 25 per cent of its wealth (Thorpe, 2015), while its external debt was the highest in the country's history (Cairncross, 1985). Approximately five million servicemen and women from 1945–47 had to be demobilised, while a new aspiration of full employment had to be balanced with an entrenched defence budget of 18 per cent (Bew, 2017).

These spending paradoxes eventually erupted during the 1950–53 Korean War, requiring 40,000 soldiers, extensive remobilisation costs and, according to Gaitskell, cuts to the NHS. The war divided the government and, eventually, helped precipitate its end. Crises only mounted throughout Attlee's premiership in a world awash with instability and power vacuums. Most pressing was the 1945 cut of US lend-lease: the economic lifeline on which Britain depended, which essentially disappeared overnight. The government was forced to negotiate an American loan ($5 billion total) with a terrible catch: sterling–dollar convertibility by mid-1947. This clause built a timebomb under Attlee's premiership – one he can scarcely be blamed for. The bomb exploded in July 1947, precipitating a sterling crisis that was fudged by coming off convertibility in August. By 1949, the pressure had become too much, and a forced devaluation from $4.03 to $2.80 was agreed.

Thorpe's conclusion that it was 'not a national disgrace, simply a recognition of changed realities' (2015, p. 123) is a fair one, even if the decision-making leading up to both ending convertibility and devaluation were rare examples of Attlee's weaker economic grip (Hennessy, 2001). To top this off, the government grappled with chronic post-war resource shortages, particularly food (with bread rationing reintro-duced in 1947) and fuel. The domestic picture was one of vulnerability and austerity due to the aftershocks of war.

The international picture was just as bleak. Imperial ambitions had caught up with the realities of a diminished Britain – producing several hurdles. Britain's position in Palestine as peacekeeper became untenable amidst violence and illegal immigration. The 1948 with-drawal came after the UN's resolution to split the state into Israel and Palestine, resulting in an invasion of Israel by four Arab armies and a bloody war. Greece's civil war, in which Britain had been supporting the monarchy against communist insurgency from 1946, was a further crisis that Britain did well to exit. On India, Attlee successfully re-linquished power with the oversight of Lord Mountbatten. This was hastened by the pernicious divisions over borders between the Hindu and Muslim communities, resulting in vast amounts of violence and 500,000 dead, but the fast withdrawal prevented a full-scale civil war. Attlee's government grappled with the fraught politics of a declining empire and in tackling them began the transition to a post-war UK, beginning to translate the reality of Britain's waning power into policy. It would take later premierships to end empire, but Attlee's decisive willingness to take tough decisions by withdrawing from significant parts of the empire set a precedent for future governments.

Despite, or perhaps because of, international crisis and the changing world order, the government effectively reinvented Britain's foreign policy. But if Attlee contributed to this reinvention by commissioning the British atomic bomb, new secret service structures and creation of the UN, it was foreign secretary Ernest Bevin who forged the begin-nings of modern European security (Bew, 2017). As the Cold War de-veloped, Bevin successfully united the European, North American and British geopolitical circles, pushing for Marshall Aid/US intervention and eventually solidifying years of alliance-building groundwork with the creation of NATO in 1949 (Hennessy, 1987). Communism may have spurred US–European co-operation, but Bevin's, and Attlee's to a lesser extent, vision and persistence were key to the creation of the post-war geopolitical settlement. With the reemergence of European conflict, Bevin's vision for European security is a similar doctrine to that on which the Foreign Office relies today. Its endurance and effectiveness are a remarkable achievement.

With the failures of 1918 and 1924, the 1945 progressive party could not afford to lose the post-war peace. Despite the constrained circumstances, Labour set a target of just three years to implement the entirety of their new social contract, based on the 1942 Beveridge report. The bills included: the Education Act 1944 and Family Allowances Act 1945 (both passed by the coalition but implemented by Labour), the National Injuries and Insurances Acts 1946, and the National Assistance and Health Service Acts of 1946. The NHS, the 'jewel' (Hennessy, 1987, p. 36) to the Labour governing crown, was serendipitously born on the third anniversary of the election victory – 5 July 1948. While issues remained over the flat-rate contribution, subsistence levels and male-dominant system, the shift towards universal public service coverage, rather than a means-tested or insurance system, and the progressive institutions these reforms solidified cannot be understated.

So, why was the Attlee government successful? Individual brilliance is one reason. A skilled Cabinet team with Aneurin Bevan, Ernest Bevin, Hugh Dalton, Stafford Cripps, Herbert Morrison and the younger ministers (Douglas Jay, Hugh Gaitskell and Harold Wilson) ensured a high-functioning and politically adept government. While managing Cabinet was Attlee's forte, he showed a consistently strong strategic judgement, whether handling food or fuel shortages, maintaining financial support through tricky American loans, withdrawing from the empire, forging European security or being bold on a new domestic settlement despite the constrained economic situation. For if there is one overriding reason for the successes of the 1945–51 period, it is Attlee. It is a lesson to anyone in politics, as he said, 'to take things as they come. One should never worry, and one should get the greatest pleasure out of things' (Bew, 2017, pp. 364–65). Quiet, calm and considered government, converse to what many believe, can be quite revolutionary.

Wilson's Premiership (1964–70)

After thirteen years of Conservative rule (1951–64), Labour returned to power and were to rule for much of the next two decades, including eight years under Harold Wilson. His first, the 1964–70 government, is the most significant for its achievements and failures, ensuring its conflicted status in Labour history. Because of Wilson's political skill and manoeuvring and sometimes ambiguous policy in government, he is regularly accused of duplicity, of his mind having contained no principles at all. Or, conversely, his entire premiership is summarised in that one line: 'The white heat of technology.'

To understand Wilson is to understand what he aimed to do – establishing the Labour Party as a mature social democratic force, able to popularise socialist policy for not just the working class but wider demographics – particularly what Anderson (1964) called the 'technical intelligentsia' (doctors, technicians, managers etc.) who have since become a core element of the Labour vote. By maintaining credible and efficient centre-left government and mixing it with a vision to reform and reposition Britain's declining international position, Wilson would establish Labour's electoral success. Before Wilson's leadership, the fundamental question was how Labour could win and govern again in a capitalist consumerist country that was producing living standard increases and progress the social democratic ideal of greater equality.

When Wilson achieved office in 1964 with a miniscule majority, he inherited a dispiriting economic picture – the core issues included a deficit in the balance of payments and an industry in need of modernisation. The Department of Economic Affairs (DEA), Wilson's vision for a modernised planned economy, failed primarily because of deflationary economics deployed in a feeble attempt to defend the pound's value. The late devaluation in 1967 wasted millions, particularly during the 1966 July crisis. The political capital won after the 97-majority landslide in 1966 offered a better moment for devaluation, which would have bought time for economic recovery before an election (Ponting, 1990). The other unfolding issue was the unions, evident in the 1966 seamen and 1967 dock strikes and near doubling in wildcat strikes over the decade.

These developments were recognised by Wilson and Employment Secretary Barbara Castle, spurring them to tackle the issue. What resulted was the 1969 'In Place of Strife' White Paper, with agenda-changing promises to reimagine union relations and curtail their power. However, James Callaghan's political manoeuvres and Labour's factionalism ensured its failure, diminishing the government's legacy and electoral prospects (Toynbee, 2020). But despite the popular narrative of national economic 'decline' through the 1960s, Wilson's first term saw unemployment remain under 2.7 per cent, inflation float around 4 per cent, only rising to 6 per cent in the late '60s, and GDP growth averaging 2.2 per cent per annum (Tomlinson, 2004). Indeed, productivity, while not increasing as much as Italy or Germany, grew at a steady 4 per cent in the late '60s while balance of payments significantly recovered from negative £712 million to a surplus of £568 million (O'Hara, 2006).

Furthermore, one must judge this record against the difficult picture Wilson inherited. Devaluation, on which Wilson's first term historically falters, is more complex than at first inspection. O'Hara (2006) contends that even if Wilson had devalued sooner, it would have required just as much deflationary economics – stunting growth and Wilson's strategy. In addition, Bretton Woods left sterling vulnerable, essentially acting as the first defence of the dollar as a secondary reserve currency and thus undergoing acute speculation when the balance of payments was in deficit. The series of crises in the global economic system were largely out of Wilson's control – none more so than the 1968 gold crisis.

Wilson also inherited a declining empire and bloated military, which he tackled by initiating the retreat from the East of Suez policy and cutting military spending targets by £400 million with a reallocation of the budget to domestic R&D rather than foreign infrastructure. Wilson's critical foreign policy mistake was ruling out (three times) military action against a white-dominated Rhodesia, giving Prime Minister Ian Smith the confidence to declare independence and survive ineffective British sanctions. Wilson's fears of a 'British Vietnam' in Rhodesia damaged his judgement – even if keeping Britain out of the Vietnam War, despite Britain's reliance on US finance and President Lyndon Johnson's pressure, was a success of his premiership. Meanwhile, while failing to achieve EEC accession in 1967 due to a second French veto, Wilson laid the groundwork for Britain's entrance into Europe.

Wilson's real successes lie in his social and public service policy. Spending on social security, health, education, housing, transport and R&D all increased annually by 6 per cent or more, while living standards continued to increase. The creation of the Open University in 1969 spoke to the core principles of Wilson: that of open access and equality of opportunity, remaining significant today in its positive effect on social mobility. Education Secretary Anthony Crosland also pursued a significant transition towards comprehensive schools (Donoghue, 2018). But the foundational changes initiated under Wilson were the social reforms pursued by Home Secretaries Roy Jenkins and, less enthusiastically, Callaghan. In 1967, abortion was legalised and male homosexual acts decriminalised in England and Wales. The death penalty was suspended in 1965, then abolished in 1969. The same year grounds for divorce were liberalised.

Other reforms, such as the Race Relations Act 1968 and Equal Pay Act 1970, laid the groundwork for future societal reforms and liberalising of attitudes, although the 1968 Commonwealth Immigration Act fails on this front. These reforms were a successful product of Wilson's 'willingness to elevate able people who opposed him' into Cabinet (Pimlott, 1992, p. 561). But Wilson had two critical failings; first, his tendency to micromanage departments – particularly over the DEA after firing the ineffective George Brown – and second, his court-style tactics in playing rivals off each other, which only spurred ministers' factionalism and rivalries such as Castle and Callaghan.

Ultimately, Wilson oversaw a flawed if underrated first term, achieving pivotal social changes, core investment in public services and national R&D, an important but failed reimagination of the state, sustained growth, high employment, surplus balance of payments, neutrality over Vietnam and an unwinding of empire and military spending. He fell short on both points and thus his most fruitful period in office fails to merit him top prime ministerial status. The core strategic mistake Wilson made was to overpromise and underdeliver. As Pimlott succinctly put it, his first government was 'too clever, too intellectual and too unrealistically theoretical' (1992, p. 565). Or, as Ponting curtly summarised in his Wilson critique, 'the promise remained unfulfilled' (1990, p. 408). If there is an overriding lesson from Wilson's first premiership, it is that the macro cannot be resisted through the ingenuity of the micro. In other words, the foundations for strong political government cannot be bypassed through sheer political will or tactical fudges. Wilson found this out the hard way through his only electoral defeat in 1970.

Wilson and Callaghan (1974–79)

Wilson's failure to pass 'In Place of Strife' posed a core problem for his party: how can Labour manage trade unions while maintaining full employment and low inflation? It was a trifecta that had ended Edward Heath's government, aggravated by an inflationary 1972 'dash for growth', flawed union/incomes policy and mistaken showdown against the miners, triggering the three-day week. After returning to power in 1974, Wilson's 'social contract' policy ended the miners' strike immediately and repealed Heath's defunct union legislation, replacing it with a more co-operative settlement – but this still fell short of a permanent fix (Pimlott, 1992).

Wilson had inherited an economy on the brink of disaster: inflation was soaring to 16 per cent, while interest rates were over 12 per cent. Oil prices had increased fourfold due to the 1973 Yom Kippur War and OPEC reaction. Major economies experienced a balance of payments crisis, laying bare Britain's deficit and weak pound, thus making its borrowing unsustainable. The public sector borrowing requirement (PSBR) soared to finance Britain's deficit (Holmes, 1985). This, in effect, helped entrench inflation as wage bargaining was transformed into a doom-loop: the social contract ensured pay rises were linked to the cost of living, which in turn triggered further inflationary wage increases (24 per cent in 1975) (Artis et al., 1992). While the £6 pay cap agreed by the TUC in 1975, as well as Chancellor Denis Healey's £3 billion cuts achieved through a confidence vote, steadied the over-extended finances, it was not enough to stave off a full-blown crisis, which came as Wilson resigned in 1976. On balance, Wilson's social contract proved too expensive, and he moved too late to control public expenditure, though an end to the three-day week and union pay demands were always going to be necessary and expensive.

The other core battle of Wilson's late years was over party unity.

The left, organising around the Bennite majority on the National Executive Council, posed a serious threat to the government's control. Wilson, ruling in a more sustainable duumvirate with Callaghan, successfully contained the left, preventing radical policies such as Tony Benn's 'alternative economic strategy' and even demoting Benn in an effort to establish authority. Without Wilson's tactful Cabinet governing, its unlikely Labour would have survived a year in office (Morgan, 1990). Wilson also handled the European fissure ingeniously, first renegotiating a better (if unsubstantial) settlement and then allowing his party and Cabinet to vote freely in a referendum – with himself and Callaghan only moderately in support of membership. The result, a 67 per cent yes vote for Europe and maintenance of Labour both in government and as a movement was, in Hennessy's (2001, p. 367) view, Wilson's most understated and lasting-impact achievement.

Wilson's twilight years were blighted by deteriorating health and a general wearing out of the Labour movement. Not only had the old left aged, but the whole government had lost a uniting endeavour to motivate or sustain the movement after years of post-war social democratic consensus. Wilson's political strategy had been broadly successful – winning four out of five elections, ushering in an era of reduced inequality, increased social mobility and fairness, greater freedoms and a better national capacity to build and innovate. But he stayed on too long, resigning in 1976 with little innovative governing ability left after two years of drift. His overall record is one of success tempered with limitations and failures, hampered by a much weaker second term.

The resulting leadership election – a first under a Labour government – saw Callaghan defeat Michael Foot 176–132 in the PLP. Callaghan entered No. 10 with an 'atrocious inheritance and a non-existent majority' (Sandbrook, 2013, p. 807). Between January and April, the Bank of England spent over $2 billion in a failed defence of the pound, which continued to fall precipitously. As the pound reduced, inflation increased due to the rise in import prices. Even after Callaghan's reductions in spending and pay freeze agreed with the TUC, sterling continued to crash into the autumn, igniting yet another crisis. Put simply, the international market had lost confidence in a country with double-digit inflation, recessional growth, overextended PSBR and sterling's reserve status. With North Sea Oil due to come online in the later 1970s, mostly because of Labour investment and Callaghan's short-term strategy to stabilise the economy, reducing inflation and thus unemployment made sense.

However, the sterling crisis, with the pound in the $1.50s, forced Callaghan's hand further. To stabilise sterling and Britain's finances, Callaghan sought a deal with the IMF for an emergency loan while simultaneously negotiating with President Ford, Secretary of State Henry Kissinger and German Chancellor Helmut Schmidt on maintaining sterling protection and unwinding its role as a reserve currency. However, the IMF loan was predicated on staggering cuts: £3 billion for 1977–78 and £4 billion 1978–79 (Morgan, 1997). This was anathema to Callaghan, Cabinet, the trade unions and the Parliamentary Labour Party. It was widely thought that Callaghan faced impending doom – the ultimate hydra of terrible economic decisions and unreconcilable factions. But it is to Callaghan's great credit that he not only negotiated the initial cuts down to £1 billion (with a £500 million selling of BP shares) but squared off four major Cabinet factions (Benn's Alternative Economic Strategy, Crosland's Keynesianism, Peter Shore's protectionism and the Treasury minister's larger cuts) and obtained the Trades Union Congress's and PLP's agreement, while also agreeing a sterling support package with the US and Germany and the unwinding of sterling as a reserve currency. By April 1978, the pound had rebounded to $1.90, and reserves were at a healthy $9 billion. It was, as Morgan stated, 'handled with immense patience and political skill' (1997, p. 551). With the union pay freeze holding, sterling crisis averted and public expenditure under control, the economy began to recover. Douglas Jay (1985, p. 162) later noted that the 1977–79 British economy was one of the few in the West to see inflation and unemployment fall.

Callaghan's premiership contained positive policy developments – particularly his Ruskin Speech, which laid the groundwork for the 'great debate', shifting education policy towards higher standards, new methods in examination, a national curriculum and professionalism in training and support. Foreign policy was also an area of considered policy, with Callaghan utilising his contacts and diplomatic skills to act as an honest broker between the US and Europe over defence spending, economic alliances and Cold War détente. Significant changes to the welfare state were also made under Callaghan, such as the replacement of both family allowances and tax allowances with the new child benefit, paid directly to the mother rather than just the father. This was in line with other gender equality reforms of the decade, such as the Equal Pay Act 1970, coming into effect. Despite crisis, Labour's 1970s rule oversaw the lowest income inequality in modern British history. This is, perhaps, the record Callaghan would be judged by had he not been constrained by crisis.

Callaghan's remarkable economic recovery created a new conundrum: when to hold the election. By December 1977, Labour had begun to lead in the polls, overturning a momentous 15 per cent deficit in just a year. By August 1978, Labour were leading by 4 per cent in the polls while all the economic indicators had aligned in a momentary 'window' that offered a plausible foundation to go to the electorate: 2.5–3 per cent GDP growth, unemployment down to 6 per cent while real disposable income increasing by 7 per cent (Morgan, 1997). What's more, Callaghan's high-risk policy of a new 5 per cent pay cap would have likely been accepted by the unions in the event of an election – both due to the fear of Thatcher and in obedience to a popular mandate. There was no guarantee that Callaghan would have won a 1978 election, but the conditions and political strategy were much stronger (especially considering his non-existent majority in the House of Commons). His failure to call it was probably his biggest error, along with the 5 per cent policy.

It is unfair that Callaghan is remembered primarily for the Winter of Discontent, in which a series of damaging strikes ranging from binmen to gravediggers were initiated against the tight 5 per cent incomes policy. The situation was exasperated by the retiring of the union old guard of Jack Jones and Hugh Scanlon, who were replaced by a new generation uninterested in high-political co-operation. It can be argued, as Hay (1996) does, that the crisis was a hyperbolic construction, which is true to a degree – there were more days lost to strike action under Thatcher in 1979 (29 million) than Callaghan (20 million). But it was the last post-war settlement crisis to be tolerated by a beleaguered electorate who, for too long, had put up with a fluctuating economy and seemingly endless industrial strife. In March 1979, Thatcher tabled a motion of no-confidence in the house, and the SNP joined with the Tories and Liberals to bring down Labour. After having no majority for nearly three years, as well as a torrid economic picture, it is astonishing that Callaghan survived so long.

Despite the final crisis, as Artis et al. argue, (1992, p. 58) Labour actually 'left the economy in a better position than it inherited' – if still fundamentally weak due to adversarial union bargaining and the constraining (and failing) aims of full employment with low inflation. Callaghan's premiership was one of humble recovery but should not be over-mythologised – especially as a period of proto-Thatcherism. Callaghan, while containing small-c conservative elements, was unabashedly, as his biographer Kenneth Morgan notes (1997), a consensus man – old Labour at heart. Nor should his premiership be seen as a viable route to salvaging the post-war consensus. Polly Toynbee (2020) purports, it was 'poetic justice or just bitter irony' that the unions triggered his fall after he had used their influence to sink 'In Place of Strife' and propel himself toward the leadership. A fairer conclusion, however, would be that the wider Labour movement, while achieving much, had become lost. The post-war settlement had reached its ideological end. What had been an immense period of success, with Attlee building the post-war state and Wilson and Callaghan fighting to extend and maintain its benefits, ended in failure. The repercussions of this split the movement and kept it out of power for nearly two decades.

New Labour, Blair and Brown (1997–2010)

The Blair premiership started fast – declaring Bank of England independence on day one (Davis and Rentoul, 2019). This chimed with Labour's economic strategy – achieving growth in the City of London and business services, which New Labour supported through light-touch regulation to compete with other financial zones, as Howard Davies, previous leader of Blair's Financial Services Authority, admitted (2022, pp. 116–25). By generating growth through the market, social democratic ideals could be progressed: bringing 1.5 million children out of poverty, rejuvenation and investment in core public services, Sure Start, the minimum wage and redistribution through tax credits (O'Hara, 2018).

It was a radical recasting of the social democratic project – implanting market techniques or structures into the public realm while accepting increased subservience to the markets in return for growth. This was more than a mere tactical accommodation; Labour embraced the Conservative agenda at a philosophical and practical level. Economic developments reflected this with further privatisations, continuation of Thatcher's union laws, decreasing percentage of GDP spending, a flatlining Gini coefficient and extended welfare means-testing. But it is unfair to decry New Labour's economic policy as completely neoliberal – social democratic tactics were prioritised after achieving growth.

However, because there was no economic strategy to embed left-leaning structures or tackle in-built market inequalities, their achievements were left vulnerable after the financial crash. This prompts the question of whether New Labour's economic legacy seems more neo-liberal than it was because their social democratic achievements were unwound in the post-2010 government. Regardless, economic growth was impressive, averaging 2.8 per cent per annum 1997–2007, while achieving a significant decline in pensioner poverty and above average income growth (2 per cent) for the bottom 34 per cent (Institute for Fiscal Services, 2024).

Blair had a lasting domestic influence on the country's constitutional settlement: establishing devolution in Scotland and Wales, creating the Supreme Court through the Constitutional Reform Act 2005 and passing the Human Rights Act 1998, and the Civil Partnerships Act 2004. However, House of Lords reform failed, while regionalism was rejected in the 2004 north-east of England referendum. Blair's greatest constitutional legacy is peace and power-sharing in Northern Ireland with the 1998 Good Friday Agreement – building on the achievements of John Major. On immigration, Blair's push for the EU 2004 accession of the eight eastern European countries resulted in high levels of net migration, oscillating between around 140,000 and 280,000 from 1997–2007 (Office for National Statistics, 2015). This facilitated economic growth and led to further European integration but created cultural and electoral problems that would hurt Labour in the 2010s.

Blair's largest impact was felt in foreign policy, the most interventionist since Attlee and Bevin. This was first articulated in his 1999 Chicago Speech, which proclaimed a 'doctrine of international community'. Blair led the decision to deploy troops in Kosovo in 1999 and Sierra Leone in 2000. Backed by the international community, both were successful and limited in their repercussions (Clarke, 2007). The post 9/11 world revolutionised domestic and foreign policy. Blair handled the new world with professionalism and deft crisis judge-ment – particularly in response to the tragic 7/7 attacks. But it was his Chicago doctrine and early success in interventionist policy that fuelled the mistaken interventions in Iraq and Afghanistan. While the tactical campaigns in both were successful, the long-term plans were wholly inadequate, and Blair was too cautious in challenging the Bush administration. In the run-up to Iraq, Hennessy (2001) contends the merging of intelligence and policy on the Joint Intelligence Committee (JIC), reached an unhealthy level, which clouded strategic judgments. Those such as Davis and Rentoul (2019) defended Blair, as did Cabi-net Secretary Robin Butler, over the JIC advice he received stating its believability, although they are markedly less convincing on why the UK felt the need to follow a flawed US strategy so acceptingly. On a fundamental level, Iraq illustrated the toxic extension of 'the special re-lationship' – even if hugging America tight made sense geopolitically, it did not justify Britan's entrance into their wars – something Wilson avoided. The whole saga completely tarnished his premiership.

Blair didn't achieve more domestically because his premiership de-scended into a power struggle with his Chancellor, Gordon Brown. From 2001 onwards, set-piece battles took place every few months, usually centralising around budgets and spending reviews, Blair's 'choice' agenda, Europe, electoral events and conferences. As one source close to Brown recalled, 'All their confrontations between 2001 and 2006 are about Gordon saying, "Why haven't you f*****g gone?"' (Rawnsley, 2010, p. 67). The largest impact of these fights was Brown's veto over Blair's attempts to join the Euro – both the Charlie Whelan 1997 leak and the co-ordinated 2003 anti-Euro campaign. The final coup attempts in 2006, co-ordinated by Brown and pushed by adviser Ed Balls, forced Blair to announce a date, after which Brown assumed the crown.

Brown had one of the strongest Chancellorship records to boast, mixed with new ideas such as the 'ministry of all talents', which promised a possible renewal of New Labour. However, events overcame a PM who had taken office at the ageing end of a government. Incumbency and economic competency were two things Brown had – and his distancing from Iraq allowed an image of change to dominate the summer of 2007. But Brown's critical mistake was not to call an election in late summer or early autumn 2007: Labour was leading in the polls by roughly 8 per cent and steady in the mid-40s, with Brown and Labour leading on every metric bar immigration and likeability (Seldon and Lodge, 2011). The drift and speculation Brown allowed to dominate, partly to destabilise David Cameron, damaged his premiership severely. In fact, Osborne's pledged inheritance tax cut and non-dom levy, matched with Cameron's accomplished party conference speech, ended up being the factors that destabilised Brown, whose poor political judgement was fuelled by his controlling and paranoid style. This situation proved deeply unfortunate; even if Labour had been returned with a lesser majority, five more years and a personal mandate for Brown could have been crucial to survive what came next.

The 2008 financial crisis proved to be a moment when Brown's expertise and dominant leadership intertwined perfectly to deliver economic stabilisation. While Brown's early responses were slow, his eventual recapitalisations and mergers, along with direct Bank of England £400 billion of quantitative easing and 315-year low interest rates, proved effective stabilisers as liquidity propped up the UK financial system. However, Brown's finest role was his coordination of the G20 and global response, including emerging economies while crafting a new voting right and securing over $1 trillion extra resources for the International Monetary Fund (IMF). Tooze (2019, p. 372) notes that 'Brown proved that he was perfectly suited to the role of Treasury secretary to the world' if not always Prime Minister. The financial crash proved that when Brown utilised his expertise and crafted a brilliant

No. 10–No. 11 team, much could be achieved. But it also ended Brown's premiership – the cost of dealing with the crisis was the association with its causes – and destroyed Labour's economic competency.

Overall, Blair was a successful premier – winning three elections, overseeing national renewal, starting important constitutional changes and re-establishing Labour as a force for government. In Hennessy (2001) and our (Seldon et al., 2024) rankings, he falls just short due to his inability to escape factional infighting, prioritising electioneering over governing and lack of economic agenda-changing impact. While Blair accepted the neoliberal consensus, there is a question of how feasible it would have been to push against it. However, Bogdanor (2007, p. 182) notes that it is fair to say that Blair's acceptance of it led to a 'narrowing if not [entirely eliminated] scope for the politics of redistribution'. His primary mistakes in Iraq, and to a lesser extent Afghanistan, are a lesson for why clear strategic judgement retains a sacrosanct place in the skillset of a PM – hubris can never infect decision-making.

For Brown, the picture is much more opaque. His premiership was one of the weakest in Labour's history. The 2008 Climate Change Act, crafted by David Miliband and passed by Ed Miliband, is Brown's most innovative and impactful policy achievement. Not calling the 2007 election looks worse in hindsight – the tactical decisions leading up to the call were incredibly rookie for a leader so seasoned in political government. Brown's premiership, for all the talk of 'a ministry of all talents', was a far cry from the individual brilliance promoted in previous Labour Cabinets. Brown's micromanagement limited any creativity or options for renewal: for Rawnsley (2010, p. 677) he was addicted to 'fighting the last war'. While there is a debate around Brown's role in fostering a deregulated City that ended up being crucial to the financial crash, his domestic handling of the crisis was accomplished. The crash marked what could have been with the Brown premiership.

However, Brown's failure to win the political-economic narrative after the crash became one of the most detrimental legacies for the New Labour period – and precipitated its reversal with austerity.

Lessons for Starmer

Drawing coherent threads from four complex and contrasting periods of Labour history will always be unsatisfactory. Much of what you may dismiss as failure or laud as success will depend on your beliefs. Drawing on the foundational threads of Labour's success, Will Hutton (2024), is compelling in his point that the Labour movement's two schools, the 'we' and the 'I' – or, brusquely, the socialist and the progressive liberal – must be united. On a basic level, and regardless of ideological position, Labour governments are immensely powerful when both schools sing from a similar hymn sheet.

The lesson taken from Attlee's period should not be one of simple unity – the party was ideologically and personally at odds with itself. The point was that Attlee controlled the differing individuals and creativity to enable a successful governing agenda. Wilson's key successes came from devolving power to Jenkins and Crosland. His key failures came when he ignored his best ministers, played them off each other or tried to micromanage them – particularly over devaluation. Callaghan's own failures came from his early corrupting power games and lack of innovation or nerve to force the unions to help save the post-war consensus and unite the movement. The Blair government's infighting and centralisation ensured its descent into a reductive coalition of the 'we' (Brown) and 'I' (Blair). An unhappy, restricted marriage of the two schools can never work – there must be an agreed creative aim and a leader magnanimous enough to empower a team to complete it. This is not to say Starmer will fail unless he returns to Hennessy's (2001, pp. 3–15) 'Platonic ideal' of Cabinet government. Delegation and devolution of power to highly capable teams with a diverse set of skills does not have to be organised into something spelt 'Cabinet'. But what helps with Cabinet government, or something unifying like it, is the political entrenchment of a movement into government – particularly one that is historically prone to faction fighting – while enabling the empowerment of capable delivery ministers.

While unity, creativity and individual talent are important, the other basic lesson is the imperative of strategic judgement. Understanding the big picture is crucial: a PM must accept the basic facts of politics before they can ever hope to change them. In three of the four periods discussed here, Labour came into office during times of economic crisis (1945, 1964 and 1974) and the other (1997) during a violently transforming world. Dealing with these acute problems is paramount – the thousands of detailed decisions a PM must make, regardless of speed or complexity, cannot lead to inaction or excuses: governing – especially for a progressive movement during demanding times – is incredibly challenging. There is no place for hubristic thinking or defeatist inaction. To make the correct strategic call consistently, over several years, is what marks the best leaders and creates the governing space for Labour's successes. Labour PMs may have historically lacked delivery on their ideological aims, but they have been broadly accomplished at making the right strategic call in difficult circumstances. This is something that should neither be forgotten nor taken for granted.

Starmer hardly needs more people offering him advice. But if there is one suggestion, it is that a reading of Labour's complex but fascinating history will enlighten ideas and methods sparingly debated and little understood. He would do well to incorporate some into his government.

Thanks to Kit Haukeland for research and editorial assistance.

Section II

New Times Foretold

4

Who Is Labour Actually Giving Voice To?

Neal Lawson, Jeremy Gilbert, John Denham and Laura Parker

Neal:

Labour kind of won against all the odds. There's a huge majority in terms of seats but not in terms of share of the vote, which was somewhere near the level that it received in 2019. Then the Tories won what looked like then a decisive eighty-seat majority, which looked like the first stage in a big realignment of British politics. The infamous Red Wall fell to the Conservatives, and we looked like we were in for a period of Tory hegemony in England and Wales and SNP hegemony in Scotland. As both the Conservative and SNP positions crumbled, Labour played a really disciplined, focused, small-c conservative game. Labour won and should be given plaudits for winning a very cautious, disciplined campaign that delivered this extraordinary majority. However, that majority has been cast as one that's a mile wide and an inch thin. We're going to find out about that over the next four or five years. Starting with you, Jeremy, how much do you think this Labour victory is built on sand? How volatile are voting alignments and allegiances?

Jeremy:

We must acknowledge that the electoral strategy pursued by the leadership was, on its own terms, successful. It was predicated on an analysis of the electoral politics of Britain, which isn't fundamentally different to the analysis Compass would make, although it proposed a very different response. The analysis said we have a completely skewed electoral system that massively weights the votes of particular constituencies. These swing voters are the kind of voters who delivered a huge majority to Boris Johnson based on relatively small changes in vote share in 2019: they are mostly older, socially conservative, relatively comfortable, socio-culturally disgruntled voters. They made a decision that by targeting those voters almost exclusively, and by presenting themselves to the broader establishment as completely unthreatening, they would be able to appeal to them.

Historically, in 1992 and 2019 you're looking at elections in which the motivation of some Tory voters to vote against Labour was crucial. Persuading those voters to stay home was critical in 1997 and 2024. On those terms, it's successful. It achieved the objective it set out. And it was based on a correct analysis. One of the assumptions proceeding from that analysis was that there would be no electoral costs to Labour alienating its core metropolitan vote and alienating young voters; in effect, alienating the entire progressive constituency, which it set out to do egregiously. It did this partly to convince the broader establishment that it wasn't a threat and could be allowed to form a government. The idea was that we wouldn't see screaming headlines persuading soft Tories to come out and vote against you on the day. All that has been successful on their terms. But the outcome has been a situation in which Labour's support is neither wide nor deep. They've got a small share of the vote. The success of the strategy was dependent on the collapse of the Tory vote and the split between the Tories and Reform.

What wasn't expected was the extent to which they alienated the progressive vote, indicated in the overall vote share and number of votes, and success of the Greens and independents. This is an extremely volatile and fragile situation. The No. 1 danger for Labour in this is there being any kind of effective realignment of politics on the right, overcoming the split between Reform and Tory votes. If that starts to happen then it's not clear what the current Labour project is. What would be the future of this project?

Laura:

I agree with that, including the question about the governing coalition. Simply to win with a skewed system obviously skews your entire political offering. To govern successfully, you can't be so all over the place. I think it's very fragile. I think one could argue that this is possibly the weakest position any incoming majority government has been in in modern times.

We've seen previously how Labour has struggled to attract the voters it needs to win without alienating others. We saw Scotland at the end of Blair, the Red Wall, and I think we're seeing something with the Green and independent vote. We are at the start of something that could continue to be another wave of Labour losing, for quite a sustained period, people it needs to keep electorally. And of course, I would argue that Labour must keep them, in terms of the politics it promotes. Clearly Reform–Farage has been critical in the past three elections, and that is probably a big question in the next election.

What does Labour do? I would argue that all roads lead to PR. At the moment, Labour doesn't want to be green, radical or redistributive. That's nonsense that's got to end. I mean, it must pick a side and govern decisively from that side. The big question mark about what Starmer now does is the extent that they back away from democratic reform, including electoral reform.

I work for Good Law Project, and we surveyed our supporters before the election to discover how they were going to vote. Only 52 per cent were intending to vote Labour. Although the vast majority said that they were optimistic about a Labour government being better than the current Tory administration, they were only mildly optimistic. They didn't think it was going to be that much better. And we're about to survey them again, and I think that they will present themselves as the kind of people Jeremy referred to: alienated progressives, radicals and liberals.

Neal:

If I was sitting in Starmer's office, I'd be saying we've got a 172-seat majority. A level of control of the party and Parliament as strong as Labour has ever had. While a uniform swing of 6 per cent against Labour would see Labour's majority go, it is very hard to see how the Tories overturn that by the next election.

John:

I've got to say that we've had four Labour leaders since 2005 and this is the first who's won an election. I know some people think we won in 2017 – apart from the technical issue of winning fewer seats and fewer votes than the Tories – but here, we've actually won. Jeremy is right. They had a strategy to do that. It was a strategy to peel away the Conservative vote from 2019, which had become split three ways. One went to Reform. Those voters were never going to vote Labour. Others came to Labour and the Lib Dems. And let's not forget that the Lib Dems massively outperformed their result in 2019 without increasing their share of the vote.

There's a lot about electoral efficiency here. The people that Labour targeted were less radical than the people they lost. They were pro-public service. They were broadly, not fanatically, patriotic. They tended to be middle class and graduates. I'm really talking about England, not the other nations. They were people who wanted a decent, more competent government. They tended to be Remainery sort of people, but not people who desperately wanted the EU issue reopened.

Two things. Jeremy hinted at this. Labour did not set out to lose as many votes to the left of the party as it lost in the end. One of the big uncertainties at the moment is what you might call the Owen Jones group of people. You had this group of people going around saying, because of all the MRP polls, that Labour is going to win so you don't have to vote for them. We do not know how many of those people would have voted Labour had they thought that Labour might lose. There's a big uncertainty about the nature of the electorate that now is to the left of Labour.

Another point on coalition fragility. I don't think this coalition is any more fragile than the Labour coalition in 1997. The big difference is it comprises far fewer voters. In 1997, Labour could lose a million working-class votes in 2001 and four million working-class votes in 2005 and still come out with an overall majority. This coalition is more like Labour's coalition in 2005, in terms of how big it is and how dependent it is on electoral efficiency. One of the real challenges is that unless you think your targeting can be so effective again at the next election, Labour needs to try to build support in government. My sense would be that the potential pool of votes that Labour could build in to this is somewhat to the more radical side of where Labour was at the election, rather than further to the right. Secondly, the people who might vote Labour were probably people who voted Liberal Democrat at the last election, and there'll be very good strategic reasons for them to do so if the electoral system remains the same. Most of the gains have got to come from somewhere to the left of the current government, and that's a real challenge for the governing strategy.

Neal:
Let's look at the progressive alliance. After 2019, this stressed the need

for some kind of collaborative approach that was blown out the water by the implosion of the Tories and the SNP. But there was a kind of progressive alliance at the election. Jeremy hinted at it a bit in the ruthless targeting from above and tactical voting from below – in terms of people knowing where to vote in the right place for the right party to inflict damage. That pincer movement was part of the efficiency of the Labour win and Lib Dems and Greens winning seats. Yet we have seen the Greens expelling people for advocating for progressive alliances, just as Labour has done in the past. Is our kind of progressive alliance dead?

Jeremy:
It's a good question. There's always been a hypothetical scenario in which the electorate becomes sufficiently educated about tactical voting that formal progressive alliances aren't needed. There's some movement in that direction, but there'd be a long way to go before we were there. The election strategy pursued by Labour was an answer to the question of how you deal with the fact that you have an electoral system that massively rewards efficient vote distribution and massively punishes inefficient vote distribution. How could a Labour Party effectively respond to the problems presented to it by an electoral system that is set up only to be a two-party system but, since the 1970s, has been effectively a multi-party system that works in favour of the Conservatives?

New Labour drew the conclusion that the only response to that situation would be to move Labour to the right of the Lib Dems, directly taking Tory votes, which – as people on the right of the party will always point out – are effectively worth twice as much as votes taken from any other party (or none). In both 1997 and 2024, Labour positioned themselves to the right of the Lib Dems. In 2024, during the campaign the Lib Dems presented themselves to the left of Labour in terms of public spending and taxes. Once that happens, Labour voters in places where Labour doesn't have a hope are much more motivated to vote tactically for the Lib Dems.

The problem, which we know from New Labour, is that such an electoral strategy risks leading to a governing project that is to all intents and purposes centre-right. The progressive alliance idea has always been partly predicated on the understanding that the only other effective response to the electoral dilemma that Labour has found itself in for decades, and the only response that could produce a progressive governing project, would be a different way of responding to the problem of how to distribute votes efficiently. And that would require a project recognising that there's a broad progressive majority that has to be mobilised across party divisions. That's still probably true, so I don't think the progressive alliance has gone away for ever as an idea.

But the Labour right have a very strong preference for their historically successful strategy of outflanking the Lib Dems to the right. As long as that's what you're doing, the party is sort of electorally obliged to pursue a programme that expresses their ideological preferences. If your whole electoral strategy is based on chasing soft Tory votes, then you're more likely to pursue the kind of soft Tory policies that the Labour right traditionally prefers over more radical ones.

Neal:
I think our mistake as Compass was to argue for the progressive alliance on the basis that Labour can't win without it. Labour can clearly win on a centre-right agenda but without mobilising a sizeable constituency needed for more transformative change.

John:
We need to be clear about what happened. I'm sitting in Winchester. The Labour Party asked me to go and work in Basingstoke, where

we won. There were no Liberal Democrats canvassing in Basingstoke because they had all been sent to Maidenhead. At the level of the official party machines, except for a handful of places largely in the West Country, Labour and the Liberal Democrats were not contesting against each other in this election, which in many ways was what many of you who've advocated for a progressive alliance want.

The second thing is the intervention of polling. We saw this massively in 2015, when you had polls pointing to a hung parliament, and the Tories didn't take Labour votes away but got people to vote for them to stop Miliband being in the pocket of Alex Salmond. Opinion polls end up shaping election results. The growth of MRP polls is doing this on a massive scale. There is lots of voter information out there. I think tactical voting has become a reality and was played by party machines.

The one thing I disagree with Jeremy on is, I don't think it would be fair to say that in this election, Labour set out to put itself to the right of the Liberal Democrats. All the opinion polls show there's almost no difference in values between the people who voted Liberal Democrat and the people who voted Labour. They're swimming in the same pond.

Secondly, people like Ed Davey, who was a great enthusiast for austerity after 2010, were implausible advocates for a radical project. What they did was pick two issues, social care and water, on which they could campaign specifically. The idea of a progressive alliance in terms of a purely electoral project looks to me less relevant than it may have been in the past. I've always been a slight sceptic about the idea of a such an alliance except as understanding that there are people in the Liberal Democrats, in Labour and in the Greens who would broadly share a same view about the potential for radical change. That's a political project. That's a non-sectarian way of looking at the issues, and something that remains a relevant thing to create the space for people to talk about outside governing structures about what happens over the next few years.

Neal:

I guess if someone from Labour HQ was on this call, they'd probably argue that their project made Labour a safe option, aiding Tories moving to the Liberal Democrats, because they weren't going to get Corbyn.

John:

We got the same vote share as we did in 2019. Would you prefer to have had the same vote share and same voters in 2019, which would have lost you the election? Because it did in 2019. If you only got a third of the vote, you might as well have them in the right place at the right time. The difficulty is that it is a small base of the electorate from which to govern and win the next election.

Neal:

It was a strategy to win an election. It wasn't a strategy to govern and change the country, and this is what we want to be at. This is the job of our part of the left: to think through how you both win and govern effectively to change the country.

Laura:

I agree with John's conclusion about the ongoing political relevance of the progressive alliance being much greater than electoral salience. Voters have MRP. There are digital apps telling people where to canvass. But regarding the politics of building the progressive left, I agree with Jeremy. I think the drum has to be banged loudly for PR, because it's one of the ways that Starmer manages his way through this. If Labour doesn't do anything about the electoral system, then it's not impossible that there's a big swing to a virulent right-wing. Starmer has shown no sign of embracing democratic reform. There's nothing about the Lords. Nothing about devolution. Nothing about PR. And none of us ever expected that there would be, but this is one of the routes out for him. Surely people are whispering in Starmer's ear about the fragility. And surely he understands that with PR, his decade of renewal is more likely? This probably has to be a bigger priority than the progressive alliance for Compass.

Neal:

John, were you surprised by the Green and independent vote? The Greens are now second in forty seats, particularly in London. How much of a threat is that to Labour?

John:

You can focus on the next UK election, but one of the things we often dismiss is the extent to which by-elections, mayoral contests and Welsh and Scottish elections can be disruptive. It's worth noting that UKIP were never any good at parliamentary elections, but they still managed to reshape the whole of politics by the impact they had on the Conservatives and then on Labour.

Firstly, the immediate issue is the possibility of either the Greens or Reform in different places becoming the place that people go to as a protest-vote party. I think you must have strategies for responding to that. Secondly, the Owen Jones argument. To what extent is the Green vote now an anti-Labour vote – 'I'm going to vote with my conscience, because I know Labour's going to win.' That will be critical in future general elections.

How does Labour try to protect its position in government? It seems to me that what's very critical is a compelling story about the nature of the country that we're in and why we're going to rebuild it in a way that works for everybody, or at least for the great majority. What worries me about the initial positioning of the government over the past few months is that there's not an obvious national story coming out, separated from the economic question. The worst thing Labour could do is chase off with one strategy for stopping people peeling off to Reform and going off with another strategy to address the Greens. The dicing and slicing of the electorate will fail. What you need is a compelling national story. What Labour needs to concentrate on is having an inclusive national story of a country that works for the common good, that will protect against losing votes to left and right.

Neal:

What do you think the left is going to do? The other thing that's happened since the election is seven members of the Campaign Group had their Labour membership suspended for six months. Where does that fit with Corbyn, trade unions, the Greens, independents and more? How is that going to coalesce – a protest or electoral challenge to Labour?

Jeremy:

It's a complicated situation, a challenging one for the left with difficult questions to answer. First, what happens to the Labour left? One of the conditions of life over the next year or so is going to be the fact Labour members who never voted for Corbyn are not going to be happy. Anecdotally, they're already not happy with a lot of what's happening. Whether that ends up having any political implications remains to be seen.

Right now, one really has to say that every criticism that's ever been made – including by ideological Blairites – of the traditional old right of the party (who are now back in control for the first time since 1979) is being borne out. They do not have a political project. They do not have a vision. Their project was to restore their positions as the rightful owners of the Labour Party. They've done that. But they have no vision for government.

What historic precedents there are don't really give us much of an idea of what will happen on the broader left. The general fragmentation of the left voter bloc between Greens, independents and the Labour left could result in a much more creative set of strategies for building flexible, mobile alliances between independents, Greens and people inside and outside Labour. A great deal is going to depend on what happens to the Green Party and I don't know really what they're thinking. I think the Greens themselves are going to have a major internal debate as to how they relate to the situation. There's probably a dominant tendency within the Green Party that thinks that how they should respond to the situation now is to keep pressing on with their aim of effectively supplanting the entire left of the Labour Party as an electoral project and vehicle. This could see them act effectively in collaboration with the right wing of the Labour Party, because they all have an interest in progressive voters and members just leaving Labour and going to the Greens. But hopefully they will be more creative and strategic than that.

If you have an electoral system like ours, but you end up in a situation in which there is Labour, Tories, Reform, Greens and independents, SNP and Plaid Cymru, all able to command significant votes, then you end up with a situation that is totally dysfunctional: nobody can assemble a majority coalition. The far right could end up in government with 20 per cent of the electorate supporting them, just like Labour now. Trying to avoid that being where we end up is going to be a task for everybody and we might find some unlikely allies in trying to prevent that situation.

Neal:

What you've just described is a world where you learn the art of negotiation between those different competing electoral groups, as opposed to them fighting each other. The tribalism, the adversarialism, the lack of any long-term strategy. It's not the diversity we're against. It's the culture and structural forms of our old politics, which prevents such diversity becoming a more ambitious, radical political project.

Laura:

John and Jeremy made me think about the challenges the Greens face. Because we mustn't just assume it is a left Green Party. They won support that cannot simply be reduced to a left vote. This requires difficult thinking. How do we force realignment? The electorate in many respects is ahead of us. You've got disgruntled Tories who want to conserve the planet, and their grandchildren are doing projects on climate change, and they're voting Green for different reasons.

So, other than banging on about PR, how do we help shape that realignment? Corbyn has come out for PR. It took him a long time. How do we see as a realignment that is already happening, rather than as a fragmentation, and get ahead of that and make it work electorally and politically?

I agree with John's point that there are various pinch points coming. It's not that we have to wait for five years and see what happens. Things could change quite significantly. I agree with Jeremy on the unprecedented nature of this moment. But how does it become a positive opportunity and not just a threat? Who are people going to rally around in Parliament? It's not going to be Corbyn and I worked for him and have huge respect. I don't see any signs of the left getting its act together.

Neal:

As you were talking, Laura, it makes me think that Labour has a 172-seat majority overturning a Tory eighty-seat majority. Governments don't fall with majorities that big, but leaders can. I think that's an area of volatility. Let's conclude on the right. We're coming to this at the tail end of a tumultuous summer in terms of the far right mobilising on the streets in England, on social media, culturally and intellectually. Is the Conservative Party going to follow Farage – or tack back to try to win back those Blue Wall seats? And what's going to be the effect on Labour progressives in terms of what's happening on the right and far right of British politics? And how scared should we be of the rise of authoritarian populism in the UK?

John:
Predicting is very difficult. Firstly, I think that if the Tory party goes towards the Farage wing, that's probably the best thing that can happen for Labour. The bigger danger is a Conservative Party that decides it wants to eat Labour's and the Lib Dem's lunch in the seats that the Conservatives lost this time round. That's quite a big task for the Tories, and it could be that the left generally is rather in the position that the right was in the 1980s, when the broadly centre-left vote was split irredeemably, and Thatcherism could do what it wanted.

There isn't a Conservative strategy that doesn't tack back towards the voters they lost this time round. From our point of view, it seems that there are opportunities here to tell the sort of national story I was talking about – if only we want to do it. I slightly disagree with Jeremy's characterisation of the Labour right as a sort of monolithic block with a simple project. Because one of the things I did in preparation for this was go back to read Rachel Reeves's Mais Lecture in March this year and compare it with Starmer's first big Downing Street speech in August.

The interesting thing about Rachel's speech is that she very presciently set out how a market economy that becomes detached from the lives of most of the people in the country produces populism of right and left – which is destructive, not constructive. She laid out an analysis way before the riots that said that if your economy is not serving the majority of people, this is what's going to happen. Labour had an opportunity to say this. It still has, though it hasn't been taken by Starmer yet.

The causes of the riots are not purely about fourteen years of bad government but, more fundamentally, the nature of the economy. If Rachel Reeves is able, before the riots even happened, to root it in the nature of the economy and to make that a case for reform, so surely should be sections of the Labour Party. I think we need to keep an eye on what's happening on the right. Our biggest threat is a Tory party moving towards the centre, but our big chance is to tell a much more rooted national story than we seem to be trying to do now.

Neal:

I think that's right, John. But the problem over the past fourteen years has been that in the absence of that national story, Reform, as you alluded to earlier, have set the tone of debate, dragging politics in their direction, dragging the Tories in their direction. Who have then dragged Labour in that direction as well. That dynamic can continue even when Labour has a big majority.

John:

One thing that needs to happen on the left is stopping our aversion of talking about the nation as a nation and what sort of country we want to be, because one of the difficulties is that liberal cosmopolitans tend to be uncomfortable about this. There's been a space for talking about a national story, and we've only been offered one part of that national story, so that's a challenge for people on the left to get into that territory, but in a progressive way.

Neal:

Jeremy, what's your thoughts on the threat of the right and the far right, and what it does to progressives?

Jeremy:

I've been saying for nearly ten years now that a simple rule of British politics is if Jeremy Corbyn can become Labour leader, anything can happen. I was talking to Andy Beckett about his book about the Labour left recently and about the fact that in 2013 Corbyn was literally the least likely member of the PLP to become the next Labour leader. John McDonnell would have seemed far more plausible; Diane Abbott would have seemed more plausible – but it was Corbyn. If that can happen, anything can happen.

We're in an extremely volatile period. After the 2019 election, we were supposed to live through a ten-year hegemony of the Tories and Johnson; that imploded and collapsed over a couple of years. From here on in, anything could happen, and under the circumstances we're all describing, there is a very real danger of the right being able to be the people who can tell a national story that enough people find compelling for them to get into power.

There is an opportunity for us to tell that compelling national story. The problem is that there isn't a plausible story you can tell about what's happened to Britain that makes an argument for mild, moderate reform at this stage. The only plausible argument you can make to people about what's happened to Britain since the 1970s, that is as compelling as the stories told by the right, is one that takes account of the scale of the disaster of the Blairite capitulation to Thatcherism and the total dysfunction of liberal democracy in Britain for decades now. And the only logical conclusion of that story would be very radical reform.

That is a story that cannot be told by Starmer or Reeves. Their whole job in terms of the wider political establishment is not telling it. Reeves can tell a story that will be convincing to 10 per cent of the electorate – highly educated, relatively secure economically. It will say we need to slowly, carefully rebalance the economy so that it starts to become more productive and work better for people. But that will not be anything like enough to win over most people or challenge the rising right. Only a more radical narrative and analysis could do that. I'm utterly sceptical that Starmer or Reeves are capable of delivering that or willing to do so if they could.

It's not inconceivable that story ends up being told by someone from the Labour right. It doesn't have to be told by someone on the party's left. But it cannot be told by someone completely committed to the ongoing factional project of alienating and excluding the left. The difference with the USA is striking. Partly because they never felt as threatened in their jobs as the Labour right did, the centrist Democratic establishment have broadly accepted the need to be seen to include elements like Bernie Sanders and his followers and to make serious rhetorical and programmatic concessions to them. It is very clear that the people currently running Labour and the government would rather die than make any such concessions. For all these reasons, I cannot see Starmer or Reeves being able to tell the story that needs to be told.

Neal:

One of the cases we've got to make for PR is the argument that under First Past the Post you can win a majority on 25 per cent of the vote and the far right across Europe would be installed in many places if they had First Past the Post. Any final thoughts on the threat of the right, what it means for Labour and the progressives? Laura, the last word is to you.

Laura:

I think we're going to have to look outside of Parliament for the answers. Starmer found his way through the riots, because it was summer, and he's going to jail his way out of this problem. But the response was completely inadequate, in terms of naming what this was about. How do we inject some courage into the party so that it's not responding in its factional control way but is responding with what the country needs in terms of solving the big crises?

Think of the contrast with the US Inflation Reduction Act and the Democratic accommodation with Sanders. That is because the Democrats have understood that they have some serious problems to contend with. I know it's American banal spin, but it gave out hope, the sense of possibility, and then listening to Starmer's August Downing Street speech, you just wanted to tear your hair out. How do we inject into the party some reflection of the real and outside world that is going to carry on turning irrespective of what Morgan McSweeney thinks about it? We failed Corbyn with the bridge between the movement and the party, because control of the party machine became the dominant force behind Corbynism.

But if the movement building had won, maybe we'd still be in the same place, but that seems to me to be where we need to bring the energy, ideas and events. There is no way that the best we can manage over the next five years is keeping the debt a bit under control and more austerity. It is not going to hold. So how do we harness that before it becomes a crisis in a positive sense? Do we just sit around waiting for a crisis? On the national story, I tear my hair out when we have something like Children in Need, the nation digging into its pockets, pensioners giving their pensions.

Starmer should stand up and talk about the generosity of the British public, their internationalism, their innate sense of fairness. They don't want kids drowning in the Mediterranean. There are national stories happening that we must encourage the party to harness. Britain's small-c conservative population digging deep for people on the other side the planet. There are moments that Starmer could lean into that do tell a different story, because that story is happening. So how do we inject the outside world, whether it's the movement building or nice folk giving to Children in Need? We didn't manage it under Corbyn. That's part of the realignment. It's not yet clear to me what that means in terms of what the PLP will do politically, whether they will have the nous to organise externally, or whether they'll all just get fed up. The one thing that is certain is that Labour is not coming back in with this majority next time around.

Neal:

A lot of ground covered – some pessimism, some optimism. In all that volatility we need to develop that national story of renewal. Compass are trying to do that with the New Settlement project. And if you can mobilise the more political elements of civil society, the challenge of climate change, NHS crisis, civil liberties, small boats, threat of the far right – all this is bubbling up and brewing. And if we can pull that stuff together into something coherent, in all the volatility, we might have a chance to do something positive and enduring.

5

Beyond Progressive Alliance to Genuine Pluralism

Molly Scott Cato

The progressive alliance was an idea of its time: a time when the left felt weak and divided and those with vision and hope sought to use a co-operative approach to block the ravages of Tory austerity. With a Labour government safely ensconced behind a historic majority in July 2024, that time is past. A better question for progressives is: what is the best strategy to make radical change when Labour's success seems to have been more about getting the nod from oligarchs, financiers and newspaper barons than popular enthusiasm? But the question for this chapter is how to establish hope that we can build a truly pluralist democracy in the UK when our government comes from a party that seems determined to shut down any diversity of opinion.

The Democracy of Buggins' Turn

We are unique among Western democracies in having a political system that is named after and truly resembles a horse race. YouGov polling indicates that the overwhelming majority of people who voted Labour at the 2024 general election did so 'to get the Tories out'. This was the reason given by 48 per cent of Labour voters, with the next most popular reason being that 'the country needs a change' (13 per cent), followed by 'I agree with their policies', at only 5 per cent. This is the depressing reality of the UK's democracy: most people vote negatively, and policies hardly feature in the election campaign or in the decision-making process of voters.

The BBC's electoral guidelines make it clear that polls should not dominate electoral coverage. Indeed, they should only be presented carefully and with sufficient context. These standards were not met in the 2024 general election campaign, which was dominated by speculation about the possible outcome, especially about how Reform might perform and the impact that this would have on the overall result. Analysis by the University of Loughborough shows that the issue dominating broadcast and print media was the electoral process itself. It absorbed more than a third of the airtime, with taxation taking up only 10 per cent, similar to corruption, while economy was at 7 per cent for broadcast and 5 per cent for press, and health was at only 4 per cent of TV time and 5 per cent for press (Deacon et al., 2024). While voters are desperately concerned about the state of our NHS, journalists are obsessed with the movements of polls. This also directs voters towards tactical decisions rather than making choices about the party best placed to create the country they want to live in.

So the electoral thought process goes something like this: 'I'm fed up and want a change, so how do I most effectively vote against the existing government? Oh, I see the polls suggest that Labour are doing well, I'll vote for them to get rid of this lot.' Or, perhaps: 'I'll vote Reform to give this lot a bloody nose.' Decisions are then made on the basis of MRP polls that use national data to predict outcomes in individual seats but have minimal information about likely outcomes in those seats or local factors influencing outcomes in real constituencies. This is highly frustrating for a party like the Green Party of England and Wales, which is forced by our majoritarian system to focus on a small number of seats, leaving Green voters grossly underrepresented in Parliament.

The data shows that Green voters were the last to make up their minds, many doing so in the last few days of the campaign, or even on election day itself. According to Tim Bale,

> Wow: over half of those who decided to vote for the Greens made up their mind in the last few days or on polling day itself. Perhaps they were just waiting to make absolutely sure that Labour were going to win anyway, rendering it safe to do so; but, really, who knows? (Twitter, 6 July 2024)

At every election, Labour's squeeze-messaging about Greens splitting the votes – which they also use in their safe seats and seats they could never hope to win – was unconvincing in the face of polls showing unprecedented leads for Labour. The fact that this is probably the most compelling reason why we now have four Green MPs is a telling indictment of a rotten system.

Both the 'two main parties' have a strong incentive to collude in this diminution of our politics to a tactical gamble. They know that if they put up with their time in opposition for long enough, their time of power will return. The pendulum of the swingometer is the most powerful metaphor in UK political life, in spite of the fact that only two-thirds of voters in 2024 chose one of those parties. And when the choice is so narrow, it is unsurprising that nearly half of eligible voters chose not to vote at all.

Commentators have noted the speed and efficiency with which one government replaced another on 5 July 2024, and this is the claimed advantage of our political system: it delivers clear majorities. But it does this at the expense of the representation of the third of voters who chose other parties. YouGov polling indicates that more than a third of Labour voters would have voted otherwise if they had not chosen to vote tactically and that the majority of those voters would have chosen the Green Party (Smith, 2024). Voters chose pluralism and would have chosen more variety if they had not been bamboozled by reporting and by the system itself to narrow their options.

Ironically, Labour's thumping majority may make it easier for the voices beyond the Westminster duopoly to be heard in this new parliament. As soon as the new parliament assembled, we saw the beginning of a collaboration forming to push for the abolition of the iniquitous two-child benefit cap. We saw organisation by left-wing Labour MPs, Greens and the pro-Gaza MPs to mobilise to put pressure on Labour. With such a large majority, discipline is not essential to win votes, and this seems to be giving Labour MPs a sense of freedom. But they will balance their moral commitment against their fear of disciplinary repercussions. Starmer has already demonstrated his inclination to be as uncompromising with the consciences of his own MPs as he is with those who prefer other parties. We wait to see how this will impact his reputation in the long term.

Supporters of the existing system also point to the way that the two main parties make coalitions internally before elections, rather than externally after elections, as happens under proportional systems. But the reality is that Labour, in particular, thrives through ruthless tribalism outside and ruthless factionalism within. We have seen the virtual elimination of Labour politicians who supported Corbyn, leaving Corbyn himself to fight and win as an independent. The original progressive alliance failed because Labour would not participate, preferring to wait their turn to be the government as one of the 'two main parties'. There is no question that this had destructive impacts on the country and on most UK citizens. If Labour had joined the alliance, we could have stopped austerity and the rollback of climate action back in 2015, not to mention never having to face the disaster of Brexit and the boost it has given to the far right.

This is perhaps the most damaging aspect of our political system: it guarantees rotational power for the two main parties. As both have demonstrated in recent years, they don't have to be inspiring or to respond to the wishes of voters. They just have to wait out their time in opposition until the electorate are finally exhausted with the other side, at which point their time for power and patronage will arrive. We have a political system without real competition and the sclerosis that right-wing commentators have sought in Whitehall or in the public sector in fact lies at the heart of the political system, where the oxygen of true pluralism barely reaches.

A majoritarian electoral system creates a system of two parties and forces uniformity within those parties. A perusal of our recent political history shows that the dominant factor in deciding which governments we have had for half a century and more is not the preferences of voters, or even who would be best for the country, but who is fighting an opposition that is divided. Thatcher's success was as much the result of Labour divisions as the popularity of her policies. I fear the next period of government is going to demonstrate the same for Labour, who are now barely distinguishable on many issues from Thatcher's policy platform.

Debate and Disagreement Is the Point of Democracy

Imagine a political system where, rather than checking the form and assessing who might win, voters entered an election campaign considering the policy proposals of the political parties and assessing which best matched their aspirations and their vision of a future society. In the context of the UK, this seems hopelessly utopian, but it really shouldn't.

The majority of people in the UK have supported public ownership of essential services, greater investment in health and social care, and higher rates of taxation for those on higher incomes for decades. Survation polling from 2023 showed that 69 per cent of people supported the public ownership of water, while the figure was as high as 78 per cent for the NHS and at 67 per cent for the railway (Shoben, 2022). Polling during the 2024 election campaign indicated that 71 per cent of the population support the introduction of a wealth tax (Conner, 2024). In 2017, a significant number of people voted for an ambitious policy platform that offered just these sorts of policies – for a short interval and imperfectly, the Corbyn-led Labour Party gave expression to progressive support for an alternative and enjoyed a brief period of popularity.

Now imagine if a Corbyn-style political party were a permanent feature of our political system, as it is in other European countries. In 2024, we had the Greens offering fiscal ambition that was similar to Corbyn's Labour, but theirs was matched with stronger protections for nature and the climate. In a pluralist democracy, these parties would not be just a minor part of the Westminster furniture but key players in governing coalitions. Having a wider range of parties and a genuine choice of policies is a necessary precondition for a functional democracy. But it isn't sufficient. We need to be more ambitious, to think about enabling constructive dialogue and debate, and not just inside political parties.

For a number of intersecting reasons, our democracy has become increasingly polarised in recent years. This is not something unique to the UK, although the Brexit vote is a striking example of the use of polarisation to achieve political change. The question of whether we should be members of the EU was used to subvert our whole political system, something evidenced in the *omertà* surrounding the question eight years after the referendum, so that we are not allowed to question it.

The hallowing of the EU referendum result as 'the will of the people' is something unique to that event. But the strategy that achieved it, the deliberate choice of divisive issues and the radicalisation of opinions on both sides so that people can no longer talk to each other, is something that has now become a widespread tactic. The 'culture wars' are just an extension of the Brexit strategy to sideline rational thought and appeal to voters' basest instincts. To radicalise them into two groups and to convince each group that the other threatens them in some essential and dangerous way.

Social media is often blamed for this polarisation, and certainly its spread through smartphones has enabled its rapid diffusion. The creation and reinforcement of thought-bubbles by profit-driven algorithms reinforces people in their righteous views and encourages them to define others as beyond any sort of debatable pale. The constant absorption of our rational minds in the trivia of 'news alerts' or the latest Twitter spat diverts us from the useful reflective thought that a flourishing democracy requires of us.

But it is the choice of politicians whether to follow this trend or to resist and challenge it that will determine whether our democracy flourishes or fails. Jeopardy or joking around are the easiest ways to gain media attention and we have seen politicians follow journalists down this road that denigrates them and drags our whole democratic system into the mire. The interview that is an ambush or picking a fight to give the audience their boost of dopamine has replaced the thoughtful attempt to inform voters about what politicians stand for.

Meanwhile, the short attention span demanded by the ten-second social media video or the 280-character tweet has served the far-right politicians who offer simple solutions to complex problems. Trying to explain the complexity of the political process, where you spend most of your time in grey areas and compromise is the point rather than a sign of betrayal, has turned into a mug's game.

A Democracy that Doesn't Deliver Cannot Hold

But it is too simple to blame technological changes for our political malaise; too simple and also untrue. The main reason that millions of working people in established democracies have lost faith in democracy is that politicians are failing to solve their problems. For decades, politicians of the traditional right and left have refused to challenge the power of corporations and the super-rich. The economic value they create is being siphoned offshore or into the bank accounts of the global 'citizens of nowhere', who they believe have politicians in their pockets.

As already discussed, in the UK the centre of gravity of political opinion is well to the left of governments that have been elected for several decades. The austerity that has driven millions into destitution and destroyed the public services we all rely on never received majority support. George Osborne skilfully exploited the Liberal Democrats to deliver it and then gamed the system to take enough seats from them to win the 2015 election outright. The dance of death with the far right that the Tories have been engaged in since then only holds interest for a minority of voters. Even many of those who vote for UKIP/Brexit/Reform (whatever its latest corporate rebranding may be) are expressing disgust rather than a positive vote for any particular platform.

'A plague on both your houses' is a strong, perhaps dominant and certainly growing electoral motivation. And not just in the UK but across the Western democracies where corporate capture and financialisation have made it impossible for governments to deliver for citizens, even should they wish to. George Galloway's 'two cheeks of the same arse' quip summarises what the lack of pluralism and real electoral competition has brought in its wake. The failures in our system are undermining people's faith in democracy itself.

Voters are desperate to choose politicians like Nigel Farage or George Galloway, who appear to offer the hope of something different and deceitfully promote simple solutions to complex problems. But the capture of the most powerful political parties by corporate interests so that the government, whether red or blue, does not improve people's lives is what enables them to do this.

Revitalising our Democracy

Revitalising our democracy and building genuine pluralism will require a change in our electoral system. But that will only be a first step. We need to build a genuinely competitive system where parties and politicians are on their toes, listening to voters and finding solutions to their problems, because if they don't, somebody else will. Without the insulation of the 'two party system', we could expect to see much better performance by both Labour and the Conservatives, and we will see a wider range of politicians from a diverse range of backgrounds bringing new interests and issues into the political arena. Pluralism would revitalise our democracy by giving space to more exciting and diverse solutions to these problems. It would allow ambitious outsiders to give the establishment politicians a run for their money.

But representation in Parliament is just one aspect of a flourishing democracy. It goes without saying that we need a written constitution, so that we are clear about our rights and so that our governments can no longer flout conventions and make up procedure on the hoof. And of course we should end the embarrassment of an unelected chamber by making the House of Lords fully democratic. But these are just changes to one aspect – the assemblies – of our democratic organisation, which should be seen as a complex ecosystem rather than just 'the Palace of Westminster'.

No democracy can flourish unless its citizens understand the power of their vote and the choices that they can make, as well as having clear and unbiased information. To achieve this, we clearly need the Electoral Commission to have stronger powers both to register political parties and to monitor electoral communications for factual accuracy. Their own website says that 'there are few restrictions on what candidates, political parties or campaigners can say in campaign materials. These restrictions include making or publishing a false statement about the personal character or conduct of a candidate or publishing offensive material.' You cannot make up nonsense about toothpaste or motor vehicles without falling foul of the Advertising Standards Authority. But political party adverts are not regulated for factual accuracy.

Citizenship education is obviously another crucial plank of a successful democracy. The government published curricula for citizenship programmes in schools in 2013, but the House of Lords was critical of the content and approach:

> We have found that citizenship education, which should be the first great opportunity for instilling and developing our values, encouraging social cohesion and creating active citizens, has been neglected. Often it is subsumed into individual development, which, whilst undoubtedly important, is not the same as learning about the political and social structure of the country, how it is governed, how laws are made and how they are enforced by an independent judiciary. Nor does it offer an opportunity of practising civic engagement in schools, local communities and beyond.
> (House of Lords, 2023)

They also criticised the fact that academies are not required to follow the requirement to include citizenship education, that it is held in low esteem and that the GCSE in citizenship and the number of teachers qualified to teach it are both declining. It goes without saying that a flourishing democracy would require much more emphasis on citizenship education and not just in schools but as part of lifelong learning. And if our aim is pluralism then it would be integral that citizenship education be based on taking alternative views seriously and modelling respectful disagreement. The ability to debate and to argue for a position that doesn't correspond with your own view is a useful antidote to the social media thought-bubbles that could become a central party of citizenship education. Perhaps it should be included as a core skill in the national curriculum?

We could also take on board widespread calls for a more deliberative approach to democracy. Parliament took some tentative steps in this direction by setting up a Climate Assembly that reported in September 2020 (Climate Assembly UK, 2020). Unsurprisingly, when given clear information and allowed to discuss the issue of climate action with experts and between themselves, citizens proposed much stronger measures than either of 'the two main parties' would risk including in their manifestos. This was also excellent training in the core skills of a democratic citizen: listening to other views and learning to balance those with your own to build consensus. But the process was undermined by the refusal of the Conservatives to follow through on these policies. In fact, they took the opposite approach, turning the climate policy agenda into a culture war and enabling fossil fuel development in the North Sea.

YouthLink Scotland is pioneering work on building engaged and participatory communities through its Participative Democracy Certificate. This is a process of training young people involved in group decision-making that 'gives participants the opportunity to acknowledge and develop their communication, decision-making and negotiation skills in the context of democratic engagement'. While it is aimed at young people and community groups, it demonstrates the importance of considering negotiation and engagement skills as something that can be learned, practised and improved upon. We should broaden this approach across our whole society.

Compass is one of several organisations in the ecosystem of

democracy organisations that are doing excellent work to encourage true democratic values. But surely such an important project cannot be left on the margins. Given the weakening of democratic support across UK society, this should be a central commitment for us all and, while government funding for inherently political projects is always problematic, we should expect financial support for citizenship programmes in all our communities.

Perhaps most importantly, building a flourishing, participatory and pluralist democracy will require us all to escape the internet for long enough to find time and space to think and then to disagree constructively with others, until we find a consensus and are able to move forward together. Let this be the challenge of the next five years: embrace difference, accommodate the views of 'the other' and think it possible that you may be mistaken.

6

An End to Fantasies: Conservatism and the Right

Robert Saunders

'It's snowing still. And freezing. However,
we haven't had an earthquake lately.'
THE HOUSE AT POOH CORNER (1928)

For the Conservative Party, it was more an exorcism than an election. On 4 July 2024, the most successful electoral force in British history suffered the worst defeat in its 200-year existence. In all parts of the country, against all shades of opposition, Conservatives found their safe seats overturned, their majorities dismantled and their ministers expelled from Parliament. Just five years earlier, after the election of 2019, it had been fashionable to talk of a 'realignment' that could entrench the Conservatives in office for a generation. Instead, without the magnetic forces of Brexit and Jeremy Corbyn to hold it together, that new alignment splintered and broke, shattering its electoral coalition and delivering an epochal reverse.

Destruction at the polls followed disintegration in office. Since the Brexit referendum in 2016, the party has had five different Prime Ministers and has lurched haphazardly from one vision of conservatism to another. Its leaders have been Leavers and Remainers; tax-cutters and fiscal hawks; populists and technocrats; village-fête conservatives and 'thrill-seeking mavericks'. It has talked of the 'small state', the 'active state', the 'deep state' and the 'big society'. It has been engulfed by scandal and overwhelmed by events, bequeathing a toxic combination of high taxes, deteriorating services, economic dysfunction and internal division. The result has been a crisis of ideas, of personnel, of competence and even of conscience. Parties do not have a divine right to survive, and the Conservatives enter opposition with a depleted front bench, a vacuum of direction and a serious competitor on the right. The challenge, as leadership candidate Kemi Badenoch wrote in the weeks after the election, was not just to 'unite', or even to win back support, but to ask, 'What are we uniting around? What are we winning for?'

Those who are *not* Conservatives – including many who will read this book – might legitimately ask why they should care. Some will actively hope that the party's crisis deepens, in a way that locks it out of government for longer and perhaps in perpetuity. Yet there are good reasons to be concerned about the party's plight. Despite the scale of their defeat, the Conservatives remain the largest opposition party, with a constitutional responsibility to scrutinise government and hold ministers to account. Whether they perform that function competently or disintegrate further into conspiratorialism, factionalism and fantasy will have consequences for the quality of government, the conduct of public debate and confidence in democratic politics among voters on the right. The Conservatives remain, at present, the most plausible alternative to Labour as a party of government, at a time when governing is likely to be especially difficult. A scenario in which, if Labour falters, there is either no viable alternative at all or one that cannot safely be entrusted with power, should alarm even those most hostile to Conservative politics.

In addressing those challenges, the party must resist three fantasies that have loomed too large in much early commentary: that defeat was less severe than at first appeared; that its failures in office were the fault of traitors and non-believers; and that there are easy solutions to the policy dilemmas that now confront it. If the party aspires not only to return to government but to develop a viable governing agenda, it must find new solutions to new challenges. That requires it, first, to be honest about the scale and seriousness of its current predicament.

Into the Void

This was the worst result in Conservative history. The party won its lowest ever share of the vote, its lowest number of MPs and lost a record number of Cabinet Ministers (House of Commons Library, 2024). Previous records were not just broken but obliterated: at 23.7 per cent, the Conservative vote share was a full seven points behind its previous nadir in 1997, and its paltry tally of 121 MPs was 22 per cent below the disaster of 1906. Conservatives now supply barely half of all opposition MPs (50.6 per cent), the lowest share for a second party since the coming of universal suffrage. (Even after 2019, Labour supplied 71 per cent of the opposition.) Liz Truss, who became the first former Prime Minister since Ramsay MacDonald to lose her seat, pulled off another record in her South-West Norfolk constituency, inspiring the largest Conservative-to-Labour swing in electoral history (25.9 per cent). This was not just a personal achievement: more than seventy seats saw swings from the Conservatives to Labour that exceeded the previous record (Ford, 2024).

The Conservatives won 6.8 million votes in 2024: less than half their tally in 2019 and their fewest since 1923, when the electorate was less than half the size. They shed support to all parties, in all parts of the country. Overall, 182 seats were lost to Labour, sixty to the Liberal Democrats, five to Reform UK, two each to the Greens and Plaid Cymru, and one to the SNP. The Conservatives retained only eleven out of fifty-eight seats in the south-west, down from forty-eight of fifty-five in 2019. They won less than a third of the seats in the south-east, compared with 88 per cent five years earlier, and surrendered more than half of their seats in the Midlands, retaining 28.9 per cent of its MPs against 78 per cent in 2019. Of the 107 seats outside England, the Conservatives now hold just five – down from twenty at the previous election. Of the 211 seats north of the Midlands, the party holds only eighteen, compared with seventy-four out of 217 in 2019.

Not for the first time, the Conservative vote in 2024 was heavily skewed by age, but its dependence on the elderly is becoming positively dangerous. The party lost to Labour among all age cohorts below the age of sixty-five; pollsters placed it either third or fifth among the 18–34 cohort and only narrowly ahead of Reform and the Lib Dems among 35–44-year-olds (Lord Ashcroft, 2024; IPSOS, 2024). Statistically, one in six of its voters is likely to die before the next election, and those voters are not being replaced among younger cohorts. The party lost across all social classes, including both its traditional supporters among business, the professions and more prosperous voters, and its newer blue-collar constituencies in the 'Red Wall'. Even those who *did* vote Conservative seemed distinctly unenthused, with more than half reporting that it was 'harder' or 'much harder than usual' to decide how to vote (Lord Ashcroft, 2024). If, as the party likes to claim, this was a 'loveless landslide' for Keir Starmer, the Conservative benches are home to a 'reluctant rump'.

Beneath the statistics lie an array of more fundamental problems. The party has torched its reputation for governing competence. From 2016 to 2024, it burned through five Prime Ministers, seven Chancellors of the Exchequer, eight Home Secretaries, seven Health Secretaries, eight Justice Secretaries, nine Education Secretaries and eleven Prisons Ministers. The quality of those appointments was not, to put it delicately, always high, and a lavish approach to the honours system reinforced a perception that ideology or factional alignment overrode competence in the distribution of offices and emoluments.

Problems with personnel were amplified by, and contributed to, failures in performance. 'Partygate' and 'the Mini-Budget' have joined 'Black Wednesday' and 'the Winter of Discontent' as terms so familiar that they barely need quotation marks. Names have great power in politics: voters who could not have explained what the ERM was in 1992, or what Liz Truss was proposing in 2022, instantly recognise those labels and know whom to blame. In the weeks after the election, a slew of reports by the National Audit Office painted a dismaying picture of deteriorating services, lack of direction and poor management of resources, culminating in spectacular overspends for declining levels of provision. Together with soaring waiting lists, a crisis in the courts system, a 'critical failure' in the prison estate, an escalating asylum backlog and spending forecasts that the Office for Budget Responsibility thought it 'generous' to describe as 'a work of fiction', it was hard not to conclude that, in significant areas of the state, the 'natural party of government' had all but abandoned governing (Inman and Elliott, 2024).

All this has left the Conservative 'brand' badly tarnished. A striking feature of Conservative election literature was its reluctance to mention the party by name, preferring to distribute fake 'newspapers' printed in the colours of almost every party except Tory blue (Mortimer, 2024). Few went as far as the Conservative candidate for High Peaks, who appeared in front of a red background labelled 'Labour for Largan', but Tories often appeared strikingly coy about the party for which they were standing (Hazell, 2024). A party whose own candidates are reluctant to be associated with it has a major reputational problem.

The party itself, once famed for its discipline, has become a byword for internal warfare. Talk of 'the five families' – a term borrowed from the New York mafia, whose relations were rarely convivial

– understated the dizzying array of factions struggling for control of the party (Guido Fawkes, 2024). 'National Conservatives', 'Popular Conservatives' and 'New Conservatives' jostled for attention with the European Research Group, the Northern Research Group, the One Nation Caucus, the Net Zero Scrutiny Group, the Common Sense Group and a 'Conservative Democratic Organisation'. The party has acquired an almost Bennite enthusiasm for purity tests and purges, intended to separate 'real' Conservatives from what Liz Truss, in a characteristically bungled acronym, called 'CHINOS: Conservatives In Name Only' (Jacobs, 2024).

As the party narrows its own appeal, it must now confront a serious challenger on the right. For most of the past century, the Conservatives occupied the right of British politics almost without competition; in 2024, by contrast, Reform UK won more than 4 million votes and 14 per cent of the poll. Though it secured just five seats, it came second in ninety-eight more and returned its most charismatic figure, Nigel Farage, for the first time. It outperformed the Conservatives among younger voters, a cohort that could grow if the party finds an equivalent to Jordan Bardella, the youthful sidekick to Marine Le Pen. Reform recruited the Conservatives' former vice-chair, Lee Anderson, and Farage himself is popular with Conservative members – repeatedly joking that he could lead the party by 2026. How to respond to the challenge of Reform – whether to oppose it, partner with it, merge with it or move on to its territory – will be one of the central strategic dilemmas for the Conservative Party over the next four years. That dilemma may become more acute if the far-right street violence seen in August 2024 recurs over the coming years.

Finally, the party risks losing its historic advantage in the press. For nearly 150 years, the Conservatives have been able to rely on a highly partisan media dominated by Tory papers: notably, the *Daily Telegraph*, the *Daily Mail*, the *Daily Express*, *The Sun*, *The Times* and their Sunday outlets. While most of those papers remain loyal, their reach is contracting. Sales of print media have declined vertiginously, and traditional outlets have been displaced, among younger voters in particular, by new media with different alignments. There is, now, a dedicated right-wing news channel, GB News, which is popular with Tory voters and members. Yet despite employing Conservative MPs as presenters, the channel is, to say the least, Reform-curious, and its viewers appear to prefer Reform to the Conservatives (Redfield and Wilton, 2024). If Reform UK endures, the Conservatives may find their long dominance of the media under threat for the first time since the 1880s.

Cold Comfort

There are some embers of hope to be found in the ashes of the Conservatives' fortunes. Bad as it was, the defeat in 2024 could have been worse. The Conservatives did not, as some polls had suggested, win fewer votes than Reform or fewer seats than the Liberal Democrats. They did not drop below 100 MPs, jeopardising their status as the official opposition. Those scenarios were not wholly fanciful: in the fortnight before the election, two pollsters put Reform within a point of the Conservatives, and two more identified a four-point gap. Such polls were outliers, but they received extensive media coverage. Thirty-two Conservatives held on with majorities of less than 2,000 – more than a quarter of their total and enough to lift the party into three figures. That transformed an extinction event into a survivable disaster. By finishing forty-nine seats ahead of the Lib Dems and more than nine percentage points ahead of Reform, the Conservatives maintained their position as the alternative party of government: an achievement that may, in time, appear as significant as Labour holding off the Liberal–SDP Alliance in 1983.

Conservatives might also find comfort in history, for the party has recovered swiftly from previous reverses. Having been crushed in 1906, it was the largest party again by 1911. The Labour majority of 1945 was wiped out by 1950, and the Conservatives returned to power a year later. More recently, the party came fifth in the European Parliament elections of 2019, registering less than 9 per cent of the vote, only to win an eighty-seat majority at Westminster barely six months later. If Labour could recover, in a single term, from disaster in 2019 to triumph in 2024, Conservatives may feel that they can repeat the trick – especially as Labour will now inherit the problems that the Conservatives have left behind.

Labour's own support appears wide rather than deep, securing just 34 per cent of the vote on an alarmingly low turnout. It holds sixty-five seats with a majority of less than 3,000, and sixty-six more with a majority below 5,000. No previous government has won a majority of *any* size on so small a percentage of the vote, and it seems unlikely that the anti-Conservative vote will be so disciplined or so highly motivated after four years of Labour government. As for Reform UK: if Farage's previous parties are any guide, it is likely to prove fractious. Whether Farage, Richard Tice and Lee Anderson will still be in the same party by the end of this parliament remains an open question, and Farage himself clearly feels the pull of American politics. That allure may strengthen if Donald Trump returns to the presidency, opening a larger stage for the Reform leader's talents. Even quite a small drop in the Reform vote could bring substantial numbers of seats back into play, including sixty where the Conservatives came second by 2,504 votes or less.

The novelty of Reform's performance can, in any case, be overstated. Reform won 4.1 million votes in 2024 with 14.3 per cent of the vote, winning five seats and coming second in ninety-eight. In 2015 its predecessor, UKIP, won 3.8 million votes and 12.6 per cent of the poll, winning one seat and coming second in 120. Broadly speaking, 'Faragism' has simply recovered the ground it has lost since the Brexit vote. Of the ninety-eight seats in which Reform is second today, eighty-nine are held by Labour, which suggests that Farage's energies may be directed as much against the new government as against the Conservatives over the coming parliament.

Yet in seeking out the silver lining, Conservatives should not lose focus on the cloud. The fracturing of the vote in 2024, across a larger menu of opposition parties, means that the Conservatives cannot simply rely on a swing back in their direction or assume that a difficult period for the government will work to their advantage. Contrary to popular mythology, parties can improve their position in government, even when times are hard: the Conservative Party increased its share of the vote at every election from 2010 to 2019 and its majority at every election between 1951 and 1959. As Labour and the Liberal Party could attest, opposition parties can as easily go backwards as forwards after a major defeat. The Conservatives held on to more than forty seats in 2024 with a margin of less than 3,000, and even a small deterioration in their position could push them below a hundred seats.

Having leaked support both to Reform on their right and the Liberal Democrats on their left, any new direction risks exacerbating the Conservatives' problems. A movement towards Reform could endanger twenty-nine seats in which the party has a lead of less than 2,000 over Labour or the Liberal Democrats. A movement towards the centre might imperil the nine seats in which Reform lies second, and a much larger number where Reform could wipe out a small majority. Even a modest recovery by the SNP would put four of the Conservatives' five Scottish seats in jeopardy, while comparisons with UKIP's performance in 2015 raise as many questions as they answer. The Conservatives met the challenge of UKIP by conceding its core demands: holding a referendum on EU membership then becoming the party of Brexit. That bolt cannot be fired again, and it served only to suspend, not extinguish, the Faragist advance.

Above all, Conservatives should not take false comfort from Labour's 'loveless landslide'. First Past the Post does not reward vote-share and parties do not set out to maximise it. Labour's strategy was focused on winning votes where they were needed – even denying party workers access to canvassing software in seats regarded either as unwinnable or in the bag – and on allowing other parties to lead the charge where they were better placed to defeat the Conservatives (Adu et al., 2024). Labour ran up spectacular swings in the places they were required, while the Lib Dems' success rested in part on two pillars: the willingness of Labour supporters to vote tactically – Lord Ashcroft's election-day poll found that 46 per cent of Lib Dem voters cast their votes 'to try and stop the party I liked least from winning', rather than 'for the party I most wanted to win' (Lord Ashcroft, 2024) – and a readiness to accept a Labour government as the consequence of an anti-Tory vote.

Fear of Labour had suppressed the Lib Dem vote in 2019; conversely, Lib Dem success in 2024 depended on its voters being comfortable with a Labour premiership (Sloman, 2020). Labour's low vote share should not conceal a much larger proportion of voters who were happy to facilitate a Labour government, not least in order to exclude the Conservatives from power. So where does the party go from here?

Looking Ahead

It is a truism that governments lose elections even when oppositions struggle to win them; and the inheritance of this government is the most parlous in generations. It follows that the Conservatives can undoubtedly win again – and if the goal is *only* to win, then the strategic dilemmas confronting the party become reducible to technocratic questions of coalition-building and electoral mathematics. Would moving left or right secure more votes? Should the party prioritise votes lost to Reform, to Labour or to the Liberal Democrats? What policies might win back the 'Red Wall' or refortify the Conservatives' traditional heartlands? Yet a focus on *how* the party might win risks obscuring the more important question, identified earlier in this chapter, of *why* the party wishes to win, and what it aspires to do in government.

It is not for those outside the party to tell it what its principles or policies should be. But if it wishes to carry out those policies, rather than simply proclaiming them and failing to deliver, it will need to take more seriously the obstacles that lie in their path. Blaming enemies and non-believers in its own ranks – variously identified as 'Blairites', 'Liberal Democrats' or 'Conservatives in Name Only' – may be psychologically satisfying, but it risks repeating the failures of the past fourteen years and feeding the disillusionment of its own supporters.

For example: Conservatives are entitled to argue that taxes are too high and should be reduced. Yet any serious tax-cutting agenda must address the structural pressures that are pushing spending upwards. These include an ageing population, which is driving up NHS and social-care costs; rising defence spending, which is reversing the 'Cold War dividend'; and the economic costs of climate disruption and geo-political instability (Hay, 2024). Those challenges will bear particularly on a party that draws much of its support from the elderly; that has been vocal in support of Ukraine; and that talks of 'Global Britain' and an 'Indo-Pacific tilt'. With Russia unravelling the Cold War settlement, China menacing Taiwan, tensions boiling in the Middle East and the continuing power of an 'America First' ideology in the United States, those pressures are more likely to increase than to abate. If the Conservatives wish to cut taxes while maintaining services for the elderly, raising defence spending and preserving the resilience to deal with climate shocks or future pandemics, they will need to think harder about what the state should *not* be doing and the areas of provision from which it should retreat.

Likewise: if the party wants to reduce immigration and asylum – which it failed to achieve in office – it will require more than tough talking and a taste for law-breaking. It will need to address the challenges for the labour force and the tax system, as the British-born population becomes increasingly elderly. It will need constructive proposals for those sectors of the economy that have become dependent on migrant labour, including agriculture, hospitality, science and the care sector. And it will require a surer understanding of the forces driving the movement of peoples across the world, some of which – such as political instability, regional conflict and climate pressure – lie beyond the control of any one nation. Addressing those challenges is likely to require international co-operation, at a time when the party is increasingly suspicious of international institutions and neuralgic about co-operation with the EU.

In addressing those challenges, the party might find inspiration in its own history. After the landslide defeat of 1945, Conservatism engaged in a striking act of intellectual renewal. The Conservative Research Department, charged by 'Rab' Butler to become the party's 'thinking machine', generated an 'Industrial Charter' (1947), 'Agricultural Charter' (1948) and statement on 'The Right Road for Britain' (1949) that laid down a new policy agenda for government. A Conservative Political Centre was established to 'wrest the initiative in the battle of ideas from the socialists', while a new educational centre, Swinton College, was established to train future Conservative activists. This work not only propelled the party back into government just six years after defeat but armed it with a governing agenda that would endure for a quarter of a century (Saunders, 2019).

In 1974, likewise, the combination of a double electoral defeat and a series of 'U-turns' in government sparked a new wave of intellectual activity. The Conservative historian Robert Blake, who was personally sympathetic to Heath, thought that his government had become 'disorientated' by its 'lack of a guiding purpose', and the years that followed produced a veritable football team of groups and publications, with names like 'Inside Right' and 'Centre Forward'. In meetings of the Selsdon Group and the Conservative Philosophy Group, in speeches by Keith Joseph, in new 'think tanks' like the Centre for Policy Studies (1974) and the Adam Smith Institute (1977), and in the pages of the *Salisbury Review*, new ideas were hammered out for new political and economic circumstances. Though it is unlikely that Margaret Thatcher ever said, 'We must have an ideology', she was keen to restore a sense of intellectual direction and to equip the party with a policy agenda that could be carried into government (Saunders, 2012).

That policy work was less in evidence from 1997 to 2010. In consequence, the party's rhetorical commitments were rarely matched by policy delivery, whether on tax, immigration, 'the big society', 'levelling up', 'a New Deal in Europe' or a Brexit settlement that neither Leavers nor Remainers seem to like. Too often, the party blamed its failure on traitors within and enemies without: whether 'lefty lawyers', 'Remainer civil servants', 'woke elites', 'the blob', the judiciary, the 'economic establishment' or 'Theresa the Remainer'. This is a tendency more commonly associated with the left, which has a long history of blaming defeats – in what might be called the 'Red Flag' theory of politics – on 'cowards' who 'flinch' and 'traitors' who 'sneer'. As history, that theory leaves a great deal to be desired; as an electoral coping mechanism, it is actively destructive. It prevents parties engaging seriously with the causes of their defeat, the challenges they face or the changing conditions under which they might have to govern.

If the Conservative Party continues to blame 'Blairo-Marxists' or 'Conservatives in Name Only' for its failures, it may still return to power. But a party that takes refuge in fantasy and conspiratorialism will struggle to govern effectively or to carry its principles into practice. In 2024, the Conservatives paid a heavy price for their loss of direction and failures in government. Like British politics more broadly, the party badly needs an end to fantasies. Otherwise, it may no longer be fantastical to envisage an end to Conservatism.

Section III

Rethinking the Economy

7

How Has the Economic Narrative Changed and Can It Be Reshaped?

Aditya Chakrabortty and Adam Tooze

Aditya:

It strikes me that looking at Keir Starmer's Labour from a transatlantic perspective we have gone beyond the traditional social democratic, New Labour- and (in the US) New Democrat-style offerings, and now we are in somewhat uncharted terrain. The 2024 election was marked by many as a change election after years of Conservative misrule, but in reality there was no contest of ideas. Neither Labour nor the Tories really had a coherent economic narrative. That applies to the labels we try to attach to competing positions, too. To have something called neoliberalism, you must also have a counter-narrative. But in this election, there was no narrative at all, no real sense of economic history.

Adam:

While the *Financial Times* was recently celebrating the end of neoliberalism, there was a sense that Labour were going to do a new iteration of 'the Third Way', a new version of Clinton–Blair or a new iteration of Brown–Obama in 2009 – the London G20 meeting, when everyone in Gordon Brown's circle was reading books about the New Deal. And the problem, of course, is that the air has gone out of the balloon on both sides of the Atlantic simultaneously. The recent US economic story looks like a theory of change that may not play out in the way people expected. In other words, there's a narrative vacuum. The external anchoring isn't working. But two elements, at least, of neoliberalism are still rock solidly in place. First, everyone knows there has to be growth, and second, everyone knows that Britain's malaise is low investment, so you've got to do something about that. But if you're also committed to not doing a Liz Truss, and you therefore constrain your fiscal options, where on earth are you going to go? You're basically going to try to do what they called PFIs (Private Finance Initiatives) and PPPs (Public Private Partnerships). So who will offer us these? Well, Larry Fink will offer them from BlackRock, and he did, in fact, endorse Starmer's candidacy. Not just a Washington consensus, but a Wall Street consensus.

The idea here is that neoliberalism, insofar as we can speak of it coherently, keeps morphing. In Britain, it moved from the IMF-style 1970s structural adjustment logic to a public enabling of private investment type logic. It's not clear how much of this is paper-tiger stuff, but that's the narrative. And in that case, this incarnation of Labour looks the ticket, right? Because it's about policing what limited public fiscal capacity you have at your disposal by de-risking private investment. And where does that come from? It comes from the global organisers of asset management capitalism. Of course, this was and is American-centric, which is another way of defining what neoliberalism has really been. Neoliberalism is a class politics. It's a set of ideas and a culture, but it's also a practice of government. So public–private partnership is the key to everything you do. It's also a geopolitics. It's about the centre of power being in the United States. It wasn't called the Washington consensus for nothing.

So at that level, this move to Rachel Reeves is basically just from big government to big corporatism with a little wash of Labour in it. Now, will it work? That is the question. Will you get, say, half a percentage point of GDP uptick in your investment and then say, 'We've ticked the box,' while in reality no difference is made to the underlying problems of the UK? This is the vacuum that Aditya describes in his writing. But on the face of it, they're going to convene an 'Investment Summit', and it will be a direct line from Boris Johnson's management of COP26 Glasgow, where they had then Bank of England boss Mark Carney doing the big dance with $133 trillion worth of oil billets that Britain was going to orchestrate towards the green energy revolution. And it all just turned to vapour.

Aditya:

There's obviously a lot in that. Labour thought, OK, that is the bargain we have to make. But this generation of politicians aren't necessarily so clear on what the quid pro quo is: how to drive a hard bargain, how to protect workers, how to get a real return and so on. Secondly, a lot of the talk about financing infrastructure is constrained around infrastructure capital spending, concentrated in energy in particular.

They've got a National Wealth Fund, which is meant to invest, to put public sector money in, with the expectation that the private sector ponies up the rest. The ratio is something like for every pound that the taxpayer chips in, the private sector puts in three pounds. The public contribution will be in the region of £7 billion. Now, when the Tories were talking about how much it would cost to decarbonise the grid in this country, it was in the region of £130 billion.

Adam:

So obviously, in terms of these sums, there is a contradiction. What you could call a neoliberal pantomime.

Aditya:

Both main parties are now obsessed with GDP growth. But no matter how much politicians go on about it, most people in Britain don't benefit that much from GDP growth, which is part of the reason why we had, in that great Brexit referendum, the cry from many that 'it's your bloody GDP, not ours'. When I started as an economics journalist some twenty years ago, Gordon Brown used to talk about possibly getting GDP growth up to 3 per cent a year. And now politicians would be delighted if they could get nearer to 2 per cent. But the real issue is 'growth where, for whom and in what'.

Adam:

New Labour had the idea that the City of London was guiding this. But 2008 proved the breakpoint, not 2010 or 2016. This means that Britain today, like every other advanced economy without a hyperactive massive financial sector bolted on to it, has this question as to how you generate real per capita growth? The inner logic of fixating on growth is that if you're also fixated on another ratio, which is debt-to-GDP, and you are inflation phobic because of the cost-of-living crisis, poverty and inequality the only thing that you can flex is the denominator of the debt-to-GDP ratio. But the broader picture poses the question as to whether the Starmer coalition, within mainstream existing policy discourse, is going to move forward on the investment side, and if so do some sort of public–private China-style 'shared growth' investment strategy, with de-risking. That looks to be the toolkit.

Then there is a malaise of deindustrialisation. The idea comes to be that only manufacturing creates improved productivity, and that is the key to growth, and growth then fixes your fiscal equation. So you say the answer is industrial policy. But that is in danger of becoming a bizarre conflation of a series of disparate moves. Take the US–China situation as a comparison. China is dominant in certain key sectors, so you come up with this odd notion that by subsidising a chip factory somewhere you're going to save the American Republic by winning the next election through creating more blue-collar jobs in Ohio, and so on. It's just classic ideology. And I think Starmer is a soft version of this.

When you actually have to translate this into policy, each link breaks down and it becomes obvious that since not that many people work in manufacturing in Britain anymore, you cannot fix the social malaise with manufacturing jobs. Should you double down on biotech or defence technology? Of course, because Britain has some real capacity in those areas. But don't imply that you can fix the social crisis by ensuring that a biotech hub around Cambridge becomes world beating. The EU relationship could enable elements of a coherent growth strategy that wouldn't require you to deliver that whole package, which is really a fantasy. And you could do the whole Institute of Fiscal Studies policy roster to dramatically improve British society without needing to do macro-policy. Create a more coherent tax system. Eliminate the most egregious malfunctions of the benefit system. These would be huge steps in the right direction for millions of people. But there's no big discourse about those step-by-step improvements, which would be so crucial – because you would then have to talk about poverty and inequality and foreground that dimension.

Aditya:
The ideological spiral leads you towards a 'growth revolution' in which you have a sense that manufacturing jobs are very important. Then you end up going for productivity, which will automatically reduce the number of manufacturing jobs you have. There is no essential join. Yet somehow it all becomes seen as a magic mix. For example, in Blythe in the north-east of England, there is an economic hole that was meant to be fixed by an electric battery factory. And Boris Johnson expected the

private sector to do its bit. He staked a lot on this factory, but he didn't manage to get it off the ground. You can see elements of the same kind of flag-waving economic policy emerging again now. Ed Miliband, the Energy Secretary, wants Britain to become an energy superpower. But we've been there before. George Osborne talked about a Northern Powerhouse. Then it was 'levelling up'. But it didn't happen. Labour's idea is that we're going to become an energy giant with strong manufacturing capacity and that will sort our chronic balance of payments problem. Yet, when I look around, the wind turbines come from Denmark, the solar panels come from China. The one thing we could really do would be retrofitting and adapting all of our buildings. That would create tons of jobs. But it's clearly not the stuff that you can get the private sector to pony up for in a way they can get returns from it. So we're not going to do that easily.

Adam:

To be fair, with the North Sea and offshore wind, Britain is genuinely ideally positioned. But as we know from Brett Christopher's work, the real problem with renewable energy is that when the wind blows in the North Sea, the price of electricity goes to zero. So, you cannot actually make any money exporting. In terms of the decarbonisation agenda, Britain can claim a leading role, but it's not a coherent economic prospectus unless you know exactly where you're going to go with it. So the real challenge for Britain is retrofitting a bunch of nineteenth-century buildings. That's a historic challenge China doesn't have but one Britain should have great expertise in.

Aditya:

Then there is this Starmer language around toolmakers. These are jobs that do not really exist in Britain anymore, yet there are tons of working-class jobs around: from delivery drivers to teaching assistants. But the Labour government is going to run into confrontation over pay in these areas, because people still feel poor after the great cost-of-living crisis shock. Now Labour have put themselves on the hook for spending cuts in the region of £20 billion a year, which is equal to the shutting of a minor government department annually. So it doesn't quite add up. You have black women and others working in care who are seriously underpaid, and there's no plan for them. There was no social care bill in the first King's Speech, despite promises. So Labour is heading for a confrontation with working-class people, though not the sepia-tinted working class of the old industrial era.

Adam:

There's a parallel with America. The Green New Deal in 2008 squarely addressed the realities that we're talking about here. The working class in the United States is diverse, female and in the service sector. And that's what needs to be organised. It is a third of the US economy. Fewer than 10 per cent of the workforce is in manufacturing, and there is a structural failure of political imagination on the centre-left that, when given a push from the right, just reflexes into a Meccano-set version of industrial policy. Because of this focus on the geopolitical competition with China, we now have this arms race in industrial policy, which is focused on things like chip factories, where the only sustainable jobs will be for super experts.

This is not a specifically British problem, it's a recurring feature of deindustrialisation going back to the Thatcher era. She waged war against certain parts of the industrial working class, notably the miners, to change the social and economic balance of Britain. The killer now is AI, which isn't just about routine jobs. It could eliminate a large part of the routine legal workforce, for example, both at the graduate level and clerical level, because AI is going to be better at drafting standard legal documents than humans are. So we're definitely in some sort of hiatus. It feels as though a really big shoe is about to drop. And we're in this weird, liminal space where it's not obvious what the contours of that future are going to be, but current economic discourses seem at odds with the realities that we're actually dealing with.

Adam:

One of those is health, where the UK clearly still chronically underspends. In the US, health as a proportion of GDP is pushing around 20 per cent. But that's a terrible system and it's largely because of waste. If you take a holistic sense of health, if you integrate care, if you think about preventative action in childhood, various types of interventions in stress families at an early stage, focus on happiness or wellness and well-being, this generates alternative measures and economic benefits from investment. As Mark Blyth has remarked, seen one way the economy is a wholly owned subsidiary of health. The entire project is about high-quality life extension, basically.

Aditya:

I'm slightly worried that we've been overly critical of Labour in their early days so far. So it would be good to look at other sides of the account. The Legatum Institute have put out a report about what the public actually want from the economy. There is a section going from one to twenty in terms of what priority they put on various components of policy; and at the top, easily, are health care, education and housing. So much of what was in that research was around the everyday economy, the condition of the high street that you go to. Everyone's high street now looks pretty much empty – so much has gone. So Rachel Reeves might be better off looking at what she wrote in 2018, rather than her rhetoric in 2024. It's about delivering the everyday economy.

Success in that, looking to a second term by connecting with voters economically, is vital – because Reform are now, by vote share, the third largest political force. Farage is a skilful politician, even if he's lazy and cynical. He'll be looking to build on that in 2029, and he will be different. We should take him seriously when he says, 'We're coming for Labour.' That's definitely what he wants to do. Right-wing populism is a threat when things fall apart, when people feel cut off. So a relevant economics is not thinking about getting in this Korean factory, or this whizzy new thing, but sorting out the basics of people's everyday lives – which in many ways don't work for too many of them at the moment. We need to refine our discussion of everyday economics for people, linking back to the cost-of-living crisis.

Adam:

I like that framing a lot. I think you might be able to bridge the gap between the everyday economics and some of 'growthmanship' language with a 'ditches' agenda. Places to dig in and work from. The obvious thing is to stop thinking of health and education as costs and start thinking of them consistently as high-value service provisions. Be in the business of exporting medical services. Britain should not have year-long waiting lists, it should be in the health export market. It has all the resources to do that. This is not inconsistent with selectively bidding for particular manufacturing technologies relevant to that and fitting them within a portfolio. And like it or not, defence is another area where Britain is still in the game. So there's no reason not to double down on those in a selective way, disagreeable as we may find some of the foreign policy that goes with it.

Political philosopher Stuart Hall was unfair to New Labour when he said it didn't have a vision of the new person it was going to create. I started my career under the Tories and ended it in Britain under Blair. And it was completely transforming, in a double sense. They followed through on Major's huge expansion of the number of kids in higher education across the UK, which is the unacknowledged social revolution of our generation. It was still extraordinarily exclusive to go to university in the 1970s, but its current form today has become generic middle class, a prospect for a very large number. What has been created is like a loyal public sector electorate. The Tories hammered this with austerity and broke it in the 2010s. So I think Labour should just go back to basics on that.

What Britain now needs is an unapologetic, unashamed, unabashed expansion of public services, but in a more progressive way: advanced public services. Positioning education and health as pillars of a better society but also as major centres of value generation. The fact that they run through the public budget is incidental to the fact that they are clearly what people want, need and care about – and that they have the capacity to generate value. It's about creating a decent society in which people are less likely to vote for reactionary politics. And it's centered on the younger and middle-aged constituency. The problem is that Starmer actually seems determined to appeal more to the 65-year-old, recently retired *Daily Mail* readers and wave the flag over everything so as to get that vote, which is not where he should be going.

Let's also talk about infrastructure, which surely ought to be a major area of investment and development, because so much of it is crumbling. There's a huge opportunity there and it's been done in the past. Privatised rail where money did not go where it was really desperately needed has not worked. Some massive high-cost prestige projects have failed. But there is real potential.

Aditya:

As Chancellor, Gordon Brown rather cleverly used his government's fiscal rule about borrowing to invest in day-to-day services, as well as what we would call infrastructure. I would hope that the Treasury under Rachel Reeves learns from that. To some extent, I have misgivings about the straightforward renationalisation of things like railways or water. I know the unions will really welcome them, because they'll find it much easier to negotiate. The current negotiation system is a facade, when it is supposed to be about talking to private train operators but actually it's government setting the terms. Clearly, that hasn't worked. Under austerity, that has meant the need to obey constrained fiscal choices, which are actually self-imposed constraints. But I worry about where the investment is going to come from. And I think it would be better if we thought about it in creative ways. Let's take trains. Why not say that anyone who moves into a narrow radius around a train station has to pay something towards upgrading infrastructure, because they're benefitting from that commuter-belt uplift to property prices?

In relation to infrastructure, we talk a lot about bridges, roads and rail, but crucially there's also social infrastructure – 'palaces for the people': libraries, parks and other facilities where people live and spend their lives. That depends upon sustainable and well-functioning local councils. We should be concerned about that, as well.

Adam:

This is where you have to bite the bullet on the fiscal side. I come out of 1980s regulation economics. Not the fancy French kind but the American industrial one. So I think the question of ownership is secondary to the question of how you manage assets. In the 1950s and 1960s, nationalisation meant that you were subject to Treasury rules, which basically didn't allow for large-scale public investment much of the time, didn't apply basic cost-benefit analysis, and rigged interest rates to favour some projects over others. You get neither democracy nor efficiency from public ownership done that way.

Much of infrastructure and green energy does generate an income stream. So harness that to various reframed types of public-private partnership. The devil is in the detail here. But when it comes to immediately remediating the huge surge in child poverty, you just have to put money in place as quickly as you can to the people who need it most. Then in the second tier, you've got to undo the damage from austerity, reversing the de-civilisation of Britain in the 2010s. That requires a central–local fiscal bargain. It's a big political undertaking, but it's crucial. So infrastructure must be put pretty squarely in the 'it will generate revenue' camp.

We are in a kind of fifty-year cycle with various types of rules. There was a reaction against 'the golden age' 1950s and 1960s settlement. We're on an ascending curve of affluence, generally speaking, though that has gone back in Britain for the last ten years. Now we are up against an environmental time constraint that we just didn't understand previously, plus a massively changed global order with the rise of China. Those are the parameters of the conversation we're in. So without going back, it is possible to relook at a lot of the initiatives that would be necessary to address the current crisis and to recognise that in many ways they originate in various types of New Left politics from the 1970s and early 1980s. That's not a bad prospectus for much of the more radical politics we need at the present moment. The challenges that came with Brexit probably got politics to this moment, and it's why the climate issue is so attractive, as with the US Green New Deal idea. It felt dynamic and historic. That is where the trajectory of progressive politics needs to head now.

Aditya:
In London, housing poverty and related issues are horrific for too many people. In the north of England there is a kind of ingrained hopelessness. Some 15 per cent of people in Britain are now on antidepressants, mood-altering drugs to get through the day. It's shocking, right? But the problem we face is that the institutions and forces needed to put this kind of creative politics back on the agenda have either been dismantled or are fragmented. My worry is that some of the best of this

iteration of Labour is led intellectually by young, progressive, university educated think tank types who are quite disembodied from the people that they would hope to speak for. That was one of the problems with a great Green New Deal. So looking back at what occurred with the Yellow Vests across Europe, you can see what happens when the left tries to do climate change without thinking enough about the class aspects of all this.

Adam:

That said, in the first few weeks of the Starmer government, they have tried to talk a language of class. So there is a shift from the Blair era, where we were all supposed to be middle class. I've been tracking the European elections quite closely, along with the British ones. And the really striking thing, as an effect of the British electoral system, is that the Starmerite coalition is less differentiated across constituencies in terms of deprivation and affluence than ever before, and it's more socially balanced than that of its analogues in Europe. It is balanced in support across social classes A to D, though a little more among higher income groups and those with higher education degrees – though that is because of young people. But compared to the Italian or French left, it has constructed an incredibly broad coalition. So I agree that what's striking about the Starmer Labour Party is its emphasis on working-class winners.

But we agree that it's an outdated and even insulting conception of what the working class in Britain actually is, which is not white, male and industrial. And that's the real myth here. So, back to the fiscal point. I'm always a little worried about the mind-forged manacles argument on this, because it licenses a particular approach to neoliberalism and a particular approach to policy that sees bad ideas as the ultimate problem. Therefore, middle-class 'people like us' can fix the problem with Modern Monetary Theory (MMT), for example. In

America, the MMTers genuinely believe that if people can have an epiphany about how money actually works, then our political problems will be solved. It's really a kind of suburban evangelicalism that has a hold in sections of society and politics but doesn't conform to how I personally think the world actually works. So I'm sceptical about that.

Looking back, Labour moved from a relatively self-confident Gordon Brown 'Golden Rule' type model, which was also non-discretionary, to a moment of adventurism and experimentation in the Miliband to Corbyn phase, where there really was a return to left Keynesianism and the Green New Deal. You could invoke the Second World War but in a quite constructive way. It was the 'whatever we can do we can afford' style Keynesianism. This was a challenging moment of opening up public possibility. Now, post-Truss, we're back to having these 'goody two-shoes' fiscal rules, and we're going to tie ourselves and everyone else up. I just hope we can get past that. And I agree with Aditya that the way we do it is to manipulate those rules by playing the old game within the Treasury and recognising that a constraint is actually of one type and not another. It's not helpful to talk about 'maxing out your credit card', it's not helpful to say you don't want to tax wealth creators. This stuff is not going to be useful in two years' time when you actually need to be thinking about borrowing more or taxing those with money a little more.

Aditya:

On the political side, and linking back to class and identity, we have to mention Gaza here. When you say of people who are not voting for you over Gaza that 'we're shaking off the fleas', that language from parts of Labour is disgusting. And what they are doing by that kind of rhetoric – which situates themselves as appealing to a white working class and against a brown working class – is they are ending up causing or exacerbating far-right policies and sectarianism. They are ending up playing in the court of Nigel Farage. That's what really worries me about this. Because there are all kinds of chancers among ethnic minorities who will say, 'Well, look, this party is no longer representing you, come over to my side. We can do deals.' My concern is Labour using this kind of 'class as a culture' position without anything about class politics or class economics. Let alone thinking about how to help people from the working class by asking the different working classes who actually live in this country. By what they do and fail to do in this area, the worry is that Labour are helping to exacerbate a communal politics, which will be particularly dangerous if the economy goes further south. So we get to 2029 with people asking the Labour government, 'Well, what have you done for me lately?'

Adam:

My real fear is that Starmer is too like Giorgia Meloni in Italy. Why? Because if you look at the macroeconomic numbers, Italy is the obvious country to compare the UK to with its stagnant economy. And because of the flag-waving. The fundamental structural material conditions of British society and economy right now are a convergence in which Brexit is the legal and political frame. What does that look like? It looks like a mythical white working-class 'national Labour', a narrow culturalism. I'm white, and obviously I don't suffer the disadvantages of being a Muslim or being a person of colour. But if you were, how on earth could you vote for this kind of party? That, of course, is where we saw a swing against Labour and where the far right are trying to sow division on territory that has been opened up for them. There can be a dark side to Blue Labour. There is a convergent, nationalist, conservative style 'common sense' across British (accurately English) politics, which Starmer seems to articulate. We must not retreat into that. The way forward is an inclusively progressive everyday political and economic agenda of the kind we have been searching for in this exchange.

8

Rethinking Economics for a Transformed and Just Future

Ann Pettifor

The global financial architecture – like the ecosystem – is teetering on the edge of collapse. Built on the ideology of global, disembedded financial markets on the one hand and the shifting sands of over-valued assets on the other, the system of financialised capitalism has leveraged vast mountains of debt and used its power to extract and exploit, to a maximum, earth's finite ecological, economic and human assets.

The system was licensed to undertake such extraction and exploitation by the deregulation era President Nixon launched in 1971, with his decision to unilaterally dismantle the Bretton Woods international financial architecture.

Today the system's foundations and structures are shaky and unstable. When trust in the valuation of $217 trillion in financial assets held by the 'shadow banking' sector evaporates – as it did in August 2007 and again in March 2020 – a volcanic eruption will follow (Financial Stability Board, 2023). Bear in mind that a significant proportion of that $217 trillion includes the world's pension savings, privatised and funnelled into private institutions like BlackRock and other asset management funds – to be 'managed'.

The Bank of England's executive director of financial stability, Andy Haldane, explained in a speech back in 2014 that private asset management companies like the Vanguard Group, BlackRock and State Street Global had scooped up and at that time managed about $87 trillion of the world's savings (that are also obligations to pay out in the future). That sum was equal to the whole of the world's income that year. By 2023, that total had risen to $112 trillion – $12 trillion more than global income (Haldane, 2014).

The risks of this delegation to the private sector of responsibility for pension payments is almost entirely one-sided, as Haldane reminded pensioners in 2014:

> …asset managers do not bear credit, market and liquidity risk on their portfolios. Currently, Blackrock has over $4 trillion of assets under management, but has only $9 billion of assets of its own. Fluctuations in asset values do not threaten the insolvency of an asset manager as they would a bank. Asset managers are, to a large extent, insolvency-remote. (Haldane, 2014)

Not so the world's pensioners.

Global Imbalances

Global debt relative to global income has soared much higher than before the great financial crisis (hereafter GFC). In 2007, the world's total debt (government, non-financial corporations and households) amounted to 198 per cent of global income (GDP) according to McKinsey Global Institute (Lund et al., 2018). That was unbalanced enough to topple the global financial system. Amazingly the basic features of the international financial architecture, including its shaking 'foundations', were kept intact after the GFC by world leaders, including Britain's Labour Party.

By 2020, global debt had reached 256 per cent of GDP (Gaspar et al., 2021). This year, global debt rose by some $1.3 trillion to a new record high of $315 trillion in Q1 2024 – 333 per cent of global GDP (Tiftik et al., 2024). These are staggeringly high imbalances that cannot be sustained. The gravest impact of these high levels of debt is on the lives and livelihoods of the poorest people of the world. Low-income countries are experiencing 'the worst debt crisis ever' according to Development Finance International – and that has implications for the security and stability of millions of innocent people at a time of climate breakdown (Elliott, 2024; Martin, 2023).

To repay public and private debts at what can only be described as today's high, usurious rates of interest requires even more intense extraction of the planet's precious scarce resources, the degradation of nature and even greater exploitation of labour, worldwide. These imbalances and injustices demand a radical rethinking of economics before, or even after, the world economy blows up and craters once again – as it did in 1929, 2007–9 and in March 2020.

By 2024, there were signs of stress in the US banking system, technology markets, commodity markets and residential and commercial property markets. Even the IMF concedes the sector has meaningful vulnerabilities, because it 'is opaque to stakeholders and is growing rapidly under limited prudential oversight. If these trends continue, private credit vulnerabilities may become systemic' (IMF Staff, 2024).

Changing the Nation's Attention

That inevitability makes the development of an alternative global economic order a matter of great urgency. But transformation is not possible as long as orthodox economics prevails, and political parties and the public are persuaded by diversion or distraction to focus on 'bread and circuses' and not on the dangerous dynamics of both the international financial system and its impact on the ecosystem. Above all, change is not possible if the public fail to understand the direct impact the system has on their daily lives and livelihoods.

When not diverted, public attention is directed by orthodox economists, officials and politicians to just one part of the economy: government budgets, or *fiscal policy*. Imbalances, instability and volatility abound within the vast, global financial edifice. And yet far less attention is paid by the economics profession to the *monetary* policies and regulations needed to prevent imbalances and crises.

While the public finances of any one government are undoubtedly important, within the towering complex of reckless globalised finance they do not pose as grave a threat to society as does the semi-detached financial system.

Money

Claudio Borio of the Bank for International Settlements noted in 2018 that

> few issues in economics have generated such heated debates as the nature of money and its role in the economy. What is money? How is it related to debt? How does it influence economic activity? The recent mainstream economic literature is an unfortunate exception. Bar a few who have sailed into these waters, money has been allowed to sink by the macroeconomics profession. And with little or no regrets.
> (Borio, 2018)

Divorcing economic theory from money has had consequences – including the myopia that prevented economists from predicting the GFC. Monetarist and other forms of economic orthodoxy treat money as peripheral – 'a veil' over real transactions between individuals, firms and governments. Money is employed, but as Keynes explained, it is treated by orthodox economists as being in some sense *neutral*. Stefan Eich explains in *The Currency of Politics* that attempts to 'depoliticise' money rely on a performative contradiction – a magician's sleight of hand – insofar as they disavow that such calls are themselves political moves within the politics of money: 'Much of what passes as "depoliticization" would be more accurately described as the de-democratisation of monetary politics, which itself ought to be subjected to democratic scrutiny' (Eich, 2022, p. xv).

This failure to address the nature of money, its systems and dynamics, gives every private financier operating in the deregulated financial system in which money is simply a 'veil' a get out of jail free card. When mainstream economists do think about money, it is in terms of a commodity. Even if they do not go so far as to argue that money is gold, silver or bitcoin, the language of finance used includes concepts like the 'fixed supply' of Bitcoin, the 'shortage' of money and an increase in the velocity of money, implying that money acts like a commodity and is finite.

Economists have known since 1705 when the genius John Law published his *Money and Trade Considered* that money originates everywhere and every time as a promise to pay – an obligation, a credit or debt (Law, 1705). In his *History of Economic Analysis*, Joseph Schumpeter's assessment of the outstanding figures in monetary economics includes John Law (1671–1729), Henry Thornton (1760–1815) and Henry Dunning MacLeod (1821–1902) (Schumpeter, 1954). In the list of academics that understood money, we can include Schumpeter himself, John Maynard Keynes, John Kenneth Galbraith and more recently the brilliant sociologist Geoffrey Ingham.

Money as a promise requires a legally enforceable contract that upholds the promise; a fixed period for repayment, a currency in which the promise is made and a rate of interest – a measure of the risk associated with the money. (Risky borrowers/clients are charged higher rates than sound borrowers. OECD governments are among the safest borrowers.)

The key point is this: all money is a human, social construct or social technology. Money and the system that maintains the issuance and credibility of money was invented and over time developed to help humans transact – buy and sell – without bartering. Above all, and as Keynes argued, the monetary system was built and is upheld in order *to enable us to do what we can do* – within the limits of the biosphere.

Economics and Economists Must Change

If we are to rethink economics, economists must end their obsession with microeconomics – and their habit of drawing macroeconomic conclusions from microeconomic reasoning. Government finances cannot be compared to household finances. Macroeconomic theory must be restored to its proper place: the analysis of aggregate, macroeconomic conditions – in other words, analysis of the economy (and the global economy) as a whole.

Second, we must restore ethics to the profession's analyses and treatment of money, credit and the rate of interest. Global, deregulated capital flows expand and empower both the commercial and the 'shadow banking' system to generate limitless quantities of credit at high, real and usurious rates of interest. This is done without regard to regulation or restraint or to the economy's limits and nature's boundaries. Economists must be reminded of 4,000 years of usury prohibition, on moral, ethical and legal grounds.

We must discredit the Ricardian dogma that economics is a science. That logical abstractions, models and equations can explain the complexity of economic and social life. We must recognise that, thanks to David Ricardo, economics developed not as a science *of* wealth but a science *for* wealth, as Nat Dyer explains in his forthcoming book *Ricardo's Dream* (Dyer, 2025). And that the economic science *for wealth* has built a global economy that serves the interests of wealth and not the interests of those, the majority, who labour by hand or brain. In expunging Ricardian economics, we need to reintegrate morality, power and history into economic theories that inform policy-making.

Economics *Sans* Money, Power and History

This rethinking cannot be confined to the widely discredited economics profession. Mainstream economics is not fit to tackle the herculean task of redesigning the world economy – given that the profession is largely culpable for the mess we're in. The reason for the profession's irrelevance is straightforward: the rigid confines of orthodox, abstract and mathematical economic theory exclude powerful forces driving today's imbalances and inequality: morality, money, power and history.

The refusal – for it is a refusal and not an inability – to integrate morality, money, power and history into economic, financial and trade theory and policies dates back to the doctrines of David Ricardo. A fabulously wealthy banker and speculator, he was, according to John Stuart Mill, 'the true founder of the abstract science of political economy' (Dyer, 2025).

We live with the consequences: today's global economy is deliberately designed to support wealth, not work, as Geoff Tily of the Trades Union Congress has argued (Tily, 2023). And in doing so, it has created imbalances that have violently disturbed the global ecosystem.

To Rethink Economics, Ensure Monetary and Fiscal Policy Work in Tandem

Britain's Labour Party joined in the raucous cheers of international financiers when Chancellor Gordon Brown announced on 6 May 1997 that the Bank of England was to be removed from effective demo-cratic oversight and made 'independent'. The decision simply made it legitimate for central bank technocrats on the government's payroll to prioritise the interests of global capital markets over the interests of the British economy. Since then, instead of fiscal and monetary policy (and institutions) operating in tandem to support government eco-nomic policy, the Bank of England operates in effective opposition to government policy.

During both the GFC of 2007–9 and the March 2020 global finan-cial meltdown, 'the world forgot' the Bank of England used bailouts, quantitative easing and loose monetary policy (i.e. low rates) to further the interests of Wall Street and City of London financiers (Smialek, 2021). The financiers whose activities in private, globalised capital mar-kets had precipitated systemic failure.

Under the recent leadership of Governor Andrew Bailey, the Bank of England governed very publicly against the interests of the 2019–24 Conservative government. The Tory chair of the Treasury Select Com-mittee, Harriett Baldwin MP, complained in the *Financial Times* that by doing so the bank was taking 'a leap in the dark' – a leap likely to incur £130 billion of losses 'to be paid for by the government':

> No major central bank has pursued QT [quantitative tightening] in this way. Both the Federal Reserve and the European Central Bank have opted only for the passive method of allowing their bonds to mature without replacement. The absence of supporting evidence on which the Treasury committee, or indeed the BoE, can predict the impact of its QT programme is why we concluded, this week, that the plans are a leap in the dark for the British economy.
> (Baldwin, 2024)

Under its monetary policy mandate, the bank is required to:

a. maintain price stability, and

b. subject to that, to support the economic policy of Her Majesty's Government, including its objectives for growth and employment (Bank of England Act 1998).

Ignoring this mandate, the bank continues to intervene in fiscal affairs under the new 2024 Labour government. It is doing so, as Professor Daniela Gabor explained, by using its invisible hand to deplete:

> Treasury coffers to boost commercial bank profits. This is the consequence of the institutional arrangement for quantitative easing, through the Asset Purchase Facility [APF] run by the Bank of England. Unique in the world, the APF has cost the UK Treasury around £38 billion in 2023 and a projected £40 billion in 2024. The Bank of England has projected that under the 'optimistic' scenario, the Treasury will pay the APF around £110 billion throughout a 2025–30 government, and net costs could reach £230 billion by 2033, beyond Labour's wildest green-spending dreams.
>
> (Gabor, 2024)

Instead of helping to provide the financing needed for the green transition, the bank will thwart the interests of the Labour government and, as things stand, continue to prioritise the interests of private, international creditors and financial institutions – including fossil interests.

The economics profession's neglect of monetary theory and policy has therefore exacted a high price from the biosphere but also from the economy and society. Its consequences for both people and planet are dire. Not so for the wealthy: the creditors, financiers and asset managers that operate and make huge capital gains from the globalised financial system and who benefit richly from taxpayer-backed central bank largesse. Their capital gains are immense when compared to the profits that more embedded capitalists make from entrepreneurial and industrial activity in the domestic economy.

Public ignorance of the financial system's activities is not accidental. The divorce of fiscal and monetary theory and policy and the separation of fiscal and monetary institutions is a direct consequence of orthodox, mainstream economic theory and policy, as I explain below.

If we are to renew economics for a just, sustainable and interdependent future, we need to alter our focus, join the dots and reintegrate monetary and fiscal theory and policy. Just as we had to adjust our focus, join the dots and integrate experience of the weather and climate. That means throwing much of what passes as orthodox economics overboard.

The Regressive Role of Inequality, Overproduction and Debt

Rethinking economics requires a frank and honest assessment of the current state of the global economy. Thanks largely to the Ricardian legacy, inequality – *between* rich and poor states and *within* rich and poor states – has reached historically unparalleled levels.

In Britain, workers have endured the worst pay squeeze for 200 years and a vast increase in insecure and low-quality work, and as a consequence, public services are in crisis. Of a devastating 15 million people in poverty, more than half are in work. The Resolution Foundation revealed that unprotected departmental current spending per head was cut by 20 per cent over the period 2010–23 (Tily, 2023). 'Financial wealth' was up by more than £800 billion to £1.9 trillion, while annual growth in dividend payments was three times the annual growth in nominal pay (up from double ahead of the crisis).

Total wealth for the top decile over this period was up 70 per cent, from £3.9 trillion to £6.6 trillion. The grotesque parading of an Indian billionaire's wedding excesses in 2024 was but one manifestation of global disparities in wealth.

To Rethink Economics, We Have to Rethink 'Free' Trade

Today's trade imbalances – with some countries enjoying massive surpluses and others in substantial deficit – have predictably led to political tensions and to the rise of protectionism and authoritarianism.

As Klein and Pettis show in *Trade Wars Are Class Wars*, inequality is immensely consequential for the global economy. Here's why: the top 1 per cent of wealth holders do not spend all they earn. There are limits to the number of superyachts, private jets and expansive estates they can buy. In contrast, the 99 per cent spend all their income, using it to keep the roof over their heads, buy food, maintain their health and send their children to university. However, as incomes have fallen in real terms, populations have come to lack the purchasing power needed to buy all that is produced by the export-oriented economy.

Far from society's purchasing power chasing too few goods and services, there are in aggregate terms too many goods and services chasing too little purchasing power. This imbalance has led to high levels of private debt, as the 99 per cent borrow money for housing, health care and food at the same time as firms (which cannot sell all they produce) borrow to compensate for falling sales.

Overproduction and Ecological Breakdown

The consequences of inequality and trade imbalances are the reverse of most conventional economic commentary: *overproduction*, high levels of private debt, and falling incomes. Experience has shown that all these elements lead to global financial crises and ecological breakdown. If we are to rethink the economic system, then ending a system of overproduction that extracts and leaches the planet's finite resources

– in order to repay debts to financiers and creditors unaccountable to society – is unsustainable and morally unacceptable.

Financial Deregulation, Shadow Banking and Debt

To rethink economics, we have to rethink the powers granted to owners of capital to move their money offshore and across borders without encountering the friction and barriers encountered by traders, travellers or migrants.

Unfettered, deregulated cross-border capital flows – that can cross borders at the speed of lightning – strip citizens and their representatives of power over key levers for managing the domestic economy. These include the power to tax large corporations and the wealthy; to manage the exchange rate of the currency; and to maintain low rates of interest for loans across the full spectrum of risk: short- and long-term loans; safe and risky loans; and in real terms (relative to inflation).

Footloose capital flows combined with a dominant US dollar can, by fixing and disrupting the exchange rate of a nation's currency, do substantial harm to producers, exporters, importers and the domestic economy. That in turn damages and raises international trade tensions. Most dangerously, private capital flows influence both central bank and market interest rates – economic levers fundamental to an economy's rate of sustainable investment.

Finally mobile capital can inflate or deflate asset prices – including prices of commodities, property and land. Sky-high property prices and rents in London, Shanghai, Accra and Bogota (to name but a few affected cities) are prime examples of what happens if too much money chases, and inflates, a fixed supply of land. The housing crisis will not be fixed by building more houses but by limiting the 'too much money' that is currently chasing a finite supply of property.

These powers are essential if democratic governments are to respond to the needs of their citizens. By stripping elected governments of vital economic power and rendering politicians impotent, orthodox economic theory has helped spur a rise in protectionism – and authoritarianism – as society clamours for protection from ruthless markets.

Given a proper understanding of money, its institutions and systems, it is entirely possible for societies worldwide to mobilise the finance needed for the transition away from the world's addiction to fossil fuels. The first task is to rescue the macroeconomics of money from the depths to which economists have allowed it to sink and to use that understanding to transform the financial system, its theory, institutions and policies.

To rethink economics requires, at the very least, rethinking the support we give to a private, globalised system that prioritises wealth over work. And in the context of climate breakdown and the collapse of nature in all its diversity, we need to understand that much work has to be done to urgently transform the global system from its excessive dependence on fossil fuels. We will have to substitute clean energy and human labour for the energy of fossil fuels. That vast workload of transformation will not be undertaken by the wealthy – the 1 per cent. It is work that will be done by the 99 per cent.

9

A New Approach to Industrial Policy

Mariana Mazzucato

Approximately ten years ago, I wrote my book *The Entrepreneurial State: Debunking Public vs. Private Sector Myths* off the back of a wave of austerity in the UK that was being implemented in the name of making the UK more competitive (Mazzucato, 2013). What I found through my research, however, is that the development of a competitive economy requires a very active state. This, in turn, necessitates an updated view on industrial policy. Broadly speaking, industrial policy can be understood as government policy or targeted intervention that intends to alter the structure of economic activity toward sectors, technologies or goals that are deemed desirable for economic growth or societal welfare. This may lead to the transformation, promotion or winding down of some sectors. Industrial strategies often combine different measures (Mazzucato, 2018).

In the past, industrial policy has focused on specific sectors or technologies ('picking winners'). Modern industrial policy should instead be oriented around bold goals that will catalyse innovation and investment across multiple sectors. These goals, or 'missions', should be aligned with critical policy priorities, in areas such as health, climate, housing and digital inclusion, enabling the government to direct innovation, investment and ultimately growth towards goals that matter to people and planet (Mazzucato, 2021). This new approach to industrial strategy recognises that decisions about how to foster growth and shape economies cannot be separated from social, environmental and health priorities (Mazzucato, 2018). The *direction* of growth matters.

Importantly, industrial policy marks a clear break from the prevailing New Public Management (NPM) approach that sees the state as having a limited role, fixing rather than shaping markets, and with little active role in innovation or directing growth.

Current Context

The competitiveness of the UK depends on the quality of the goods and services it produces. This is fundamentally linked to the technological, institutional and organisational innovations that transform production, distribution and consumption. Linking industrial policy measures to a system-wide transformation is therefore key.

The UK has a comparatively weak industrial base. Since the 1990s, the UK's manufacturing sector has experienced a more rapid decline in output compared to other European countries as well as the average of high-income countries. Whereas UK manufacturing value added represented around 16 per cent of GDP in the 1990s, it only accounts for 8 per cent today. Additionally, financial instruments such as public venture capital, loans and guarantees (excluding export finance and COVID-19 interventions) represented just 0.1 per cent of the UK's GDP in 2021 – compared to an average of 0.7 per cent, and over 1.5 per cent in countries like France and Italy. The UK's strengths lie primarily in its service sector – not just financial services but professional services, design, the creative sector, education and legal services.

The UK has regressed on climate policies and is falling short of the ambitious goals of the Glasgow Climate pact, for example, moving back the phase-out date of petrol cars, approving a new coal mine, and supporting additional oil and gas exploration within the UK.

Additionally, the UK's response to significant international green industrial strategy initiatives, such as the US Inflation Reduction Act or the EU's Green Deal Industrial Plan, has been lacklustre. These initiatives are attracting green investments, emphasising the urgency for the UK to reaffirm its commitment to climate leadership.

At the COP26 summit, the UK set ambitious goals for 2030 in its Nationally Determined Contribution (NDC), aiming for a minimum 68 per cent reduction in territorial emissions compared to 1990 levels. To realise this goal, emissions reduction efforts outside the power sector need to accelerate nearly fourfold. However, ongoing delays in policy formulation and execution have made achieving the NDC targets increasingly difficult. It is imperative for the UK to articulate a clear strategy focused on the achievement of its NDC goals that will catalyse a cross-sectoral transition towards net zero industries and technologies.

Industrial Policy around the World
In recent years, industrial policy has become increasingly popular with governments around the world as a tool to respond to grand challenges such as climate change, the COVID-19 pandemic, related supply chain issues and inflation, as well as geopolitical tensions. In the US, the Inflation Reduction Act, CHIPS and Science Act and Infrastructure Investment and Jobs Act are playing a catalytic role in stimulating private investment. Similarly, the EU has implemented the EU Green Deal Industrial Plan and European Chips Act. These industrial policies aim not only to catalyse growth, but – to some extent – they also seek to direct growth to shape economies that are greener, more inclusive and more resilient. The UK cannot afford to lag behind or to engage in piecemeal industrial policy. It needs an ambitious, joined-up industrial strategy with a clear vision to compete in the current global context.

A New Framing of the State

To realise the full potential of industrial policy, a new framing of the role of the state in directing growth and shaping markets is needed. This contrasts with the more established view of the role of the state as, at best, fixing market failures. A sustainable and inclusive economy requires a renewed social contract; in particular, one that is premised on the state approaching public-private collaboration with a view to maximising public value, undergirded by a new 'economics of the common good'.

There are five principles that can help to shape the economics of the common good. The first, purpose and directionality, is about promoting outcomes-oriented policies that are in the common interest. The second, co-creation and participation, is about allowing citizens and stakeholders to participate in debate, discussion and consensus-building that brings different voices to the table. The third, collective learning and knowledge-sharing, can support true purpose-oriented partnerships that drive collective intelligence. The fourth, access for all and reward-sharing, speaks to the importance of sharing the benefits of innovation and investment with all the risk-takers in the economy, whether through equity schemes, royalties, pricing or collective funds. The fifth, transparency and accountability, can ensure public legitimacy and engagement by enforcing commitments among all actors and by aligning evaluation mechanisms. To implement these principles in practice, governments must invest in their capacity to engage effectively with businesses and civil society (Mazzucato, 2023a).

Setting a clear direction, through bold goals or 'missions', for industrial policy is important. Governing how the resulting innovation and investment is structured is equally important. Conditionalities are key tools for governing innovation and investment in the interests of the common good, and for changing the behaviour of firms to ensure they are not privatising the gains secured through public investment.

Conditions can be embedded in the contracts that grant businesses access to public sector grants, loans and equity investments, and in the terms of tax benefits and other incentives, to ensure that these deals maximise public value (Mazzucato, 2018; Mazzucato and Rodrik, 2023). Conditionalities can prioritise:

- *Access*: ensuring equitable and affordable access to the resulting products and services (dependent on areas like pricing and intellectual property rights).
- *Directionality*: directing firms' activities towards socially desirable goals (e.g. net zero).
- *Profit-sharing*: requiring profitable firms to share returns (e.g. via royalties or equity with government).
- *Reinvestment*: requiring reinvestment of profits into productive activities (e.g., R&D or worker training).

Mission-Oriented Industrial Policy

Conventional approaches to industrial strategy involve both 'horizontal' policies that seek to improve conditions across the national economy and 'vertical' policies that target interventions in specific areas. Mission-oriented industrial policy shifts the vertical dimension from a focus on sectors to a focus on problems that draw on many different sectors. Instead of 'picking winners', mission-oriented policy is about 'picking the willing' (Mazzucato, 2021).

Mission maps can help visualise the missions, sectors, and projects required to tackle grand challenges. Grand challenges are difficult but important, systemic, and society-wide problems that do not have obvious solutions. Missions are concrete goals that, if achieved, will help to tackle a grand challenge. They set a clear direction for the different actors and sectors whose investment, innovation and effort is required to develop solutions. Sectors are the economic sectors that need to be involved in developing solutions to specific missions, generally in collaboration with one another. Projects are clearly articulated activities or programmes that address part of the broader mission – for example, an R&D programme focused on developing a new product, service or process that could contribute to mission success.

Growth should not be treated as the goal of economic policy but rather as an outcome of well-designed missions. Missions can help steer innovation and investment in the direction of solving societal challenges while also generating technological spill-overs, boosting productivity, creating jobs and generating economic growth. Through a mission-oriented approach, the government can turn challenges into business opportunities and investment pathways. Through industrial policy measures, the UK government can make strategic interventions in the economy to drive competitiveness and, through market-opportunity creation, crowd different forms of finance (such as venture capital) into priority areas. Importantly, missions foster cross-sectoral collaboration, innovation and investment that is focused on solving problems; these are areas where the government has the levers to shape market opportunities that benefit business as well as people and the planet (Mazzucato, 2021).

Missions can lead to a multiplier effect, with an initial public investment generating an amplified impact on GDP by crowding in private investment and innovation. Public investment should focus on generating additionality: incentivising investment that otherwise would not have occurred. Previous evidence has shown a greater multiplier for investments (that is, greater impact on GDP growth, from an initial level of public investment) guided by mission-oriented policies that respond to grand socio-economic and environmental challenges and engage different sectors across the economy (Deleidi, De Lipis, Mazzucato et al., 2019). Shifting from using a static multiplier to more dynamic evaluation methodologies can help governments capture the spillovers generated by and multiplicative effects of mission-oriented public investment.

A mission-oriented approach is not a top-down process. It requires fostering dynamic engagement across society and across sectors to nurture multiple, bottom-up solutions to solving big challenges.

The Oxford–AstraZeneca Vaccine: An Example

The creation of COVID-19 vaccines offers a good example of how an ambitious goal can catalyse investment and innovation, leading to economic as well as public health gains. In the UK, the success of the Ox–AZ vaccine, developed within a year, was possible through the contributions of scientists, venture capitalists, manufacturing experts, regulators, civil servants and volunteers, each playing a pivotal role at various points in the supply chain. This example underscores the effectiveness of a mission-oriented approach in mobilising the capabilities of the public, private and third sectors and in bringing key policy tools – including public procurement, R&D investments, public finance, regulation etc. – into alignment with the mission goal. A case study by the Industrial Strategy Council reveals that government involvement was instrumental at every phase of the Ox–AZ vaccine supply chain. Importantly, the Ox–AZ vaccine (in contrast to other COVID-19 vaccines) was also designed with clear conditions on public investments to ensure access and affordability (WHO Council on the Economics of Health for All, 2023).

Tools, Institutions and Capabilities

To implement a mission-oriented approach to industrial strategy in practice, governments must invest in redesigned tools such as procurement, institutions such as public development banks, and in dynamic capabilities. Mission-oriented industrial strategy constitutes a radical shift and requires a commensurate state transformation (Mazzucato, 2023b).

Public procurement, which represents 12 per cent of GDP in OECD countries, is an effective tool for shaping markets that align with mission-oriented industrial strategy. The UK government spent £306 billion on procuring goods and services in 2020–21. There is a significant opportunity to leverage this spending to create a market pull for innovation and investment that aligns with mission goals. Mission-oriented procurement requires a broader notion of *public value* – which goes beyond the more accepted *social value* framework. This would mean that, rather than providing a static analysis at a single point in time, commissioners would take into account the potential for different providers to contribute towards long-term mission goals and aim to proactively shape the market in that direction. Green public procurement can be seen as a special case of mission-oriented stimulus, whereby public organisations expand markets for sustainable products.

Patient public finance is critical to successful industrial policy. In addition to government spending through budget and fiscal reviews, patient public finance can also stem from sovereign wealth funds and development banks. The governance frameworks guiding these public financial institutions typically insulate them from the pressures of generating immediate returns. This unique position enables them to commit resources to long-term, transformative endeavours, offering a vital source of capital for projects that necessitate extended timelines to mature and yield benefits. A mission-oriented, long-term lens can be applied to public financial institutions at all levels of government, turning governments into investors of first resort rather than lenders of last resort. One local level example is Camden's new Community Wealth Fund, which the Institute for Innovation and Public Purpose informed.

Successful execution of mission-oriented industrial policy will require investment and reform within the civil service to bolster the state's capacity to co-ordinate across ministries and to actively and confidently shape markets and direct growth. Industrial policy measures must be guided by a new understanding of the role of the state in driving broad-scale economic transformation and by investments in the dynamic capabilities required to implement this transformation (Kattel and Mazzucato, 2018). This requires a shift away from austerity measures and away from an over-reliance on large consulting firms, which undercut the capacity of the civil service to solve problems and drive ambitious policy agendas forward (Mazzucato and Collington, 2023).

This chapter is excerpted, with permission, from evidence submitted by Mariana Mazzucato to the UK government's Trade and Industry Committee for its inquiry into industrial policy, concluding in February 2024.

10

Evolving Labour's Work Strategy: Humanising Work, Keeping It Flexible and Enhancing Networks

Julia Hobsbawm

How should Labour respond to a world where the way work is done is changing at incredible scale and speed – and the way that people *feel* about working life is changing just as fast? The tides of COVID-19 have now receded, leaving attitudes to work and capacity to work fundamentally altered. One-fifth of all UK adults of working age are now classified as 'economically inactive' (Office for National Statistics, 2024), which means they are unwilling or unable to work as they did before. Even without this startling fact, work is undeniably undergoing a great re-evaluation across every generation.

This is also a world that bears no relation in terms of the technology of jobs, skills and society to the one left by Labour in 2010. Cast your mind back to when 'Cleggmania' was a famous phrase and no one had heard of Brexit. The wheels of the world of work turned in an analogue way, despite the gathering pace of the digital world. Back then, cloud meant sky, not information storage. In 2010, e-commerce sales were 18 per cent (Office for National Statistics, 2012), unlike today, when 90 per cent of British consumers have bought something online

(Macnaught, 2024). Back in the rose-garden days of the Cameron-led coalition government, the World Economic Forum hadn't yet coined the phrase 'Fourth Industrial Revolution' and Zoom had not been invented. Today's acute anxiety about surveillance at work did not exist, no one monitored keystrokes or swipe-ins – and of course, everyone was always in the office.

And besides, the last time that Labour held office, the equalising but polarising nature of social media was yet to happen – as was the integration of social media platforms and the arrival of apps that can give every workplace a digital profile, presence and voice. We were still awaiting the first corporate scandal caused by Twitter. In 2013, a young PR executive tweeted a thoughtless post just before jumping on a plane. By the time she landed (no airborne internet access then) she was a trending hashtag – #hasjustinelandedyet – and lost her job. Of course, back then, viral did not mean the network effects of the internet – or a communicable airborne virus called coronavirus. This time, it is different.

Labour's response to these quantum shifts could occur through taking a new approach beyond addressing economic inequalities – welcome and necessary though the Employment Rights Bill is. Labour needs to adopt a systematic approach which cuts across any, and all, departments that touch on work (basically all of them). Specifically, it should prioritise three interconnected areas. The first is *humanised work* – namely how to keep the human job, skill and experience front and centre of an increasingly machine age in which automation and the personification of so-called digital co-workers (Marks, 2024) abound.

Secondly, it should include *flexible work*, because the dominant form of work in developed economies is moving away from anything resembling the 9–5 tradition, and an all-collar class of worker is emerging that is termed 'the Flexetariat' (Hobsbawm, 2022a). This reflects not only rising preferences on where and when to work but also the rise of rotational, shift and independent work. By 2025, as much as 40 per cent of the global workforce will be freelance – with all the associated potential advantages and disadvantages (Gerson and Gratton, 2024).

Thirdly: *networked work*. The importance of social capital, connection, loneliness and their impact on well-being and performance are all now well understood (Hertz, 2020). In distributed workforces, in which people are in the same place at the same time less and less often, and in a world where social skills – ranging from the basics of making eye contact to being able to reach the right people to get stuff done – are critical, having strong networks at the heart of any organisation will be vital (Ibarra and Hunter, 2007).

The Human in the Machine

The human must be front and centre of the machine age. Every government department should dust off the shelf the *Taylor Review of Modern Working Practices*, by Matthew Taylor, a Labour grandee who cut his teeth in the No. 10 policy unit (Taylor, 2017). Commissioned under a Conservative government in 2016 by Theresa May, it sets out a blueprint for 'Good Work' which acknowledges the uneasy and complex dance we all now make with tech with which to design, deliver and conduct working life.

We live in a world experiencing more upheaval than at any time since automation and the assembly line a century ago. Not only are white-collar workers experiencing the windy chill of technological transformation previously reserved for their blue-collar colleagues, but AI's impact is far greater than the headline-grabbing large language warrior ChatGPT. This explains Labour's stop-gap announcement within a month of taking office of an investment of £30 million to cover 100 AI-related projects – affecting everything from how NHS prescriptions are dispensed to health and safety in the construction industry (UK Research and Innovation, 2024).

Ensuring that AI and technology's new capabilities help rather than harm human work prospects and experience is a tremendous challenge. Addressing the technological impact on work requires not only regulating matters such as surveillance or a whole suite of deemed risks (TUC, 2024) but the repudiation of a rising narrative, heavily promoted by Silicon Valley, that work is somehow not such a big deal, and that life would be so much more fun if robots and AI assistants did it for us. Let's not forget that Rishi Sunak appeared awestruck (possibly dumbstruck) when Elon Musk famously told him at Bletchley Park that 'you can have a job if you want for personal satisfaction, but AI will do everything' (Kleinman and Seddon, 2023).

The UK is the third largest AI market in the world after the US and China (International Trade Administration, 2023). It is unsurprising that there was no AI in the first raft of legislation when Labour took office, because it will be challenging to unpick the difference between regulating the privacy, security and data collection aspect of AI at work and the fact that we want and need the merits of AI (Towers, 2024).

Policy-makers, however, are clear that AI must be embraced: Ursula von der Leyen, President of the European Commission, told the audience of the World Economic Forum at Davos in January 2024 that 'our future competitiveness depends on AI adoption in our daily businesses, and Europe must up its game and show the way to responsible use of AI. That is AI that enhances human capabilities, improves productivity and serves society' (European Commission, 2024).

A phrase that both worries and reassures has emerged recently – 'keeping the human in the loop'. The challenge, of course, is to do just that and to remember that the application of AI by businesses and government to serve and service customers and consumers is a political and management issue, not a technological one. That is not, though, the way that government departments think. Nor is there a minister responsible for arguably the most important role in any boardroom right now – Human Resources. Human Resources as a function has had to absorb digital technology faster than any others: Josh Bersin, the leading HR analyst, estimates that the average large company has 'eighty employee facing systems, and each one stores large volumes of important data to help manage its own area' (Bersin, 2023).

All too often the digital implementation involves at-scale disconnection. One-way video applications that are not responded to and the rise to an average of forty-four days to apply for a job and go through the process (Semuels, 2023) are signs of a system that has humans using technology in the worst way possible. Government should be addressing this granular aspect because it impacts on well-being. I'm not surprised that Gallup estimates the cost of problems with low employee engagement globally at $8.8 trillion per annum (Dennison, 2024). This is why humanised work should be enshrined in Labour's strategy.

Hybrid Haves and Hybrid Have-Nots

If the politics of technology is as divisive as it is pervasive, so too are arguments around flexibility. In *The Nowhere Office*, I predicted that flexibility was a latent need and desire across the workforce, which, like a genie released from the bottle, would not 'go back' (Hobsbawm, 2021). This prediction proved correct. I based my working assumptions on a close analysis of datasets but also a lengthy career in consulting, running businesses and talking to people about work. It was clear to me for years that 'the office' was every bit as difficult a workplace, differently of course, as a factory floor, and that a myth had built around the idea that the bigger and fancier the office, the more karaoke evenings and beanbags, the better the working experience.

I direct you back to the Gallup data on engagement. Those of us looking at the evidence have known for years that all was not well in the workplace. Well before COVID-19, 12 million working days a year were lost to stress, accounting for 45 per cent of all days lost due to ill health (Hobsbawm, 2017).

Post-pandemic, inevitably the public imagination has seized on flexibility as the main expression of the desire for freedom, autonomy and control over working life. This is practical: the Nobel laureate Claudia Goldin writes expressly about the negative impact on high-flying women's careers when they have children (Ramaswamy, 2023) – what she calls 'the motherhood penalty'. The well-documented difficulties of women having to work through the pandemic and simultaneously manage being 'at work' online while organising their children's schooling are almost too painful to remember.

Women have been at the forefront of net gains, however, of a new culture in which flexible working in the UK has become far more widespread post-pandemic: almost three-quarters of UK employers now offer hybrid or remote work, with 44 per cent offering a form of 'structured hybrid' work and 38 per cent requiring two to three days in the office (Flex Index, 2024).

It is worth remembering that the story of flexible work is, and always has been, a Labour one, even though the final push came, thanks to post-pandemic pressure, from the Conservative-led Flexible Working Bill introduced in 2024 (UK Parliament, 2023). It goes back, however, to the very origin of the Labour movement.

As I have previously argued, concerns about too much work – and not enough rest and leisure – hampering productivity go back to the beginnings of industrialisation, when observers noticed a link between excess work hours, exhausted employees and declining productivity. The nineteenth-century Welsh textile manufacturer and philanthropist Robert Owen called for eight hours' labour, eight hours' recreation, eight hours' rest (becoming a defining feature of socialism in response to business resistance). By 1886, this slogan had crossed the Atlantic to the Knights of Labor Assemblies, and by 1890, the international trade union movement had placed the number of hours people worked each day at the centre of its push for workers' rights.

Fast forward to a quarter of a century ago, when Tony Blair's government first coined the term 'work–life balance' in Parliament in 2000, when Dame Margaret Hodge, then an MP, stood up in the Commons and declared on behalf of the government that 'achieving a good balance between work and the rest of our lives is central to the agenda of the government, and to that of the British public' (Hansard, 2000).

Flexibility is now enshrined as a need by workers – the Chartered Institute for Professional Development (CIPD) estimated that 4 million UK employees changed jobs due to lack of flexibility and 71 per cent say that a flexible working pattern 'is important to them' (CIPD, 2023).

A key challenge is to acknowledge that there is no one-size-fits-all version of hybrid working – a phrase that is a catch-all for multiple modes of working that are not of a linear, same-time-same-place format – and to address the problem of hybrid haves and have-nots in an economy that, in some jobs, still requires an in-person presence in varying degrees. The question is which jobs – and when? And what are the politics of assuming that everyone needs to be always in work and available, when times have so clearly changed? And how will offices need to be repurposed or rebuilt to accommodate the new trends, as is being successfully done already in cities like Manchester?

It is difficult to argue that work that could be done on a laptop at home must be done in an office. Research shows that 69 per cent of people believe they are required to come to work 'due to traditional expectations' (Owl Labs, 2023), and the older generation tend to have a distinct bias towards presenteeism.

A brief word on the four-day week, and specifically the campaign for full-pay shorter working hours. There are many claims that it works, but there is deep irony in the idea that the desire for flexibility can be met by imposing rigidity (Four Day Week Campaign, 2024). Regardless of whether some think that work culture is harmed by hybrid as opposed to full-on presence, which is arguably much harder to manage (and thus costs more), the Flexetariat era is here. Labour will need to think through such incentives as a 'presenteeism premium' (Hobsbawm, 2022b) when grappling with the national mood, but doing so makes more sense when framed against consistently telling the story of work's past, present and future.

Labour should be using the 2025 anniversary of introducing work–life balance into Hansard as a springboard to demonstrate how it led before and will lead again on core issues such as when we work – as well, of course, as where. Flexible work matters.

Networked Work

The third and final cornerstone of Labour's ambition to transform work and working life, and to reflect current times, should be to champion networks and networked work. Labour should take this opportunity to reject the notion that networks are elitist and unmeritocratic. The evidence suggests that while systems to democratise access to jobs and careers with such techniques as 'blind hiring' matter and can help, networks are a sure-fire way to make your own progress in life.

Never has there been a more necessary time for networks in the history of work. Networks are a vital counterpoint to the rising inequality of the system of work – where you need more and more skills, more and more ways through 'the system' of application, and greater interpersonal talent to be, in the parlance, 'your best self'.

As someone who has argued strenuously for years that fostering network capability is both morally right and cost-effective strategically, it was heartening to read recently on the website of No Worker Left

Behind, an American campaign for workplace advancement through community, that:

> the myth of meritocracy in professional networks is being deconstructed by a growing awareness of the value of diversity and inclusivity in the workplace. By fostering networking practices that prioritize these values, we can create a labor market that truly rewards talent, ambition, and, above all, fairness.
> (No Worker Left Behind, 2024)

Mark Granovetter's 'The Strength of Weak Ties', the most famous essay ever written about networks at work, showed the power of word of mouth (Granovetter, 1973). This is partly an argument for how people find work in an increasingly contract- and freelance-based world, where no matter how good the employment rights protections are, the ability to make good and quick connections in perhaps several workplaces at once will matter a great deal.

But, additionally, as fewer people work in the same shift pattern, and more work in different time zones and different locations, the value of forming networks increases, because people are more mobile – quite literally. People working fully remotely (digital nomads) tripled during the pandemic and now sits at around 40 million people worldwide, and sixty-six different countries now offer digital nomad visas, ranging from Antigua to Taiwan.

There is one more key aspect to networks that is already happening and making an impact on the workplace – trade unions. ONS data shows that 90,000 people joined a trade union in 2023, bucking the recent downward trend (TUC, 2024). Trade unions fight for workers' rights but are also a very powerful network. In these atomised times, belonging matters hugely. In times when work puts workers under pressure and tries to avoid collective bargaining, professional loneliness can also be costly.

The United State of Work

Of any government, it should be a Labour one that understands the deep connection that people have to work, not just economically but socially and culturally. Work's DNA is traced throughout art and popular culture. From Charlie Chaplin films to Diego Rivera's street murals; even Edward Hopper's early years were spent illustrating for the *Bulletin of the New York Edison Company* and magazines called *Hotel Management*.

Labour's frontline policy document pre-election was entitled 'Labour's Plan to Make Work Pay: Delivering a New Deal for Working People' (Labour Party, 2024). It emulates the scale and ambition of Roosevelt's New Deal, aiming for an infrastructure and jobs national growth plan. In doing so, it unconsciously channelled the spirit of one of the most popular mass entertainment work songs ever: the New Deal-era Disney tune 'Heigh Ho!'

But 'Heigh Ho!', as it was used during the New Deal era, also illustrates that the United States has set the story of work for the world for a century – in everything the world uses to live and work on – from computing and finance, banking corporate real estate and communications to HR. Studs Terkel's classic book *Working* came out half a century ago and told the stories of people's working life: 'Work is about a search for daily meaning as well as daily bread, for recognition as well as cash, for astonishment rather than torpor; in short, for a sort of life rather than a Monday through Friday sort of dying' (Terkel, 1974).

Except this time it is different. The global workplace is now partly in its own region-specific state of work (for example, India has a different approach to flexibility than France or Germany), but it's also partly in a new 'United State of Work', in which everyone is connected by similar threats and opportunities – changing values, technology, lifestyles, demographics. None of the old ways of working quite do the job.

With its strong history in underpinning industrial and post-industrial work, Labour needs to reclaim from America the story of work and start to become the leader in explaining work's changes and work's history – and the story of work. Because it is very much our national story. There is no global centre dedicated equally to the story of work and the data of work. Labour's Britain should become the brain bank of work's past, present and future.

Restoring Public Life and the Public Sphere

11

Challenging the Corrosion of the Public Sphere and Media Debate

Gavin Esler

A month before Prime Minister Rishi Sunak was soaked by rain while announcing the date of the 2024 British general election, everyone knew it was coming. A select few in Sunak's inner circle were told the precise date. Some used this insider information to bet on the date, sure they would win, creating a mini scandal all across the British media. The rumoured election date had been in November 2024, but a suspicious spike in betting pointed correctly to 4 July.

The media frenzy became emblematic of the decline of standards in British public life. Most British citizens have never read a political manifesto. Most of us would fail to summarise accurately competing economic policies or plans to reinvigorate public services. But every one of us is a judge of character. We understand that – just like the notorious Downing Street drinks parties during coronavirus lockdown – the betting scandal was corrosive of our democracy. It involved one rule for cosy insiders 'in the know' and another for the ignorant mugs who as citizens pay the politicians' wages – you, me, the rest of us. It was just another headline-grabbing example of the corrosion of the public sphere in the UK in the 2020s because it turned on the poor judgement and conduct of people we need to trust at the centre of British political power. That trust has been severely diminished.

In the past two decades, we have witnessed the increasing significance of so-called 'think tanks', often located in Tufton Street close to the Houses of Parliament. Their financing is often impenetrable, but their function is clear. Their best-known 'researchers' and 'experts' are offered influential columns in right-wing magazines and newspapers. The think tankers appear frequently on current affairs shows on the BBC and other reputable broadcasters. Often they appear to act as lobbyists for right-wing and commercial causes. While open about their trenchant views, they remain suspiciously opaque about who pays their wages and for their supposed 'research'.

Meanwhile new media organisations, including GB News, provide a lucrative platform for sitting MPs and others on the right and far right of politics, despite repeated complaints to the regulator Ofcom about political bias. Yet the corrosion of trust goes far beyond a betting scandal or the conduct of a few suspect individuals, media companies and impenetrably funded organisations. It gets to the heart of lies, incompetence and the politics of distraction in British public life.

The first hint the Conservative Party was warming up for an election came with an odd advertisement on social media. It was low-budget 'take our country back' weaponised nostalgia, the kind that worked during the Brexit campaign, a montage of modern British triumphs wrapped in the Union flag. The sales pitch was a reminder to voters that after fourteen years of Conservative governments – and despite potholes, train strikes, inflation, the impossibility of finding an NHS dentist, various scandals and other standard complaints of daily life – we were not just *Great* Britain but, in some unspecified way, world leading.

'Don't let the doomsters and naysayers trick you into talking down our country,' the ad advised. British triumphs were illustrated by a photograph of Rishi Sunak alongside the England football team; King Charles III; two fighter jets; a cargo ship; an Aston Martin; and the assertion that 'Britain is the second most powerful country in the world'. That claim was – at best – nonsense, apparently based on 'voluntary' responses to a survey by a consulting firm most of us have never heard of. Every part of the ad was flawed, beginning with the implication that affection for the England football team as a symbol of British greatness is shared by voters in Wales, Scotland and Northern Ireland. The Aston Martin car company is owned by a Canadian; the F35 fighter is American; the other featured aircraft was a Eurofighter Typhoon, developed by a European consortium. The container ship is MSC *Zoe*, built in South Korea and Swiss-owned. King Charles is (yes!) British… although his (immigrant) forebears changed their name from the German Saxe-Coburg-Gotha to Windsor in 1917 during the First World War. The use of Britain's head of state in party political propaganda is a breach of protocol. The ad was withdrawn.

Apart from ignorance, deceit and the subtext that voters must be too stupid to notice, the core assumption here is that the British political audience finds nostalgia for the UK as 'the second most powerful country' in the world bankable political currency in 2024. Back in 1947, Sir Henry Tizard, an acclaimed scientist and adviser to Clement Attlee's government, explicitly warned that imperial delusions corrode realistic thinking in the public sphere and therefore blight Britain's future as a middle-ranking power. Tizard declared:

> We persist in regarding ourselves as a great power, capable of everything and only temporarily handicapped by economic difficulties. We are not a great power and never will be again. We are a great nation, but if we continue to behave like a great power we shall soon cease to be a great nation.
> (Hennessy, 1989)

The yearning for world-beating, great-power Britain to 'stand alone' frequently resurrects itself in our 21st-century media and political culture. Politicised nostalgia is always corrosive. No society can plan rationally for the future based on delusions in the present about an imagined past. Beyond the 'take our country *back*' Brexit slogan (never forward), Boris Johnson, as both a journalist and as Prime Minister, is emblematic of the problem by combining patriotic delusions of British grandeur with personal delusions of competence. In 2019, when asked what his economic policy might be, he responded, 'Boosterism!' This was his phrase for putting unspecified 'rocket boosters' on the economy as a way of 'turbocharging' it. Back in the real world, Britain turbocharged decline. One marker was health outcomes. In 2010, Sir Michael Marmot revealed that from 1997 until 2010 there had been life-changing improvements in health outcomes in England. But by 2020, when Marmot updated his review, he discovered health outcomes had gone into reverse. We spent much more of our lives in poor health. Health outcomes for women in deprived areas of England were particularly bad: 'For the first time in more than 100 years life expectancy has failed to increase across the country, and for the poorest 10 per cent of women it has actually declined' (Marmot et al., 2020).

The disjunction between boosterish Johnsonian rhetoric and the dismal reality of our daily experience was itself corrosive. The pre-election ad told us we were miraculously the 'second most powerful country in the world' whereas the Marmot report offered facts that confirmed our personal experience: that the United Kingdom was at least in one important measure significantly deteriorating. Despite the Britain-boosters in Westminster and their accomplices in some newspapers, talk radio and supposed 'think tanks', the people of the UK noticed decline in our personal lives as well as public life. We experienced a struggling NHS, near-bankrupt universities, unaffordable housing, crumbling schools, train strikes, doctors' strikes and other systemic failures that made us moan, groan and roll our eyes. Rocket boosters were attached, but mostly to price rises, NHS waiting lists and the use of food banks. Government propaganda about 'world leading' Britain didn't mention hunger. The largest food bank network, the Trussell Trust, had thirty-five food banks in 2010–11, 650 in 2013–14, nearly 1,300 in 2019–20, and 1,699 in 2023–24 (Sosenko et al., 2022). After fourteen years in office, perhaps the Conservative Party had little option except to conduct the 2024 general election in the spirit of an old Marx Brothers joke: 'Who're you gonna believe? Me? Or your own eyes?' The British people believed their own eyes.

The corrosion of public life in any society begins with the disjunction between government propaganda and the reality of life as citizens experience it. The Conservative Home Secretary in 2010 boasted of cutting 20,000 police officers in England and Wales. In July 2019, a different Conservative Home Secretary announced plans to recruit an *additional* 20,000 police officers to fill gaps – gaps created by the earlier cuts. They promised to build forty new hospitals over the next decade. They didn't. And that's fortunate, because staff shortages meant the phantom new hospitals would have had non-existent doctors and nurses. Alice in Wonderland — jam tomorrow, jam yesterday but never jam today – is fairytale politics at its worst, although the gap between propaganda and performance is not exceptional to Britain. Democracies worldwide, the United States, France, Italy, Germany, the Netherlands and others, have all seen what the American scholar Larry Diamond calls a 'democratic recession'. But Britain was exceptionally turbulent. We had five failed Conservative PMs in six years following the self-harm of the Brexit vote in 2016. Post-Brexit turbulence contributed to the self-destruction of the Conservative Party and to a wider loss of trust in British political culture. We had been bombarded with false promises, half-truths, lies (infamously, on the Brexit bus), mis-statements, ignorance and even illegal behaviour.

Taking the public for fools works in the short term, but the corrosion of trust is long lasting.

Trust and System Failure

From the summer of 2023 to the 2024 general election, I spoke at dozens of public meetings and discussions in Scotland, Wales, Northern Ireland and England. Different audiences shared a common sense that something was seriously wrong. There was outrage that political leaders expected that British people had not noticed deceptions in public life. The *Washington Post* calculated that Donald Trump told 30,000 lies in his four years in the White House. No such helpful metric exists in the UK media. But by June 2024, the British Social Attitudes survey reported that 'people's trust in governments and politicians, and confidence in their systems of government, is as low now as it has ever been over the past fifty years, if not lower' (Curtice et al., 2024). The survey noted that British trust levels 'have collapsed since 2021' undermined by lies, the failure of Brexit, the cost-of-living crisis and the egregious and scandalous misbehaviour of some politicians with a 'corrosive effect'. John Curtice concluded that 'the next government will … need to address the concerns of a public that is as doubtful as it has ever been about the trustworthiness and efficacy of the country's system of government' (*The Guardian*, 2024).

Curtice's phrasing is subtle. It is not the trustworthiness of *a* government or *the* government, but our *system of government* that is problematic. Britain's democratic recession is a systemic failure. It goes beyond well-publicised sins of individual politicians. That was confirmed rather than cured by Labour's 2024 'landslide' election victory. Labour promised 'change'. But changing policies and putting new faces on Westminster's green benches does not change loss of faith in the system. The 'landslide' vote instead demonstrated the problem truly is systemic. Labour won two-thirds (64 per cent) of the seats in the House of Commons with only a third (34 per cent) of the vote, and an astonishing 40 per cent of the UK electorate chose not to vote. If apathy were a political party, it would be in government. Imagine 40 per cent of schoolchildren don't turn up for lessons, or 40 per cent of British soldiers refuse to fight? We would be appalled. Yet 40 per cent of potential voters not voting is shrugged off as the new normal.

Labour gained more than 200 seats and has a majority of 172. Yet the 2024 Labour vote was just one per cent higher than during the party's massive *defeat* in December 2019, because for decades both Labour and the Conservatives have benefitted from the peculiarities of our traditional two-party structure, even though the UK is no longer a two-party democracy. The new parliament is composed of Labour, Conservatives, Lib Dems, Reform, SNP, Plaid Cymru, Greens, Sinn Féin and various Ulster unionists. These parties and others compete in a First Past the Post voting system for national elections of a type found in no other European country except Belarus, a pro-Russian dictatorship. Proportional representation is good enough for Parliaments in Scotland, Wales and Northern Ireland, but not for England or the UK in a general election.

Beyond these messy contradictions about what democracy means in one part of the UK being different from another, active political party membership appeals to fewer and fewer of us. In the early 1950s there were around 2.8 million Conservative Party and one million Labour Party members. But by 2022, Conservative membership was just 170,000. Only 81,000 party members voted for Liz Truss, who became our Prime Minister – that's fewer than the 90,000 of us who saw Bruce Springsteen play at Wembley one night in July 2024. By March 2024, Labour claimed 366,000 party members, but the decline in active membership of the UK's two biggest political parties runs parallel with the decline in enthusiasm for voting. Until 1970, more than 75 per cent of the British electorate voted in post-war elections. That fell to 67.3 per cent in 2019 then 59.7 per cent in 2024.

In 2024, Labour, as we noted, took a third of the vote yet won two thirds of the seats. The Conservatives took 24 per cent, Reform 14 per cent, the Liberal Democrats 12 per cent, the Greens 7 per cent. Apathy scored 40 per cent, a symptom of democratic recession to the point of 'demosclerosis'. That's defined by the American author Jonathan Rauch as democracy's progressive loss of the ability to adapt to fix problems (1994). Britain's demosclerosis is caused by a failure to adapt a political system rooted in nineteenth-century ideas of empire to succeed in the multi-polar, multi-party world of the twenty-first century. Yet low voter turnout should not be understood merely as a cause of the corrosion of the British public sphere. It is also a symptom of it. Politicians trying desperately to cut through to voters in our failing system (in the jargon, to 'excite the base') often do not seek to solve problems. They create them. One technique is inciting 'culture wars', offering the politics of distraction, providing noisy entertainment to break the mould of 'politics as usual'. That creates headlines but not solutions. The result is often to persuade voters not to vote because politicians 'are all the same' and 'my vote doesn't matter'. Of course, politicians are not 'all the same', but the politics of distraction is easier than developing achievable policies.

Performative Cruelty: Immigration and Britain's Elites

Immigration was a core issue in 2024 and a key driver for Brexit voters in 2016. In 2010, Prime Minister David Cameron promised to cut net migration to fewer than 100,000 a year. He failed. His Home Secretary Theresa May promised a 'hostile environment'. Net migration continued to rise. By 2022, Rishi Sunak sidestepped the repeated failures on legal migration to focus on those he described as 'illegal'. Boat people numbers are so low as a percentage of all migration they could be an accounting error. In the twelve months to December 2023, approximately 1.22 million people migrated to the United Kingdom, while 532,000 emigrated away from the country, resulting in a net migration figure of 685,000. That same year just 29,000 came to the UK on small boats across the English Channel, 2.3 per cent of the total migrant numbers. The Sunak government, unable or unwilling to address the real issue of UK labour shortages fuelling migration, focused on 'Stop the Boats'. The eye-catching yet unachievable promise was to send failed asylum seekers to Rwanda, a destination apparently plucked at random by Boris Johnson in 2022. The result for Sunak was not merely a deliberately divisive row involving politicians, the media commentariat, the courts and human rights groups. It was a humiliating demonstration of British government incompetence even on their chosen battleground. Days after the 2024 election, an opinion survey revealed that voters of all parties, including Conservatives, were clear why Sunak lost: 'By an incredibly wide margin, voters attribute the Conservatives' loss to incompetence rather than being too right wing or too left wing. Three-quarters of Conservative switchers, regardless of whether they defected to Labour, the Liberal Democrats or Reform UK, cite incompetence as the key reason' (More in Common, 2024).

Sunak's Rwanda distraction proved costly in cash as well as credibility. The National Audit Office (NAO) reported 'a fixed cost of £370 million, plus an additional £120 million once 300 people are relocated to Rwanda' (Walsh and Sumption, 2024). Britain paid one migrant £3,000 to go to Rwanda at the end of April 2024. The policy was then halted in the run-up to the general election. Ten days after the British election, Paul Kagame was re-elected Rwanda's President with a remarkable 99 per cent of the vote. Popular fellow, apparently. The failure of this, the government's most loudly trumpeted and divisive policy, contributed both to the Sunak-as-incompetent narrative and to the further corrosion of trust in government.

There was some good news. Diversity in Britain's political life was more obvious than ever before. The 2024 UK Parliament now has a record number of 264 women MPs, 40 per cent of the total. Rishi Sunak, the Mayor of London Sadiq Khan and the leader of Scottish Labour Anas Sarwar all have family backgrounds in Asia. Arab newspapers noted a new British MP of Yemeni background elected in Sheffield, Abtisam Mohamed. The new British Foreign Secretary, David Lammy, was the first black Briton to study at Harvard Law School. Whatever our divisions, Britain in 2024 appeared a stable, tolerant democracy with its exceptions and challenges (such as the swathe of riots in English towns and cities in the summer of 2024).

British cultural soft power extended around the world even as hard power diminished. Cambridge University could boast more Nobel laureates than any country in the world, except the United States and the UK itself. The BBC retains respect worldwide. So does our legal system. We continue to produce some of the greatest writers, storytellers and Hollywood franchises (*Harry Potter*, *James Bond*, Tolkien). From opera and the Proms to punk and pop, British music spans the globe. ONS surveys consistently show that around three quarters of the British population is 'trusting of most other people'. This figure is 'higher than the average among the OECD countries who participated in the survey'. But only

one-third (35 per cent) of the UK population reported that they trust their national government, lower than the average across the OECD countries (41 per cent). Half (49 per cent) of the UK population said they did not trust the national government ... The integrity of politicians and officials was an important driver of trust, with most people (around two

thirds) stating that officials abiding by the same rules as everybody else was a factor in how much they trust the national government.
(ONS, 2023)

The politicians 'abiding by the same rules' caveat came up repeatedly in the election betting scandal and other examples of peculiar behaviour from those who sought to govern us. As the 2024 campaign was about to begin, a 36-year-old Conservative MP called William Wragg revealed he had sent intimate pictures of himself to a stranger he met on a gay dating site. Wragg allegedly passed on contact details of MP colleagues to the stranger. A sitting MP, Sir Philip Davies, neither confirmed nor denied putting a bet of £8,000 on losing his own seat. Sir Philip Davies' wife, Esther McVey, had a ministerial post as 'Minister for Common Sense'. Davies lost his seat. William Wragg also called himself a 'Common Sense Conservative', a description apparently inconsistent with reality. But the corrosion of public life evident in these scandals is not that which is illegal. It is that which some citizens drawn into party politics appear to consider acceptable.

'How do we end up with such people?' a neighbour complained to me. One answer is that Conservative and Labour membership, as we noted, doesn't reflect the population. Their combined membership of half a million is less than one per cent of the population, whereas – for example – the National Trust for England has 5.3 million members. Political leaders emerge from a small, self-selected group. They are therefore unlikely to be 'like us', the wider public. A third of our Prime Ministers – twenty out of fifty-eight – were educated at the same school – Eton. Half – thirty – were undergraduates at the same university – Oxford (Keir Starmer studied law at the University of Leeds, though he did study later at Oxford). A survey from 2017 claimed that one in ten British people 'always' read political manifestos. More credibly, 67 per cent of people in the same survey claim they *never* read a manifesto or don't know what a manifesto is (BMG Research, 2017). The collapse in viewing figures for TV election debates tells a similar story. In 2010, the first election debate between Gordon Brown, Nick Clegg and David Cameron averaged 9.4 million viewers, a 37 per cent share of the TV audience. By 2019 just 6.8 million viewers watched then Prime Minister Boris Johnson and Labour leader Jeremy Corbyn. By the first debate of June 2024 the audience dropped again to 4.8 million and continued to decline. For context, a peak of 23.8 million UK viewers watched England lose to Spain in the 2024 European Championship final.

Media Literacy and Remaking the Public Sphere

The overarching question, therefore, is what can we do about the corrosion of British public life? Here are a few suggestions. First, recognise the problem. Second, voters and citizens need to become media literate. We need critically to examine what we read in newspapers and hear or see in other media. Who is telling me this? Why? Who pays their salary? Is this fact or opinion? Does this solve a problem or create one? Why should I trust this? Third and most importantly, we need to recognise that disenchantment with political leaders is not primarily about failed individuals. It is about a failing system that promotes mediocrity, tolerates failure and often does not represent the diversity and talent in British life. (Ask yourself: 'How do you get to be Liz Truss?')

The British media could be part of the solution as well as part of the problem. The media landscape facing Labour in 2024 and beyond is the Good, the Bad and the Ugly. The Ugly is the prevalence on social media of rumours, lies, bots, deliberate deceit and malefactors of great wealth, those who stir the public debate with selfish or malicious intent. Foreign actors, those who seek to influence or undermine democracy, have also been a factor in recent campaigns across the world. The Bad is that we live in 'information silos'. We pick up news, newspapers and other media that tend to reinforce rather than overturn our prejudices. Influential British newspapers are owned by people who are not resident in the UK for tax purposes. Some media sources and influencers, including supposed 'think tanks', may be connected to those who might be considered – in Theodore Roosevelt's famous phrase – 'malefactors of great wealth'. Labour will enjoy a short media honeymoon. But – as we discovered in the Blair–Brown years – Conservative-supporting newspapers, other media organisations and those opaque right-wing 'think tanks' will look for evidence – or convenient fictions – with which to hang Labour MPs, the wider government and Keir Starmer in particular. We can also predict that by improving relations with Europe, Labour will be accused in sections of the commentariat of 'undermining' the supposed 'will of the British people', however incoherently expressed in the Brexit referendum.

The Good news is that we have never in living memory had such diverse media and information choices. Any British person with access to the internet can consult online British radio, TV and newspaper resources and also those from abroad. Britain's 'dead trees' print media is much less significant nowadays. Although some newspapers have established an important presence on social media, print newspaper sales have collapsed. Many titles no longer report sales figures publicly. The GB News experiment proves that pumping millions of pounds into an amateurish right-wing TV channel with a tiny viewership can give a platform to selected politicians through clips on social media, but it is an expensive toy. The regulator Ofcom can expect to be revamped for this new media world. And we should also celebrate the extension of personal choice.

Upstart publications such as *Byline Times* and the *New European*, plus the plethora of podcasts and other newsworthy material, plus immediate access online to foreign publications, all provide diverse debate and some optimism for the future. We should teach media literacy in schools, since some of the current media landscape reflects the old computing phrase 'Garbage In, Garbage Out'. A misinformed democracy is an accident waiting to happen. Systemic change is necessary. Above all, we need to debunk our nostalgic delusions. Tizard was right. The UK is not a great power. We will cease to be a great nation if we continue to extol a 'traditional' political system dressed up in the incomprehensibility of an uncodified constitution.

The Victorian historian Lord Macaulay described the British constitution as 'pure gold' compared to the 'paper money' of lesser countries. Yet paying bills in pure gold, and even relying on 'paper money', is of the past, not the future. No country – certainly not the United States or our nearest neighbours in Europe – has an impeccable, trouble-free constitution. But all modern democracies have a basic rule book, including dozens of constitutions written by British scholars for Commonwealth and other countries. The 40 per cent of British voters who don't vote are a measure of democratic failure. The corrosion in British public life corrodes our private lives too, especially when we promote incompetent politicians who mistake self-confidence for competence.

An undereducated, disconsolate and apathetic workforce in a troubled and vastly unequal economy does, however, suit some in positions of influence and power. It softens us up for the politics of distraction and tabloid headlines pretending to be solutions – *Stop The Boats! Take Our Country Back! War on Woke!* An educated, media-literate and well-paid workforce is therefore democracy's secret weapon. It is an antidote to the culture wars and political clickbait. It can begin with understanding that the United Kingdom's democracy has many strengths, but we are not 'the envy of the world'.

We are, however, a developed and relatively stable power with a wonderful history and a great and diverse culture. We are creative. We trust one another. We really do have a history of solving problems…

eventually. And so perhaps we should gain confidence in the wisdom of an American diplomat, George Kennan, back in 1947, that same sober year Henry Tizard tried to offer his corrective to British exceptionalism. In the pessimism at the beginning of the Cold War confrontation with the Soviet Union, Kennan wrote that 'to avoid destruction', the United States 'need only measure up to its own best traditions and prove itself worthy of preservation as a great nation' (1947). It was sound advice for America in the 1940s. It is sound advice for rebuilding our public sphere in the United Kingdom in the 2020s.

12

Making Sense of Culture Wars and Why the Struggle for the Past Matters

Alan Lester

It was a relief to hear Lisa Nandy, the new Culture Secretary, promise that 'the culture war is over' (Walker, 2024). Along with many others, those of us trying to raise awareness of important truths about Britain's colonial past and its legacies are thoroughly sick of it. But it would be a mistake to interpret the last government's divisive interventions on history and heritage as a trivial distraction from the 'real' issues. This aspect of the culture war is a proxy war over one of the most 'wicked problems' confronting our society – persistent racism and the disparities in well-being that arise from it. The new government has some hard choices to make if it wants to deter the recurrence of populist tactics designed to deny, deflect from or opportunistically seize upon these disparities. It will have to do more than just declare peace and hope for the best.

The drowning of Edward Colston's statue in Bristol's harbour made certain questions unavoidable in a Britain still coming to terms with the loss of its imperial role. How can we develop a coherent sense of national heritage when one Briton's celebratory history is another's traumatic history? What kind of history-telling can recognise a divisive past while pointing towards a reparative future? Most urgently, how do we tackle the key inheritance of 400 years of colonialism, a malleable racism that continues to generate inequalities of opportunity and outcome?

The History

Let me first address the arguments reiterated by apologists for the British Empire over the last few years. Empires have been the norm in history. Other empires have also been brutal. Britain's was possible only with indigenous collaboration. Resistance to it was fractured by 'tribal', religious and other distinctions. Its violence was directed against white/European enemies as well as people of colour. Some of its benefits accrued to colonised black and Brown people. Its slave trade was possible only with the assistance of Africans. Trans-Atlantic slavery was not the only form of slavery. Britons are no more villainous than anyone else. British colonists left an infrastructural and institutional legacy from which postcolonial societies have benefitted. Specialist historians can confirm much of this, albeit with certain qualifications. But there is another, blatantly obvious truth about the British Empire that its defenders will never admit, and it shapes our society more profoundly than railways and Parliaments overseas: the British Empire was the most powerful vehicle of white supremacy in history. The culture war over history has been all about the denial of this fact and its implications (Lester, 2024a).

Even the fact that British colonial activities 'out there' shaped modern Britain 'back here' has been widely disavowed for a long time. Despite what most of us were taught at school, Britain's unprecedented Industrial Revolution was not an entirely domestic affair. It was owed in no small measure to slavery and the colonisation of India. 'The key manufacturing regions of the Industrial Revolution relied on access to Atlantic port cities, principally Liverpool, London, Glasgow and Bristol, and to the capital and credit that they generated' through slavery. Plantation management stimulated investments and shipping innovations with knock-on effects for the mortgage and insurance markets and 'linked provincial merchants, manufacturers and banks with the resources of the London money market' (Berg and Hudson, 2023, pp. 9–10). From the late eighteenth-century, the East India Company's exploitation of India 'began to match the enormous extraction of wealth that Britain had historically achieved from the slave-based sugar plantations of the West Indies. Together, the combined surplus in 1801 was equivalent to over 86 per cent of Britain's entire capital formation from domestic savings' (Robins, 2012, p. 206).

Paying British shareholder dividends from rent charged to Indians and using taxes raised in India to purchase commodities that Britons could sell internationally created a continuing 'drain' of capital from India to Britain, while some of the UK's largest transnational companies have their origins in the extraction of resources and labour enforced by colonial regimes (Lester, 2024a).

Even after the government had abolished slavery, British society continued to be associated with it. Much of the compensation payment awarded by the British government to some 40,000 slave owners when their human 'property' was freed in 1834 and amounting to 40 per cent of annual government revenue, flowed into the industrial, infrastructural and financial sectors, sustaining Britain's head-start in industrialisation. At the same time, enslaved black people were 're-leased' into a free-labour market with no access to land and no assets (Hall, 2002, Draper, 2009).

Antislavery did not translate to antiracism. Britain abolished the slave trade in 1807 and the zeal to suppress slavery elsewhere drove patriotic justification for the annexation of further swathes of African territory. Arguments in favour of free trade were used to support the enforced smuggling of narcotics from British India into China during the two Opium Wars of the nineteenth century, with the accompanying demonisation of Chinese people, and there were widespread calls for the 'extermination' of Indians after the uprising of 1857 (Lester et al., 2021).

Before slavery was abolished, men like John Gladstone were already sourcing 'cheap', indentured Indian labour to replace emancipated Africans. Within the half-century *after* the abolition of slavery, British colonists and locally recruited soldiers had decimated Native Americans and Aboriginal Australians; subjected the Xhosa to eight wars of colonial expansion in southern Africa; exploited the Mughal collapse to conquer much of India; and fought three wars against Māori in New Zealand. In 1896, Colonel Callwell wrote a guide for British soldiers on 'campaigns of conquest and annexation', explaining that 'uncivilized races attribute leniency to timidity. A system [of warfare] adapted to [Europe] is out of place among fanatics and savages, who must be thoroughly brought to book and cowed or they will rise again' (Callwell, 1906, pp. 31–2, 23–5, 148). British troops fought over sixty such campaigns in the second half of the nineteenth century alone.

Colonised peoples' experiences under colonial rule varied tremendously. At one extreme, Indigenous societies were all but annihilated in Canada and Australia, where millions of British migrants settled, initially by disease and violence, and then by policies taking children away from Indigenous parents and placing them in foster homes and residential schools. At the other extreme, Indian economic and caste elites accepted the role of junior partner with British rulers to extract wealth from the peasantry. They participated in the empire's global circuits of trade and prospered under the relative political stability of the Raj (Roy, 2020). However, in every colony, white supremacy was maintained, frequently through the suppression of rebellion. When the Colonial Office advised on the distribution of imperial military resources in 1860, its formula was based on each colony's ratio of white colonists to 'natives' in recognition of the intrinsic nature of the British Empire as racially stratified rule without consent (Lester et al., 2021).

Postcolonial Continuities

In contrast to the inequalities inherited from, say, the Roman Empire, which have dissipated over the intervening 1,600 years, those created by colonial exploitation are discernible eight generations later. The reasons for the ongoing harm include the racialised nature of the Atlantic system of slavery in which only black people were enslaved, the 'explanations' of racial difference invented to justify it (racism), and the fact that when the Atlantic system was ended, it was slave owners who were compensated, while enslaved people were 'released' without assets to pass on through subsequent generations.

Fourteen generations of Britons have been conditioned to think of Britain as a white country that governed lesser subjects of colour overseas. That conditioning was confronted by a new reality when hundreds of thousands more black and Asian subjects began to move to Britain just three generations ago. As the empire folded in on itself, there was no decisive rupture or reckoning with prevailing views on racial difference. In 1968 Enoch Powell articulated the rapid shift from an imperialist to a Little (white) Englander mentality, foreseeing 'rivers of blood' if more black and Brown colonial subjects were allowed to settle in the metropole. From 1948, citizens of colour exercising their right to live in the UK were often met with abuse and, almost universally, with everyday discrimination. Those who were not relatively wealthy elites were confined to poorer 'ghetto' housing, schooling and occupation, not through cultural preference, but through harassment and exclusion (Patel, 2021).

Both Labour and Conservative governments responded with increasingly restrictive and racially discriminatory immigration legislation, but just as Atlantic slavery had unintentionally 'unified' diverse

African peoples through their uprooting and 'insertion into the plantation economy', so the experience of racism encountered within Britain forged more integrated black British identities (Hall, 2021, pp. 261–2).

Black-led campaigns like the Bristol Bus Boycotts achieved legislative victories including the Race Relations Act of 1965. But inquiry after inquiry finds that racial discrimination is still structural and institutional regardless of equal civil rights. When David Lammy launched his review of inequalities in the criminal justice system in 2016, he said, 'It was riots in Brixton that led to the Scarman report in 1981. It was the murder of Stephen Lawrence that eventually produced the Macpherson report in 1999. It was more riots in Bradford, Burnley and Oldham that led to the Cantle report in 2001.' Still, he was hopeful 'that we have an opportunity to take another step forward in Britain' (Lammy, 2016). By 2020 his disillusionment was palpable: 'We do not need another review, or report, or commission to tell us what to do. I personally made thirty-five recommendations … It is time for action on the countless reviews, reports and commissions on race that have already been completed' (Lammy, 2020).

Caribbean and British black employees still earn consistently less than white employees (ONS, 2022). Around 17 per cent of the total British population live in social rented housing, but this figure is 48 per cent for black, black British or Caribbean. The highest percentage of people who are unemployed is also in this category, and especially among those aged 16–24 (ONS, 2021). Black offenders are more likely to be remanded in custody and to receive higher sentence lengths than white offenders, for the same offences. People classified as black are 3 per cent of the population but account for 18 per cent of stop and searches, 9 per cent of arrests, 11 per cent of prosecutions, 10 per cent of convictions, 12 per cent of custodial remands, 10 per cent of criminal sentences and 13 per cent of the prison population. Thirty-two per cent of children in prison are black (Ministry of Justice, 2021).

The Windrush scandal was further evidence that no amount of government inquiry would address racial inequalities inherited from centuries of white supremacy. As the official report explained, it had happened in part 'because of the public's and officials' poor understanding of Britain's colonial history, the history of inward and outward migration, and the history of black Britons'.

> Those wrongly caught in the dragnet of the hostile environment were the children of men and women who had been encouraged to migrate to post-war Britain ... These people with their centuries' long links to Britain and British history, were suddenly classified as illegal immigrants in the country they had called home for decades.
> (Olusoga, 2021, p. 532)

When the protests following the murder of George Floyd spread across what Paul Gilroy (1995) has called the 'Black Atlantic' to the UK in June 2020, 'there was a terrible symmetry' with the riots of the early 1980s, both taking place in 'cities that had been enriched by the slave trade and the sugar business'. As David Olusoga notes, the current generation of antiracist activists' 'determination to acknowledge and confront black British history and draw it into the mainstream is new and may well shape our relationship with our national history in the coming decades' (Olusoga, 2021, pp. 517, 534).

The Backlash

The first salvoes of a backlash against any such reshaping of our relationship with this history pre-dated Colston's toppling. In 2016, when students at Oxford campaigned to remove the statue of Cecil Rhodes above the entrance to Oriel College, Nigel Biggar, a theologian, embarked upon a determined revival of intellectual justifications for Rhodes's imperialism. In the wake of the divisive Brexit referendum, the scene was set for Boris Johnson's government to see electoral opportunity in the Black Lives Matter protests. In their immediate aftermath, Housing Secretary Robert Jenrick declared, 'We will save Britain's statues from the woke militants who want to censor our past.' A representative of Culture Secretary Oliver Dowden said that the minister wanted to tell Britain's leading museums, galleries and heritage organisations that they 'must defend our culture and history from the noisy minority of activists constantly trying to do Britain down'. Biggar admitted that 'those like me who think that the "anti-colonialist" narrative is wrong and politically damaging are delighted that the Government is supportive' (Biggar, 2023).

Boris Johnson appointed a commission to report on issues of racial inequity. Rather than identifying structural racism as previous reports had done, the Sewell report argued that black Britons of Caribbean descent had failed to appreciate that 'the system is [no longer] deliberately rigged against' them. The commissioners decided in advance that any racial disparities in the data would either simply be left as 'unexplained' or be explained only on 'neutral' grounds such as 'geography', 'class' or 'sex', as if these are entirely discrete from race (Portes, 2021). The report did not uncover structural racism because it did not allow it as a possibility.

As the report was being aired, over fifty Conservative MPs formed the Common Sense group. Chaired by Sir John Hayes and formed in part of 'red wall' MPs, it described Black Lives Matter as 'an extreme cultural and political group … fuelled by ignorance and an arrogant determination to erase the past and dictate the future', with 'an intolerant woke dogma'. The group's first targets, though, were an academic and a charity (Common Sense, 2021).

Professor Corinne Fowler had co-authored a report using peer-reviewed research to identify National Trust properties' connections with colonial activities of various kinds. Initially it received little attention, but in November 2020, Jacob Rees-Mogg condemned the report in Parliament and members of the Common Sense group signed a letter to the *Telegraph* accusing the National Trust of being 'coloured by cultural Marxist dogma, colloquially known as the "woke agenda"' (Fowler, 2021). The private limited company Restore Trust was founded to continue the campaign against the charity. It has tried three times to get its candidates elected to the National Trust's council, gaining widespread coverage for a story accusing even National Trust scones of being 'woke' (Swerling, 1 April 2024).

Determined to resist greater awareness of colonial history, the *Telegraph* has continued to spread disinformation. Most recently, it previewed Fowler's book *Our Island Stories* without the reviewer having read a word of it (he even got the title wrong) and spread the false claim that teaching guidelines now equate the British Empire with Nazi Germany (Lester 2024b). In August 2021, a group of scholars including Robert Tombs, Andrew Roberts and Nigel Biggar banded together to create History Reclaimed. It too has since registered as a private company. Tombs, a retired specialist in French and English history, and David Abulafia, a specialist in the early modern Mediterranean, now supply a stream of articles to the *Telegraph* with titles such as 'The Rewriting of History Has Taken a Sinister Turn'; 'Time for Historians to Fight Back against the Ideologues Who Want to Tear Down the Past', and 'Woke Activists, Take Note: There Is No Public Appetite for Erasing British History'.

Perhaps the most telling of their headlines was 'The "Antiracist" Mission to Destroy Britain Is Working – and We Have Surrendered'. It takes but a moment to appreciate the kind of Britain that would be destroyed by *anti*-racism.

A new element was added to the barrage of historical negation in April 2024, when Suella Braverman and the Institute of Economic Affairs insisted that slavery and colonial exploitation had made no contribution to Britain's economic growth. Braverman used the IEA's superficial and cherry-picked 'research' to argue that since the 'UK's wealth isn't from white privilege and colonialism' the call from former colonies for reparations is misguided (Lester, 2024c).

How Britain Needs to Change

Britishness is being reimagined in the wake of empire, just as it always has been. The governments' choice is whether to encourage, facilitate, tolerate or resist the varieties of reinvention.

Stuart Hall helpfully contrasted two ways of redefining cultural identity. One is to try to find 'the common historical experiences and shared cultural codes which provide us, as "one people," with stable, unchanging and continuous frames of reference and meaning, beneath the shifting divisions and vicissitudes of our actual history'. The other is 'a quite different practice … – not the rediscovery but the production of identity … Not an identity grounded in the archaeology, but in the retelling of the past.' This more progressive definition:

> recognises that, as well as the many points of similarity, there are also critical points of deep and significant difference which constitute 'what we really are' or rather – since history has intervened – 'we have become'. We cannot speak for very long, with any exactness, about 'one experience, one identity,' without acknowledging its other side – the ruptures and discontinuities which constitute, precisely the … 'uniqueness'.
> (Hall, 2021, pp. 259–60)

Teaching about the divergent experiences of colonialism, and the multiple identities that have come to constitute Britishness as a result of it, is not only a means of understanding the past but also the vehicle enabling us to move on from it. We need to teach colonial history not as something 'we' did to 'them', but as something done to those of us formerly described as 'other'. The new government should embark upon symbolic, rhetorical and material changes to reflect an emerging British identity comprised of many interwoven trajectories.

Even though the threat to imperial statues was exaggerated, the Conservative government's Retain and Explain policy is, for the most part, unobjectionable in principle. In practice, though, it must mean more than just Retain. The former government's Heritage Advisory Board insists upon many layers of consultation and delay before any explanation can be added, but statues can be reimagined as guides to those diverse trajectories shaping contemporary Britishness. An example is the new interpretation board for Redvers Buller's statue in Exeter, which follows his military career through the British Empire to link British communities from India, China, Canada, West Africa, Egypt, Sudan and South Africa (Lester, 2023).

The heritage organisations responsible for our country houses, museums and archives must be freed to interpret the relevant past at arm's length from government. The government should promote a vision of a postcolonial and multiracial Britain in which black historical experience is no longer refuted.

When right-wing think tanks supply misinformation about history, regulated broadcasters and especially the BBC must no longer treat them as if they provide disinterested expertise. We have seen during the COVID-19 crisis and in discussions of climate change that the pursuit of 'balance' risks generating a false equivalence between scientific consensus and fringe denialism. In regulated media coverage of colonial history, tendentious culture warriors' falsifications should not be weighed equally with the work of professional historians, whose work abides by ethical research codes and is subject to peer review. History is no more just one person's opinion versus another's than is science.

The government should disown the Sewell report, but there is no need for a new commission on racial disparity. The data is there already.

Recommendations from previous inquiries should be implemented. More fundamentally though, the government should recognise that the persistent regeneration of racial disparities has never yet been tackled. Addressing those disparities means listening to the demands of anti-racist activists for structural change, rather than dismissing them as a threat to social order. The reforms required will not be structural unless they are shaped by those demanding them.

The government should consider the analysis behind Black Lives Matter's call for a new kind of 'abolition', of a system that continues to police, criminalise and punish black people disproportionately. The demands of the first wave of abolitionists to dismantle slavery were seen as far too radical to be taken seriously in the 1790s. Within them, though, lay the 'common sense' of future liberals and centrists. The new abolitionists of the Black Atlantic argue for a partial deflection of resources from the endless cycle of ethnic minority policing, surveillance and imprisonment into investments on behalf of communities affected by poverty and racism (Gilmore, 2022).

In the international arena, demands for reparations are not going to recede because the UK government buries its head in the sand. Along with the most effective humanitarian interventions in history, reparations can be self-interested. The UK government should take the lead on the existential threat facing us all. Fossil-fuel driven colonial expansion initiated the mounting challenge of climate change, and leadership in this area, enabling low-carbon technology transfer especially to former colonies affected by trans-Atlantic slavery, will grant the UK a global role in which its citizens can take renewed pride. As Ruth Wilson Gilmore insists, the new Abolitionism 'has to take seriously the problem of environmental harm, environmental racism, and environmental degradation ... and it has to be international. It has to stretch across borders so that we can consolidate our strength, our experience and our vision' (Gilmore, 2022, p. 22).

13

The Radical Way: A Path to a 21st-Century Welfare State

Hilary Cottam

'… tell them not to feel sorry for me – that's not what it's about. I have to start changing things for the better and for the kids too. Things are looking good already. Things need to change so that it doesn't happen to other people too.'

Tara, a mother of four children in Swindon, was full of hope. It was the early 2000s, her life was back on track: she had steady work, her house had been repaired and her children – one of whom had been in care – were living at home and back in school. It still wasn't easy. If you have grown up in poverty or with abuse, if every day you have to make calculations to stretch a small budget and, if on some days the demons descend, you might always need a safe place to turn from time to time. But Tara had been part of a new approach to family work called Life and, with immense personal courage and sustained professional support, she was on a new life path (Cottam, 2018).

Tara is still well and her now grown-up children are also thriving, but in the intervening years, the infrastructure of support that enabled her to change paths and flourish has unravelled in ways that neither of us could have imagined. Poverty has escalated, homelessness has become endemic, children have been taken into care in steeply rising numbers (despite the evidence of damaging outcomes) and work has increasingly failed to provide security or stability (Curtis, 2022; Machin, 2024; Rowntree, 2024; Savage, 2021).

Raw Honesty

When Keir Starmer assumed office and convened the press on 6 July 2024, he spoke powerfully, from and to the heart, about duty and the ethics of public service. And he talked about something else: the need for 'raw honesty'.

Raw honesty, for those of us whose work is rooted in communities and who see injustices of race, class and poverty every day, means two things. First, a recognition of how bad things are: let's not pretend. Second, a recognition that the old ways don't work; that the task is much bigger than one of simply repairing a broken twentieth-century social infrastructure, an infrastructure that served us well but which was designed with a very different economy and society in mind.

What is specific and different about this moment? This is the question (borrowed from Gramsci) the cultural theorist Stuart Hall suggested we ask if we want to make change. 'Think about problems', Hall urged, 'not as you'd like them to be, not as you think they were ten years ago, not as they're written about in sacred texts, but as they really are' (Taylor, 2007).

The Context of Hope and Challenge

Today's context is one of radical uncertainty. 'We are standing on unstable ground' is a phrase that repeats, as I have journeyed with my work in recent years from Barking to Barnsley, Barrow to Kilmarnock. The precarity of work and the disintegration of our social safety net has left so many of us, from very different walks of life, feeling anxious and unsure.

A technological revolution, an ecological crisis (driving among other things levels of migration that will grow exponentially), demographic trends, an exhaustion with deep injustice: these are deep and tangled shifts that are creating exponential change within our societies and our economies, within our cultures and our minds.

The challenge is clear: to flourish, we need a 21st-century welfare state that can respond to this conjuncture, a set of systems that can help us transition and thrive in a new context, just as the twentieth-century welfare state so successfully enabled us to transition into an era of carbon-based mass production. We need a government that can tell a story of vision; a story that speaks with honesty about the possibilities and challenges; that can make sense of what is happening by showing us a new path, in which each and every one of us has a place. And we need a set of renewed institutions that can provide us with the capabilities, skills and human connections we need today: new forms of learning, health systems that can tend to our minds and bodies, family support, neighbourhood places and perhaps above all, new forms of care that remind us that we are not alone, that we are and can be capable.

It could be a time of hope. Many were not served by the economies and social systems we are leaving behind. Rupture, however painful, creates opportunity and spaces for the new to grow. In response to crisis, everywhere new ways of living have already taken root. These include new approaches to health, to care, to learning and to neighbourhood life. The new is at the margins, fragile and often invisible to those with power at the centre, but these new approaches contain the seeds of a new welfare system (Cottam, 2020).

Care: The Heart of 21st-Century Welfare

The new government have told us they will not address care in the short term. They argue there is no money. They will instead create a commission of inquiry. This strategy is an admission that, viewed through the lens of twentieth-century welfare, care is intractable, an issue to be moved sideways, perhaps returned to later. In the past twenty-five years, there has been a commission or inquiry into care almost every eighteen months (twelve government papers, five independent reviews and one royal commission). It seems unlikely that another commission will find anything new. It's also clear that another way forward is at hand, one that would start with a different formulation of the challenge, leading to some very different answers and wider lessons for a new welfare state.

Reframing Care

In 'official' British, this usually means a narrow conversation about services, and in particular the crisis in adult social care. We are living longer lives, which is something to celebrate, but we also need care in our older age as we develop complex conditions that make independent living harder, if not impossible. How to pay for such services and where to find the care workers when one in ten adult social care positions stand vacant (King's Fund, 2024)?

Care, however, is not just about older people. Firstly, the fastest-growing group of people with care needs are young adults. Secondly, care is life-wide: we need care as young children, at different points when we face challenges or disabilities and in older age. It is our need for care (and to care) that makes us human; an ancient need that is deeply wired within us.

'Who is going to care about us and how will we care about each other?' A young graduate I met in Grimsby demanded. 'There is a hole in our society… There is "care", but no one feels cared for,' a friend responded, with visible distress. This small group of young people were not yet parents or of an age where their own parents need care, but uninvited (we were collaborating on a project about work), they talked with heat and passion about the subject.

A hole where care should be causes our sense of instability, leaving us to juggle impossible social and economic contradictions. Care is not simply about one life stage, and nor is it just a question of budgets or service provision. Care is the thread that binds us, that underpins the functioning (or not) of our families, our workplaces and our schools. Care is the connection that makes our democracy function. Care is the foundation of a 21st-century welfare state, and the design of new systems cannot wait.

Start at Work

In the communities where I work, the challenges of care are frequently referred to as 'the juggle, juggle'. Unofficial stories about care start not with services but with the need to rethink the boundaries between paid work (production) and unpaid work (reproduction).

Most of us would like to care for each other – for our families, our friends, for the nature on our doorstep. Of course, we don't want to be left only caring, but this is too often the choice: care or work. One in four British adults – 11 million people are trying to care for someone around their work. A further 5 million have given up working altogether to care for family members, finding the tensions impossible to juggle. Many of those not 'working' are over fifty and caring; the same individuals the government berate and try to encourage to work without understanding this impossible tension or the role of being an unpaid carer (Kenway, 2023).

Labour's New Deal for Working People has the potential to be a critical care intervention. Predictable flexibility and secure work contracts, both of which the deal address, make it possible to plan time to care. Other small things can make a difference too: having your mobile phone with you so you can be contacted in an emergency will often determine if a working mother, for example, will take a job. In this country and globally, there is mounting evidence that shows workplaces that allow flexibility for care attract a committed, stable and talented workforce (Cottam, 2025). This new government can and should ask employers to step up and commit to a care charter.

Strengthen Community Infrastructure

Over a decade ago I started a group of community organisations called Circle. A cross between a concierge service and a social club, Circles are local organisations for those over fifty offering on-demand, practical help and strong social connection – things to do with people you like. Data on the first 10,000 members showed a 26 per cent reduction in the unnecessary reliance on formal services; an 88 per cent increase in social activity; 25 per cent increase in volunteering; and a 20 per cent reduction in hospital readmissions. Local authority savings in the first two years of operation were in excess of £2 million net of innovation costs. Further savings accrued to health partners and today Circles continue to provide strong social support across the Greater Manchester region (Cottam, 2018).

Across Britain, we find similar work. In Barrow, Women's Community Matters is a place to sit and rest, to find help with a struggling teenager, refuge from a violent partner or support with an ailing parent. One organisation in a local network called The Barrow Way, the doors are always open. There is no threshold, no need to prove how bad things are or how little you have; if you turn up, you are in the right place, and you will be cared for. All these community-rooted organisations are threadbare. Leaders in particular must do extraordinary work to motivate teams and to raise funds as needs escalate and resources become ever tighter. But this community infrastructure is the spine of an affordable 21st-century care system.

In most cases the support on offer will not be called care, it will not follow a menu, it will not have the resource to track every outcome, it will not 'do' anything to you, but it will provide the social glue, the solidarity and support that we all need in different ways to thrive in the places that we live. Finance is already available for this infrastructure, but it is fragmented in innovation pots, tied to resource-hungry bidding processes and centrally dictated policies. The role of government must be to liberate resource and consolidate funds in the hands of coalitions of community groups with ten-year horizons. This cannot wait.

Care Services

Sometimes, we do need a little more. We need expert help. When this happens, we want the professional care service to similarly feel human, co-operative, fluid and flexible. Unfortunately, when we finally find our way to the top of a waiting list, we are invariably greeted by a very different culture, one which is closed, inflexible and unresponsive. Whether our challenge is finding support for a beloved parent or a teenager in mental distress, or if like Tara we are beset by financial, social and psychological challenges, our professional welfare systems too often leave us feeling bereft, angry and uncared for.

Life, the service that worked with Tara, challenged incumbent approaches with impressive results, in the most challenging of circumstances. Across the local authorities where the service was designed, professionals from a range of services came together as one team, with one mission and one budget, to support each family into a life that they would like to lead. The role of the team was to stand beside the family, working at the family's pace and to their priorities. Tara needed a new washing machine, so her children were not bullied at school. With the washing machine in place, truancy officers were no longer needed and, with a bit of space at home, Tara could start to face some deeper challenges. For those without experience of family support services, it might be hard to understand how different this logic is to traditional approaches where professionals trip over each other, each with a menu and script that must be followed, regardless of circumstances and competing interests; 'stop smoking', 'get a job'; these might – and were – all things Tara wanted to do, but as commands barked from above, nothing changed.

The Life programme gave experienced professionals the licence and time to work as they knew they could and should – to be caring and challenging – with transformative results. Results were immediate in terms of family outcomes (evictions avoided, children back in school, adjustments to protection registers). Savings were significant: in excess of £250,000 for each group of six families (Cottam, 2018). What might happen if we allowed our care services similarly to decide how to work and at what rhythm?

In the Netherlands in the early 2000s, Jos de Blok, a Dutch nurse, watched in dismay as a series of market reforms were introduced into Dutch primary health and care systems, ostensibly to create 'efficiency'. Where once there had been professional autonomy, the ability to pop in on someone and to decide where time and budgets would be spent, now there were time sheets, risk registers and a menu of services and external consultants to audit each process.

Jos left his work and with four colleagues started to experiment. They divided neighbourhood needs between them, working co-operatively on a daily basis. They believed good care is about two principles: a continuous relationship with individuals and families, and a commitment to fostering autonomy at whatever age we might be. Buurtzorg is the organisation that grew out of this experiment. Today, Buurtzorg employs over 10,000 nurses and carers and provides 25 per cent of care within the Netherlands. Nurses and carers still work small, autonomous teams. Coaching is on hand if teams run into trouble but there is no middle management and Buurtzorg headquarters are found in a modest non-descript building. There are only forty-five people in the back office because resources: people, time and money are concentrated at the front line. The approach improves care and saves time and money. A Buurtzorg client requires almost 40 per cent less hours of care than a similar person within the more traditional systems and there is a two thirds reduction in the need for expensive hospitalisations (Buurtzorg, 2024).

There can be no good care (and no good public service) without well-paid work. With no external investors demanding dividends, with no middle management or large back office, at Buurtzorg there is money to fund good salaries. Decent pay allied to professional autonomy has drastically reduced staff absenteeism and turnover. Jos de Blok talks about a psychological contract in which frontline workers are trusted to steward resources and to use their creativity to respond to the needs in front of them.

'Every pair of hands comes with a free brain,' the chief executive of Toyota is reputed to have remarked when asked what drove the company's global success; theirs was a strategy based on worker participation, with every worker empowered both to stop the production line in case of faults and to generate new ideas. In Britain, every public service worker comes with a free imagination. Carers, teachers, social workers, doctors: they know what needs to change, and how, but they rarely have the power to make any systemic decision, let alone control the budget for their school, community or service. Twenty-first-century public services require a radical decentralisation in word and deed and given care's pivotal role in every aspect of our lives, this is where we should start.

Radical Help: The Design Code

In my book *Radical Help*, I describe five experiments (including Life and Circle) that show how we might take care of each other in this very different century, from cradle to grave. Tens of thousands of citizens were involved with the experiments. Independent evaluations show that social outcomes were much improved and the experiments saved money (Cottam, 2018). In Wigan, for example, where the approach and culture were developed and implemented across the authority, healthy life expectancy improved by seven years in the poorest wards, £200 million financial savings were made while satisfaction with public services continued to improve (King's Fund, 2019).

Many leaders – in local government and community organisations, in Britain and in other nations, have taken up the ideas in *Radical Help* and made changes from which we can learn further. In central government, the response until now has been more complicated. At least two senior civil servants left their jobs, believing that the thesis was right but that they could only do the work required outside the constraints of state departments. Others professed their commitment but quietly confessed they had not much idea about how to make such change in practice. (They could and should pick up the phone to leaders in local government such as Donna Hall the former Chief Executive at Wigan, who led transformative practice across their towns and authorities.)

The truth is that shifting our mindsets and our systems to create new forms of welfare will not be without difficulties, but the experiments in Radical Help show it can be done. Radical, as Angela Davis taught us, means going back to the root of things. In the context of welfare systems today, this means returning to the welfare state's foundational question: what do we need to flourish in times of transition?

Today we look back through rose-tinted spectacles at stories of the welfare state's foundation. The truth is it was a struggle. Not every professional was on board. Doctors in particular were reluctant to be part of a new national body, but realising that they would not be paid unless they acquiesced, they joined the NHS. Civil servants were terrified of the costs and tried to block what they could, while William

Beveridge, the author of the 1942 Beveridge report, widely considered to be the welfare state's founding document, was seen by his peers to be rather too maverick and visionary and was never offered the state job he dreamed of within the new welfare system.

To move forward, we need a shared design code, and in *Radical Help*, I describe a set of six principles that if followed (and resourced) would enable us to move from twentieth-century welfare systems (threadbare, transactional and failing) to 21st-century systems of support (shared, relational and generative). These principles have been tested multiple times in multiple settings across Britain and have been shown to bring about transformation. They could be used to guide the transformation now.

First, recover a sense of purpose: create a bigger vision. We need to tell a new story about the role of public services and the welfare state. When we need help, it is not a failing or an embarrassment; it is not an unfortunate cost. The tending of each other and the places we are from is what makes us human, and it is a pre-condition for all flourishing. The rubbing of shoulders in the GP surgery, the school, the library and the park is how we get to know each other and forge our common future.

Second, we need to grow a core set of capabilities for every citizen. Current systems are an elaborate attempt to ration, manage and fix our needs. In a complex world where the reality is uncertain, such an attempt is futile. We need to grow our skills and our collective capabilities to look after and care for one another in new ways that keep us close to our homes and the things we love.

Third, 21st-century systems are all about relationships – our need for and the value of our connections to one another. A 21st-century design must move away from an industrial idea that the support we seek comes from abstract rights or a workforce with more certificates, towards valorising professional and community experience and shared human support.

Fourth, we need to connect multiple forms of resource. Our welfare economy is still significant, but resources are scarce because we have drawn artificial boundaries between budgets and wider resources, and we have allowed for unlimited extraction of those resources by global investors. Twenty-first-century welfare must be rooted in a new social economy where surplus is reinvested within the social system.

Fifth, we must create possibility. Our designs and thinking have been hampered by a risk mindset, but scholarship, including that of orthodox economists, increasingly shows that risk-based models are not appropriate. The current and foreseeable context remains one of radical uncertainty, where outcomes cannot be pre-empted and the emphasis on risk squeezes out trust (amplifying risk) and human care. Inverting risk-based models entails a mindset that seeks open learning over audit.

Sixth, and most importantly, our commitment must be to 'take care of everyone'. No matter our stage of life or our role within a care system, we must feel taken care of, in order to care for one another. For too long we have drawn borders between those requiring help and those giving help – but all of us require support in different ways and in different stages.

Our challenge is to move what is currently thriving but marginal to the centre. This is a challenge of political will. It will be easier for our new ministers to sit at the centre and attempt to command change: to extract more care workers from abroad, to dictate new safety rules and training standards, to believe in AI rather than the imaginative public professionals. These are the established muscles and grooves of power. But as the last Labour government discovered to their cost, these ways of working neither bring, us the public, along nor create lasting change. The urgent alternative is to think laterally, to network and grow what already exists within a new social economy.

The labour movement has its own radical roots and traditions, of strong communitarian solidarity and invention, of people and places that, like Tara, don't want pity but have ideas and new ways or working that can meet the current moment. 'Raw honesty' means recognising our troubles and the depth of the challenge. It also means being alive to the longing we share to live differently and to what has already been created and could be strengthened.

'[This is] a time for revolutions, not for patching,' Beveridge grandly declared in the opening pages of his blueprint for the twentieth-century welfare state (Beveridge, 1942). Standing in a bombed-out London and a bankrupt country, he set out a bold vision. British people then, like today, were ready – they longed for something new, and together people, public servants and political leaders set about implementing one of the deepest social transformations the world has ever seen. We need to do the same, starting with a raw and honest understanding of the challenges and the promises of our current context.

14

Can Art and Culture Really Create Opportunity in Hard Times?

Dave O'Brien and Orian Brook

'For too long, for too many people, the story we tell ourselves, about ourselves as a nation, has not reflected them, their communities or their lives. This is how polarisation, division and isolation thrive. In recent years, we have found multiple ways to divide ourselves from one another and lost that sense of a self-confident, outward-looking country that values its own people in every part of the UK. Changing that is the mission of this department.'
SECRETARY OF STATE FOR CULTURE, MEDIA AND SPORT,
LISA NANDY

Lisa Nandy's remarks were widely quoted in the days following Labour's 2024 election victory. The comments make it clear that cultural policy has a place at the very heart of the government's agenda. They also indicate that, at present, the cultural sector, and its associated creative industries, are not delivering for specific communities or for the nation.

Fulfilling this promise, for culture to heal divisions and contribute to a more self-confident country, is a huge task. This chapter thinks through some of the challenges and Labour's likely approach and offers reflections on the likelihood of their success.

Culture and Creative Industries in 2024: The State of Play

Labour takes power at a difficult time for the cultural sector (Gilmore et al., 2024). The impact of the pandemic still scars workforces and audiences. Technological change offers to radically reform the audience experience at the same time as it threatens to replace key cultural occupations. Funding, and business models, are uncertain at the end of a long period of contracting local, regional and national government support, as well as a cost-of-living crisis.

Many of these crises are hard to separate from broader crises of the British state. The struggles for public sector funding, from national government and devolved administrations through to local authorities, are not unique to cultural policy. Low pay and insecurity are as much a feature of care work and the service sector as they are visual and performing arts or music. The housing crisis impacts vast proportions of society at the same time as it closes studio, rehearsal and cultural venues.

Labour confronts a sector struggling with a polycrisis, with individual problems reinforcing each other. The polycrisis for culture brings into sharp relief the nature of inequality in the arts and the broader creative industries (Brook et al., 2024). This is a long-standing and persistent problem.

The statistics do not need to be restated in detail here. Struggles for Asian and black artists to access funding, recognition and prestigious positions were subjects of debate in the 1970s and continue today. Despite efforts to address a lack of diversity, industry reports on film and theatre continue to note the ongoing presence of exclusionary practices and hostile environments. The story of social class and the workforce tells a similar tale. Discussion of the absence of those from working-class backgrounds in the cultural sector has intensified in recent years, yet the dominance of those from middle-class backgrounds has been an issue for at least fifty years, if not longer.

Many of these workforce diversity and inequality issues are closely connected to inequalities in the education system. As the 2024 Campaign for the Arts/University of Warwick's *State of the Arts* report noted, early years access to arts education in all four UK nations is highly unequal. In state schools in England, there has been a huge decline in numbers taking GCSEs and A-levels in specific creative subjects, a decline mirrored in teacher numbers.

Access to arts in schools then has a knock-on impact on creative subjects in higher education (HE). As well suffering on the front line of Conservative Party 'culture wars', specific creative subjects saw funding cuts on top of the precarious position for funding home undergraduate courses.

At the same time, creative HE subjects are highly unequal, with differences in entry and graduate outcomes based on ethnicity, gender and social class. Higher education is the central route into creative occupations and industries. Inequalities in creative HE are an important, but not the only, driver of inequalities in the creative workforce.

Education is also important in the cultivation and development of individual's cultural interests and cultural tastes. Declining access to arts and culture in and out of schools has implications for future audiences. Future audiences are also shaped by a set of much broader social inequalities, for example parental wealth and geographical distance to arts venues. Having a range of cultural interests and tastes are also implicated in success in many fields of work, not only creative occupations.

Workforce, education and audience inequalities are by no means an exhaustive list of problems for the new government. Indeed, these inequalities were exacerbated by the pandemic. For example, the pandemic hit access to education extremely hard, with clear inequalities in educational outcomes still present today, with the latest exam results showing deprivation-related attainment gaps higher than before the pandemic.

The pandemic hit creative workers, particularly those who were freelancers. Even in sectors that returned to work quickly, for example film and television, subsequent industry retrenchment has seen a widespread under- and unemployment crisis for film and TV workers in the UK.

Finally, the pandemic reinforced existing patterns of tastes. Despite lockdowns and a boom in digital modes of consumption, much of the population's cultural engagement and participation remained the same. Indeed, in a cruel irony, those disabled citizens who had long wanted better digital offers catering to their cultural interests were re-marginalised as the arts sector rushed back to 'business as usual'.

Labour's Cultural Policy

How will Labour address this long list of pressing problems? In theory we know a great deal about Labour's priorities for the cultural sector. 'Creating Growth: Labour's Plan for the Arts, Culture and Creative Industries' (Labour Party, 2024b), and the 2024 Labour Manifesto (Labour Party, 2024a) itself both contained information on cultural policy.

These documents sit alongside Labour's 'five missions' for government (Labour Party, 2024c). Two of these – Growth and Opportunities – have obvious connections to the cultural and creative sector. The rise of the arts-in-health movement; the long tradition of the use of culture in criminal justice settings; and the increasing importance of the climate emergency to organisations' and individuals' practice might also connect cultural policy to the remaining three missions.

To govern is to choose. It is unlikely that cultural policy could be *central* to, for example, the complex task of the NHS treating the extensive backlog of people waiting for treatment. This is notwithstanding the positive effects cultural engagement may have for health outcomes.

Rather, Labour's manifesto and subsequent ministerial comments suggest a dual focus. There is culture's contribution to economic growth, as evidenced by the very title of its cultural policy manifesto. Second, culture's contribution to breaking down barriers to opportunity, as evidenced in ministerial statements and speeches since the election victory.

Growth and Opportunity are tricky subjects for culture. Growth has been associated with debates over the very purpose of culture in society. Narratives of the economic contribution of the sector to jobs and GDP have also been contested, particularly in the context over the relevance and accuracy, or otherwise, of economic statistics. Opportunity carries with it the historic and ongoing interrelationship between culture and social and economic inequalities already described in this chapter. Moreover, Opportunity raises the tricky question of whether arts and culture are genuinely contributing to widening opportunity and social fairness.

Inequalities in the creative workforce suggest, at best, a huge task to make cultural jobs open to all. More generally, in contemporary British society the correct tastes can be a form of currency. For many elite professions, for example law or politics, hiring is a form of cultural matching.

How, then, might culture deliver for Growth and Opportunity? The key will be to closely connect the two missions to each other and to cultural policy. There is good evidence that 'hits', for example commercially successful computer games, are dependent on diverse teams; a more diverse workforce is thus likely to mean new products, new audiences and new markets. This is the case even in artforms that are grappling with the difficulties of attracting pre-pandemic levels of attendance and engagement. A commitment to diversifying the workforce is shared by almost every institution and key voice in almost every artform and creative industry.

More 'Opportunity' can, therefore, generate 'Growth'. The converse is likely also correct, whereby limited opportunities will limit the growth potential for the sector. We can see this in the struggles of artforms to find new audiences or commercial cultural products to find new markets. As a huge variety of research has shown, *assumptions* about what should be commissioned, what should be programmed, what should be marketed, alongside assumptions of *who* and *how*, limit the potential of the cultural sector.

What is certain is that neither opportunity nor growth can be delivered by the existing approach to cultural policy. Demanding an exhausted and underfunded cultural sector delivers a radical transformation to its workforce and audience, while offering continuity in the policy and funding system, is at best unrealistic. At worst it may be cruel to shift failures of political vision onto an already struggling sector.

Conclusion: What Story Will We Tell Ourselves?

Cultural policy is sometimes described as a battle between two competing visions. One, most associated with the democratisation of culture, has been to take the existing offer of institutions and practitioners, across a range of artforms, and ensure they are open and accessible to all individuals and communities.

The democratisation of culture has traditionally, albeit with debates and nuances, been the approach in the UK. The approach runs through policies including free entry to museums, education and careers programmes, funding for music and cultural festivals and support for British filmmakers. It is present within the BBC's role in society, and it shaped the birth of Channel 4.

An alternative, and sometimes seen as oppositional, approach has been a commitment to cultural democracy. Here the making of culture – rather than just its consumption – is opened up, often with a view to involving communities who have traditionally been excluded or underrepresented. Its roots are perhaps critical of artistic and cultural institutions, in terms of what is commissioned or collected, who attends and who is absent, and, fundamentally, how decisions are made.

Cultural democracy has also long had advocates in the UK, although it has never been the dominant approach to policy. Neither it, nor the democratisation of culture, are perfect paradigms. Both have seen extensive, and sometimes vitriolic, criticism.

Looking at their manifesto documents, it seems that Labour's cultural policy, with a focus on 'access', is firmly within the democratisation of culture. Perhaps this will work, if it addresses the collapse of conditions for the cultural and creative sectors *and* if it is connected to a broader social and economic policy agenda.

A broader social and economic policy agenda will need to fix the welfare system, so there is a genuine safety net for social protection rather than the current punitive benefits system; transitions to net zero need to go hand-in-hand with a functioning transport system, making green work and social life possible, particularly in the north of England and in rural Scotland, Wales and Northern Ireland; the economic geography of the country needs to be rebalanced, so London and the south-east of England no longer dominate and regions can thrive; and the housing crisis must be addressed.

All of these social and economic policy agendas would be transformative for culture. A functioning welfare system would make freelance work much less of a risk for individuals without existing wealth; solving the housing crisis will not only benefit individual creatives but will have impacts on venues and spaces too; a functioning and sustainable transport system will mean less pressure to move to London, along with the possibility of support for emerging, rural, creative clusters.

Yet even if this sort of revolution is realised (and we should be sceptical in the context of Labour's approach to public finances and public investment) there is the risk that the policies outlined in Labour's manifesto documents will not be enough to deliver Nandy's laudable vision of a new story to tell ourselves.

While there are references to a broader conception of access to culture in Labour's policy documents, they are still shaped by the aim of democratising culture. This democratisation of culture approach struggled to transform art, culture and creative industries even when the UK was a more equal society. If that is all Labour is proposing, then its prospects are bleak in the context of the currently collapsing British state.

Indeed, there is a distinct irony in Nandy's aim of placing cultural policy at the centre of Labour's policy agenda. The importance of policy agendas such as those on housing, welfare and transport means the cultural sector cannot be successful without more general social and economic policy successes. It remains to be seen whether social and economic policy can be successful without culture.

15

Can the UK's Broken Political System and Culture Be Remade?

Sue Goss

Successful governments understand how power works. That should be obvious. But the recent dysfunction at the heart of the UK government meant billions were wasted on policy initiatives that either didn't happen or didn't work. Some were just dangerously wrong, such as the privatisation of the probation service (see Dunt, 2024), but even well-intentioned policies, such as subsidies for home insulation, caused distress and cost ordinary householders thousands because of the shoddy way they were implemented (Conway, 2024). Allocated funding has gone unspent, initiatives have been announced with no capacity to implement them and objectives have failed because no one put in the effort to sort out how they would work in practice.

Among the challenges for an incoming government is the recreation of the basic competence necessary for governing well. The Prime Minister is not the CEO of a company, with ministers as heads of department. In Whitehall, no lessons are taught, no homes built, no suicides prevented, no operations performed. It is a place of talking and, pre-eminently, of writing. Announcements, reviews or strategy documents do not, of themselves, achieve anything. There are no simple levers that incoming ministers can pull to 'deliver'. Policies are implemented through a complex system of many stakeholders with different motivations and interests. Delivery requires energetic and committed leadership on the ground, not just at the top. Government isn't a single organisation but a complex system, and it is through understanding how to use the power of systems that a different culture of government could come. A government that understood its own workings, its strengths and weaknesses and its resources and constraints, would be truly powerful.

Luckily, Sir Keir Starmer has managed an organisation and has experience of running things. Luckily also, several of Labour's leaders have been thinking hard about the 'how' of policy as well as the content. The new government has had time to think and prepare and has been listening to a wide range of voices. Labour has an opportunity to create a more open, devolved, democratic and effective government.

There are promising signs of a different approach, with ministers already working collaboratively. The articulation of 'mission-led government' has been sparse, but the launch document criticised 'a top-down, target-led approach': 'This command-and-control management technique is good at raising poor performance to a minimum standard, but the model is less capable of allowing systems to adapt to meet ambitious goals and encourage the innovative locally-led approaches that are often needed to drive excellence' (Labour Party, 2023, p. 4).

The language is about empowering, supporting and engaging a wide range of public, private and civil society players. Most surprising, perhaps, has been the speed of engagement with other layers of government, the meeting with metro-mayors, the announcement of a new council of the nations and the regions, and the commitment to devolution to sub-regions and local government.

All this is positive. A leadership team capable of working collaboratively across and between the layers of government would have a fighting chance of meeting the challenges the government will face. But for many incoming ministers, this thinking is new. For the civil service, this will require a huge shift in mindset. The destructive culture of Whitehall and Westminster is hugely subversive of good intentions.

Reasons for Success (Or Not)
Labour in the past did not spend much time understanding the reasons for the successes and failures of successive governments. And yet, without that understanding, and a realistic 'theory of change', random policy initiatives are unlikely to succeed. In 1945, Labour inherited a war-machine capable of delivering top-down change, staffed by people with experience of rapid delivery. When setting up huge, centralised organisations, such as the Coal Board, Iron and Steel Corporation, British Electricity Authority, British Railways and the NHS, Attlee's government could draw on the mechanisms created for a war economy. That sort of power no longer exists in government, and even if it did, would not be appropriate for a modern democracy.

Subsequent Labour governments were able to build on emerging and maturing social institutions, such as the BBC, the New Town Corporations, the National Parks Authority, the Housing Corporation and Housing Associations. But they also created a network of new institutions where new thinking was needed. In the 1960s and '70s, institutions such as the Land Commission, ACAS, the Open University, the Manpower Services Commission, the Health and Safety Executive, the Equal Opportunities Commission, as well as expanded powers for local government in education and social care, created a network of delivery organisations sharing the values and goals of government.

However, frustration with an old-fashioned and elitist civil service was never far away. The Blair government of 1997 tried to tilt the civil service away from policy-making and towards 'delivery'. It absorbed the neoliberal critique of central and local government bureaucracy as inefficient and sclerotic and instituted a series of measures to introduce private sector 'efficiency' into government. The most important of these were the introduction of departmental PSAs (three-year Public Service Agreements, backed up with a delivery agreement with the Treasury), the Prime Minister's Delivery Unit headed by Michael Barber, and Sir Peter Gershon's proposals for restructuring departments, leading to significant cuts in civil service numbers across the country. Relationships with local government were made more transactional through a series of measures to modernise local government such as Best Value, a new role for the audit commission, Local Public Service Agreements and the concept of 'earned autonomy' – local government had to prove itself to government to gain access to additional resources.

The results of all these reforms were mixed. They brought greater focus on a narrow range of results and 'efficiency' savings, but in doing so, centralised decision-making created too many confusing targets and disempowered local government (Martins and Bovaird, 2005). It will be interesting to see whether 'enforcers' brought in with experience from the Blair government bring a return to New Labour centralisation or learning about the problems encountered in those years.

Since 2010, the pressure to make government function *like* the private sector has given way to replacing the civil service *with* the private sector. The shift towards externalisation has accelerated. Repeated pressures to cut civil service costs has led to the hollowing out of capacity and the stripping away of expertise and experience. The use of private consultancies has grown hugely, not just to offer technical advice, but to manage and deliver government programmes. Home Office consultancy spend increased by 788 per cent during the run-up to Brexit. Between 2017 and 2020, government spending on consultants increased to £450 million, related in large part to Brexit. The pandemic only accelerated the trend. Serco had contracts from the

Department of Health and Social Care by autumn of 2020 estimated at £410 million (Mazzucato and Collington, 2024). Mariana Mazzucato and Rosie Collington argue that outsourcing is often far costlier than alternatives, wasting the in-house specialist skills that already exist and accumulating new knowledge and experience not within the civil service itself but within consultancies, who use it to sell on to other clients.

And since 2015, the chaos in the Tory party has sharply accelerated the decline of government's ability to govern. The bewildering turnover of ministers has meant that no individual stays long enough to see through the delivery of the policies they announce.

Rory Stewart describes this:

> I had not yet finished my plan for the British environment before I was put in charge of development programmes in Syria, Yemen, Afghanistan, Bangladesh and Pakistan. Before I had a chance to visit Pakistan, I was transferred to Africa. My Africa strategy had not yet been signed off when I was made minister of state at the Ministry of Justice … Before I had finished my work on prison violence, I became secretary of state for international development. My knowledge of these portfolios was absurdly limited. And this was true of most of us.
> (Stewart, 2024)

This would not be so bad if it were not combined with the bewildering turnover of senior civil servants through a system that rewards and promotes generalists, encouraging them to move every eighteen months to two years instead of rewarding the accumulation of specialist knowledge. Combine that with the constant abolition, reshuffling and rebranding of government departments, and the rapid closing down by incoming ministers of the initiatives and projects of their predecessors, and we have a system with almost no institutional memory. 'There is very little sign', Geoff Mulgan is quoted as saying, 'that either government or opposition is even dimly aware of what was done before.' He gives the example of the disbanding of the highly successful Rough Sleepers Unit and the almost total loss of organisational memory about what had worked and why (Dunt, 2024).

Then there is the vast growth in SPADs: special political advisers. Initially, special advisers were brought in with specialist skill or knowledge, but over time they have been replaced by highly political advisers who shrink the bubble around a minister, removing challenge and distancing those civil servants who might have relevant knowledge. Civil servants have steadily lost authority and become increasingly deferential to ministers. Teaching a leadership programme involving senior civil servants, it was frightening to hear one civil servant ask, 'What should I do when I explain to my minister that something can't work, and he replies, "I don't care, do it anyway."'

All these trends have dangerously weakened the capacity of government at the centre to transfer learning from one crisis (or success) to the next, to adapt to changing demand and circumstances, or to plan for the future.

The Shift to Collaboration

Recognition of the dysfunction in Whitehall frees the new government to think creatively. Hopefully, it will liberate a drive towards a wider engagement with the public, private and voluntary sectors, with the resources of universities, charities and civil society organisations. Government can employ the expertise and agency of existing independent bodies, and if necessary, creating new social institutions with the value base, independence and expertise needed to implement change.

The UK government doesn't have to get stuck with our idiosyncratic and dated government processes – nor does it have to invent everything from scratch. A collaborative approach to government would begin with joining the networks of likeminded governments that are tackling similar problems. Ministers can begin to rebuild relationships with European governments through learning about their achievements in areas where we need to change. For example, in 2018 a partnership of 'well-being economy governments' was formed, involving the governments of Scotland, Iceland, New Zealand, Wales and Finland, with Canada actively participating. This is a collaboration of national and regional governments interested in 'sharing expertise and transferrable policy practice' to achieve progress towards UN sustainable development goals. New Zealand launched the first 'well-being budget' (WEGO, 2024). The UK could work with international partners to develop innovative approaches to developing our own well-being economy.

We could follow the example of other governments building long-term thinking into their policymaking, such as the Welsh Government's Well-being for Future Generations Act, or Finland's Committee for the Future, and Germany's Parliamentary Council on Sustainable Development.

While expertise is scarce in Whitehall, there is plenty of expertise elsewhere. Many organisations are developing policies to implement change. Coalitions of charities, faith groups, trades unions and local authorities such as the End Child Poverty Coalition and End Hunger UK, and coalitions of people with lived experience of poverty such as Poverty2Solutions, are co-creating solutions to complex social problems. Think tanks, academics and others have developed detailed policy proposals: for example the Joseph Rowntree Foundation and Trussel Trust on income guarantees, Compass on universal basic income and democratic reform, Law Society on reform of courts, Resolution Foundation on economic change, B CORP on measuring the economy differently, TUC on just transition to net-zero, Wealth Commission on tax reform, and so many others, Fairness Foundation,

Nesta, Unlock Democracy, Sortition Foundation, IPPR, Demos – the list goes on and on.

Keir Starmer has been quick to acknowledge that we are a union of four nations and build mechanisms for regular co-operation between them. He has already announced the setting up of a Council of the Nations and Regions, one of the recommendations from the Brown Commission (Commission on the UK's Future, 2022, p. 102). Such a council could be transformative in sharing thinking and decision-making – learning about how things work locally and co-creating solutions. But it will be important to find ways that England is represented in these discussions. John Denham has set out ideas for creating an English machinery of government to allow this to happen, including a process for ensuring English votes for English laws through 'English only' sittings of Parliament (Denham, 2022; Denham and Rycroft, 2023).

Devolution for Real

As the Brown Commission points out, the UK is uniquely centralised. 'No other large country takes so many political, fiscal and economic decisions at the centre' (Commission on the UK's Future, 2022, p. 37). The resources of local government have been dangerously reduced, and the powers of local government weakened over decades. We depend on crucial local services: schools, children's services, social care, parks, libraries, waste, arts and culture. Yet one in five local authorities are at risk of virtual bankruptcy. Cuts of up to 40 per cent in funding have led to alarming falls in the provision of many services, not to mention a growing crisis in children's services and social care.

Reversing this involves both transferring powers and strengthening the financial and legal basis of local government. Instead of being dependent on central government initiatives, local government needs freedom to innovate in economic and social policy, as well as adequate sources of taxation, investment and finance. The new government proposes devolution 'deals', including a local growth plan, and promises three-year funding settlements. Over time, we need to shift to a more comprehensive devolution settlement. Unlock Democracy and Compass have published a report analysing five recent proposals for how this might work, including a rewiring of the funding system (Davies and Giovannini, 2024).

The new government has focused its attention on the role of regions and sub-regions in economic policy: 'Local and sub-regional decision-making often possesses better information about their local economies and a more developed capacity for working with local businesses and institutions' (Labour Party, 2024, p. 7).

Integrated transport in London and Manchester has demonstrated what can be achieved with a regional focus. Combined authorities and metro-mayors will play a major part in the government's growth plans, with powers over housing, planning and economic decision-making, shifting to the regional and sub-regional level.

But devolution is not simply about the economy but about recreating a decent life for citizens. Our sense of belonging and community is not derived from a sub-region; it comes from our villages and towns. For too long, devolution has been to bigger and bigger administrations. The county of Kent has a higher population than several US states. The role of unitary and district councils should be acknowledged and supported, since it is only at a truly local level that problems of health, social care, housing, employment and poverty can be understood as interdependent and responded to holistically. It is local government that can engage with the energy and creativity of thousands of voluntary organisations and community groups actively tackling social problems in brilliant, practical ways. It's the voluntary and community sector that provides warm hubs, food banks, community cafes, drop-in centres, school uniform exchanges, baby banks, peer mental health support, visits to the lonely, sports clubs, community choirs, gardening groups, litter-picking and sewage testing – the list is endless. The best solutions are crafted by those who will live with the consequences. These organisations need to be part of the conversation, co-creating workable solutions.

Much will depend on the way that Whitehall works with local and regional government. One of the innovations of the Blair government was to commission academic evaluations of the impact of many parallel initiatives to 'improve' local government. The tragedy is that by the time these reported in 2010, the coalition government had taken over, the commissioning department had been abolished and the civil servants scattered, and the report was received by shiny new civil servants who had barely heard of the initiatives.

The findings, however, were unequivocal and still offer clear guidance to ministers. Firstly, national programmes are helpful in focusing attention and accelerating progress, but change always requires local leadership, accurate data and access to ways to rethink and redesign services at local level. Second, national drivers are most effective when they are consistent over time. Constant change and redirection from the centre gets in the way. Centrally imposed targets are far less likely to drive effective change than those negotiated and agreed with localities. Most initiatives take two to five years to be implemented – few central government initiatives last eighteen months. Third, the model of 'pilot and roll-out' carries problems, since the high-level sponsorship, shared learning and the enthusiasm of volunteer authorities can't be replicated in roll-out. Once the experiment and learning switches to a mindset of 'programme delivery', innovation and effectiveness decrease sharply (Martins and Bovaird, 2005). A crucial element of success is the creation of spaces for real-time shared thinking between senior civil servants and local leaders.

Rethinking the Centre

A good government would concentrate policy at the centre on those things that only central government can do. Government needs to return to shaping the overall policy environment, the economy and social institutions that will improve our society. Crucially, this involves two sorts of real power – firstly to raise and redistribute resources, and second, the power to regulate and control. Government investment can play a crucial role in setting a direction for technological change, shaping markets and supporting innovation. But, as Mariana Mazzucato has argued, the 'entrepreneurial state' does not need to continue to simply shoulder all the risk, while allowing the privatisation of reward (Mazzucato, 2023). It is the role of government to ensure that workers and citizens share in the economic success driven by taxpayer investment. Government should begin to take rewards for risky investment through taking a stake in companies that require investment, as well as by developing wealth funds and setting conditions that require companies to pay their taxes fairly. Innovation is a collective process involving many different stakeholders, and government needs to play an active role at all stages, including rebalancing the economy so that tax-breaks and subsidies match real investment and risk-bearing.

Government regulatory and legislative powers can create the conditions in which desirable actions are encouraged and harmful actions are penalised. Used well, they can change the social and economic climate, removing obstacles to radical approaches and enabling other public, private and civil society actors to create the sustainable economy and caring society we need. These powers are consistently underused, while governments fritter away attention and resource on short-term initiatives. The hectic schedule of Westminster pressurises ministers towards headline-grabbing, quick-fix solutions. But the crucial work is not designing detailed policies but creating the infrastructure that enables collaborative solution-finding to flourish.

In Finland, policy-makers, academics and government have been working to craft an approach they call 'humble government' (Demos Helsinki, 2021). They argue that conventional policy-making works well for maintaining routine state functions but is poor at solving complex social problems. The current approach, they argue, suffers from political short-termism, a siloed institutional structure, a culture of infallibility and a failure to understand how societies work. Humble government works from the assumption that ministers don't have the answers. Instead, they invite a broad range of people with first-hand knowledge of the problem to join in a deliberative problem-solving process. Local and central government and civil society organisations collaborate to begin experimentation once they have reached a 'thin consensus' about common direction and initial exploratory approaches. As learning develops, the consensus can thicken, as some approaches are seen to work better and others are discarded. Top-down direction is replaced by a continuous process of learning – resetting goals in the light of new information as it arises from the ground.

The crucial role for government is often the convening and supporting of practice exchange, spreading best practice, removing obstacles as they are identified and putting resources behind the most effective delivery.

Rebuilding Whitehall

All this requires a highly competent but very different civil service, a network of organisations focused on learning with access to good research, constantly learning about the impact of policy change elsewhere and evaluating the effectiveness of policy change at home. We need to invest in the capacity for learning and co-ordination, developing experience and skill among government staff to give wise advice. Civil servants should be encouraged to stay in a role long enough to see through the implementation of policies. Government departments need people with specialist expertise and people who understand the context and history of social and economic problems, as well as what has been tried before. Instead of constantly rebranding departments, cross-departmental teams should bring together different perspectives. Those at the centre of any policy initiative should create space to work through, with those on the ground who will live with the consequences, the obstacles and risks, and the right pressures and incentives to make it work. Skills in listening and relationship-building need to be linked to a strong shared sense of public values, an understanding of the Nolan principles, and the courage (as well as the safety) needed to tell truth to power.

The involvement of consultancies should be drastically reduced and limited to those with specialist experience that cannot easily be replicated. Senior and specialist staff need to move easily between sectors, bringing private sector, local government and civil society experience into government and enabling civil servants to learn from other organisations. Stronger links to universities could build academically credible, longitudinal studies of the impacts of different government interventions.

Creating New Institutions

The past fourteen years offer proof, if it were needed, that private sector delivery is not more effective or efficient than socially owned alternatives. In some cases, nationalisation or local government ownership may be the best way to improve services, in others the best solution may be properly resourced enforcement, or working with social enterprises, or the creation of arm's-length, values-driven social institutions, able to work effectively across sectors. Again, there is much to learn from other modern democratic governments. If we are to achieve social change, government will need to work through delivery organisations that share values of integrity, public service and sustainability and are not simply after a quick buck.

Creating a Democratic Culture

As well as working with local government and civil society, a modern democracy needs to create a direct relationship with citizens and communities. Democratisation is as much a mindset as it is a process. It assumes that many voices will be better at solving complex problems than a single one, that people have a right to be part of conversations about their own experiences and that the autonomy and freedom to shape our own lives is a human right. Democratic practice involves being eager to listen to different views, however challenging they are to our own assumptions.

In recent years there has been a renaissance of deliberative democracy. Some, like citizens' juries, are small-scale, for local decisions. Others – such as citizens' assemblies – have been responsible for serious shifts in policy. The landmark legislation in Ireland that legalised equal marriage and removed the ban on abortion resulted from recommendations by citizens' assemblies. Closer to home, the UK's national Climate Assembly broke new ground in helping politicians think through the practicalities of their commitment to net zero by 2050 (Climate Assembly UK, 2020). Citizens' assemblies are not simply a method for consulting citizens; they involve them in the work of political decision-making. Everyone learns something: politicians often emerge with a renewed respect for their constituents, while citizens develop an understanding of how to make trade-offs and how hard prioritisation can be.

There are a myriad of organisations promoting and developing participatory democracy, such as Involve, Demos, Democratic Society, the Apolitical Foundation, Unlock Democracy, Collaborate, Shared Future CIC and the Sortition Foundation. A future government could seek support from all these organisations in extending democratic experimentation.

A flourishing democracy can only happen if citizens feel it is possible, and worthwhile, to participate. National government at all levels needs to tackle the poverty and disadvantage that prevents people from taking part. Again, the new government has indicated that it will tackle voter exclusion through automatic voter registration – a good start. The best local government leaders are working with local communities, encouraging self-organising and building the infrastructure that makes that possible. A vibrant locality would be one in which local councils, residents and businesses work together to solve shared problems. Local government is also developing a role in convening safe and tolerant spaces for dialogue and deliberation, setting the rules and tone of the conversation and modelling the behaviours that make agreement possible.

We have not, as a society, championed collaboration. We think we want 'strong leaders', when in fact they are often part of the problem. We need *collaborative* leaders, and so we have to learn to work with them. If we are to participate well in citizens' assemblies, in discussions, in community organisations, we all need to develop skills in listening, facilitating and co-creating. Training in collaborative leadership skills could be part of a creative adult education offer, part of training and development within business and part of the support offered to local community organisations. The experience of more democratic workplaces, where staff have a say in direction and are able to shape their own work, can strengthen our democratic muscles. We need to upskill our children, from primary school onwards, enabling them to practise democracy by working collaboratively to address their own dilemmas. Across civil society, we need to equip ourselves to play an active role and to create a democratic infrastructure that makes meaningful participation possible.

The media have a role to play. We need media that support, rather than undermine, our democracy. Public service broadcasting becomes more important than ever, as well as regulation that enhances our ability to tell fact from fiction, with effective sanctions for lying, fake news and deliberate misinformation.

Compassion in Politics has campaigned tirelessly for a different sort of politics, one that is professional, respectful and builds consensus. The new government has already responded with a promise of an independent ethics and integrity commission (Labour Party, 2024). But we, as citizens, also need to behave differently. We must find ways to roll back a toxic online culture and to prevent the bullying of people who think differently than us. If good people are dissuaded from standing for office by relentless intimidation, our democracy is weakened. If we don't uphold the values of tolerance, respect and seek mutual understanding, the angry voices of populist demagogues get louder. The 2024 riots in England show how dangerous a culture of hate can become. The work of demonstrating solidarity and standing up for tolerance and inclusion goes on. A democratic culture is not just about what government does. It is about what we all do.

Section V

Reconfiguring Nations and Identities

16

The Three Stories of Labour Britain: Past, Recent Past and Possible Future

Gerry Hassan

Labour is a national party again, having won the popular vote in England, Scotland and Wales in 2024 for the first time since 2001. This makes Labour the party of the union. But it begs the question: whose union?

In the past, Labour has successfully articulated stories about Britain based on a vision of the future, hope and agency. This was, at its core, the main domestic message of the Labour Party at its most persuasive. It is the account of Britain that, in past generations, gave working-class people a belief in collective action and that opportunity would be widened for them and future generations – in the context of a fairer, more equal Britain, where unearned privilege and wealth were seen to be in retreat.

This peak Labour story chimes with much of the Britain in the 1945–75 era. It is an account many of us learned directly from parents and grandparents, who handed down memories of the 1930s, Tory laissez-faire and unemployment and said, in the words of historian Peter Hennessy, 'never again' (1992). In the contested 1970s, my parents, both born in Dundee in 1933, clung to this idea of Britain as the country debated European Economic Community (EEC) membership in the 1975 referendum, Scotland and Wales considered devolution in 1979 and the parameters of the post-war consensus began to be pulled apart. For the record, my parents were against the EEC ('a capitalist club') and against Scottish devolution ('Britain is the future'), as like many of their generation they clung to a progressive idea of Britain well into the 1980s.

This vision of 'Labour Britain' was of a place where government and the state could aid a more equal, fairer country. The central state would use its power and resources to redistribute income and wealth, drive change and help people and communities to flourish and live good lives. There was an enlightenment, even liberation, in its vision – while the reality was more bureaucratic, centralist, wedded to the UK's laggard economy and eventually held back by long-term economic problems.

This chapter explores the historical nature of Labour's understanding of the British state and the rise and fall of the 'Labour nation', and sketches out the possible contours of a future Labour and progressive politics that addresses the UK, British state and Britishness. It surveys the landscape post-2024 election within a longer timeframe, in so doing outlining three different stories of Britain and Britishness.

Story One: The Rise of the Labour Nation Post-1945

'Labour's relentless British nationalism from Attlee to Starmer has assumed that British national economic, social and political renewal can be delivered using the institutions of the centralised British state, and that England can be governed as "Britain" without its own national democratic representative voice or national policy space.'

SIMON LEE, ACADEMIC (2024)

Labour's embrace of the British state is usually located in 1945, Clement Attlee and the post-war Labour government. In some accounts, this is extended back to May 1940 and the entry of Attlee and Labour into the wartime coalition government headed by Churchill. A longer backstory would map the evolution of Labour thinking. Relevant in this is the rise of Fabian evolutionary socialism and gradualism, the defeat of the 1926 General Strike and 1931 humiliation of Labour at the hands of Ramsay MacDonald, the emergence of Keynesian economics and its challenge to classical economics in the 1930s. All of this occurred before Labour entered government in 1940 (Hassan and Shaw, 2019).

Moreover, as well as these developments, Labour's inner culture, worldview and DNA adopted a belief in a British road to socialism that saw the state as neutral and not in class terms. This was informed by Fabianism, by Labour's belief in planning and experts and by the legacy of the Liberal Party, which influenced Labour.

These factors also reinforced the idea that Labour had been incorporated into the dominant story of Britain. This story proposes that the UK, unlike many of our continental neighbours, adapted and changed peacefully through much of its history, its embrace of democracy, civil liberties and the rule of law happening without revolution, rupture and mass violence. This is an elite, partial and selective account of Britain, disingenuous and dishonest, but with much cachet even to the present. And it is illuminating that Labour, the party of organised labour and working classes, choose to buy into the dominant story of Britain written and told by and for the interests of the ruling classes.

This has been presented by conventional accounts as one of the great success stories of the British establishment – incorporating and taming the Labour Party. The other side of the story is less told. This is the marginalisation and defeat of other radical currents in Labour in the 1920s and 1930s, all of which challenged Fabianism and its British statism as guild socialists and syndicalists. These radical currents are worthy of reclamation, and we should draw from Labour's anti-statist perspectives for inspiration. Baroness Pauline Bryan observes that 'trade unionists, local councillors, activists in their communities … recognised that they needed their own organisations to defend themselves from the state which had long represented the landowners and was now coming under the tightening grip of capitalism' (2024).

The year 1945 was the culmination of the above: the convergence of a host of trends that furthered Labour's transformation into one of the central pillars of the British state. This had a profound lasting impact on British politics, as well as on assumptions and expectations about government that lasted for decades, but most of all it fundamentally changed Labour's way of doing things, its understanding of Britain and its way of seeing and manifesting power.

Labour Britain post-1945 projected a vision of a united, homogeneous Britain that was part aspiration, part ideal and future destination. In this, divisions and barriers had to be overcome, but belief remained in an idea of Britain where a powerful central state saw its role as to advance the good society and redistribution, to encourage greater equality and to challenge vested interests – a 'One Nation Labour', before Ed Miliband toyed with the slogan in his leadership.

This was driven by active government and a state underpinned by the codes and conventions of British constitutional practice, including parliamentary sovereignty, First Past the Post, Crown powers of the executive and a lack of checks and balances on Westminster and Whitehall. This contributed to a political central authority that had few formal constraints and that Labour, at its peak, saw as advantageous to progressing far-reaching change. The lack of democracy at the heart of the UK state was therefore seen as something that would be helpful in securing change while being part of Labour's silences about the nature of the British constitution, power and limited democracy.

The optimism and hope of this era was underpinned by Britain's experience in the Second World War and the folklore of 1940–41. Government action, state intervention, planning and the input of experts would all contribute to a new kind of statecraft, economy and society – a 'New Britain', which would put the anarchy of the market, indifference of laissez-faire and the inefficiency of competition behind us in the name of a new social contract – which would liberate people and in the name of science and evidence produce greater economic growth and prosperity for all (Addison, 1975; 2010).

The idea of a homogeneous Britain was an illusion and a future dream. This was a concept of Britain whereby national politics was about class and not place, region or nation, which was given validation by the 1951 election, where Labour and Tories won 96.8 per cent of the popular vote while underneath other differences and distinctions remained.

For example, peak Labour bought into the concept of unitary state Britain, which underpinned a homogeneous country and omnipotent centre (Hassan, 2019; 2024). However, the UK has never been a unitary state; rather, this misunderstood the nature of the unions that created the UK and the nature of the UK. The UK has, throughout its history, comprised various component territories, such as Scotland post-1707, which never legally disappeared and remained a nation with its own laws and institutions. Wales had a different experience, being subsumed in the legal notion of 'England' in the sixteenth century but reappearing as a legal entity sometime between 1920 (the disestablishment of the Church of England in Wales) and 1964 (the creation of the Welsh Office) (Paterson and Wyn Jones, 1999, p. 174).

Hence, the UK is a union state of four territories and nations which has had its current boundaries since 1922 and legal name since 1927. Yet the power and reach of the UK as a unitary state has informed political culture and institutions, totems as parliamentary sovereignty and the Labour and Tory parties.

The Tories, for most of the twentieth century, interpreted this in a more pragmatic manner than Labour, particularly from 1945–79. In the late 1940s and early 1950s, the Tories regularly railed against Labour centralisation, its belief in Whitehall experts and its riding roughshod over Scottish traditions and sentiment. Churchill, in a much-cited 1950 Edinburgh speech in that year's election, warned against Labour centralisation, declaring that Scotland should not be forced against its will into 'the serfdom of socialism'; Harold Macmillan in 1954 portrayed the union as flexible and based on consent: 'The union of the wedding ring – not of the handcuff' (Mitchell, 1990, p. 50; Conservative and Unionist Party, 1955, p. 308).

The Tories presented the union in the light of how they saw the state, localism and civic tradition: a diverse ecology informed by tradition that upheld liberty and acted as a bulwark against bureaucracy. Labour's version of the union was the opposite: counterposing the bad old interwar years of unemployment and poverty with the 'Brave New World' of planning and Keynesianism, which gave impetus to a powerful state driving change across the UK in the name of modernity and progress.

This Labour version of the union and story of Britain came stuttering to a halt, first challenged as the Wilson government of 1964–70 experienced economic difficulties, and then fundamentally opposed under the Wilson and Callaghan governments of 1974–79. There were many reasons for this – the relative decline of the UK economy, structural weaknesses and fault lines in British capitalism, the dominance of finance capitalism, the UK's global responsibilities and the nature of the UK economy beyond the UK's shores.

Added to these and the failure to address them was the nature of the UK central state and the reality that successive Labour governments tried to advance the 'New Jerusalem' on the foundations of the unreformed British state. Not only did this have all the shibboleths previously mentioned, but it was also shaped in Whitehall by a mandarin class of amateurs, a 'gentleman class' who believed in the 'good-chap theory of government' (Hennessy, 1995, p. 137). This was not a secure setting to build a programme of socialist change and modernisation, when the central state had been shaped by laissez-faire economics, colonialism and the UK's military and global expeditions.

Maybe Labour's mission to remake Britain as a social democratic country would always fail, considering the obstacles it faced. But it stood next to no chance of building social democracy on top of a Victoriana state, which at its heart remained an empire and warfare nation (Edgerton, 2005; 2018).

Story Two: The Fall of the Labour Nation

'New Labour never understood that Britishness is itself plural, expressing itself differently in the nations and regions. Instead, it saw Britishness as a single, superordinate entity above the various national and cultural divisions. Talk of British values just annoys people as they know perfectly well that these are universal values. The flag waving was profoundly un-British and the talk of duties to go with rights always had a whiff of authoritarianism.'
MICHAEL KEATING, ACADEMIC (2024)

As the post-war consensus unravelled in the 1970s and was trashed by the Thatcher government from 1979 onwards, Labour struggled to find a voice and direction. Moreover, Labour's idea of Britain, its notion of what the state should do and the future Britain it was aiding completely collapsed, leaving the party confused and lost.

In the post-1979 era, as the Conservative governments transformed the UK and remade the role of the state, Labour struggled to find the right response. In the immediate years after 1979, the party tried desperately to cling to the remnants of the previous order and idea of the state. Therefore, in the 1983 election, Labour spoke an explicit language of conservation and restoration, seeing the Thatcher era as an aberration that could be reversed and the UK pre-1979 as something that could be returned to.

When it became clear after Labour's emphatic defeat in 1983 that the Tories would be in office for an extended period, Labour had to rethink its core assumptions. In short, it undermined the party's innate belief in progress, that it was creating a better country, its idea of the role of the state and, ultimately, the stories of Britain that underpinned this thinking.

Labour's adaption involved retreating from Keynesianism; accepting large parts of Thatcherism; rowing back on state intervention; and embracing anew a regional strategy for England and devolution for Scotland and Wales (Jones and Keating, 1985). Yet at the same time, while this could be seen as a strategy, first under Neil Kinnock then under Tony Blair in opposition, it was adaptive and incomplete, often not making explicit what it was disregarding from the old order and the shape of the new it was trying to create.

This approach continued when Labour entered office in 1997, setting out an agenda to further social democratic ends in an environment defined by the Thatcherite legacy, much of which Labour accepted and left in place. The melding of different traditions saw Labour retain the core means by which it did politics at the centre – parliamentary sovereignty, FPTP and the power of the executive, while adding on to these a set of constitutional reforms mostly but not exclusively about the political system beyond the central state (Hassan, 2007). Thus, devolution to Scotland, Wales and Northern Ireland, the creation of London and English mayors and English regional development agencies saw the so-called 'periphery' of the UK transformed. However, the way the political centre governed and built relationships with the rest of the UK remained the same.

This balance between maintaining the core state and constitutional reform was always going to have one winner: the assertion of the former. The New Labour state could do progressive things (the national minimum wage, the Sure Start programme, tackling child poverty), while the values and relations that the state embodied were increasingly at odds with this: corporate consultancy, outsourcing, marketisation, seeing private sector involvement in the public sector as what constituted 'reform'. The uneasy alliance within New Labour was replicated in the inner sanctums of the state, with the dominant forces and entrenched interests at the heart of government championing a worldview of the new elites and insider classes at odds with social democracy.

All of this contributed to a New Labour story of Britain that was flawed. This mostly manifested in Gordon Brown's repeated attempts to tell a progressive story of Britishness that wedded devolution and constitutional change with his socialism by stealth, as well as his morphing of the central state. Often presented at the time as Brown's attempt to find an overarching credo to give mission to his rationale to become Prime Minister, it was about more than this; it was about trying to find a new story of Britain and social democracy in very different times from peak Labour.

Brown's version of Britishness had and has supporters, Iain McLean, for example, reflecting post-election that 'Gordon Brown had a clear conception of Britishness based on the social union and the constitutional settlement of 1707' (McLean, 2024). Brown at times seemed to endorse the Whig history of Britain – linear, seamless progress towards greater rights, the extension of democracy and the rule of law, now located on a contemporary story of the modern UK as the most successful multicultural, multinational state in human history, which did seem a mixture of British exceptionalism and hyperbole (Lee, 2007; Brown, 2014).

Ultimately, this could not give voice to a new story of Labour Britain, and by the time Labour fell from office in 2010, this Blairite and Brownite way of doing statecraft had been widely discredited. But this does not mean that Labour in opposition, first under Ed Miliband and then Jeremy Corbyn, could fully reject the New Labour era and construct a new interpretation of the British state. Rather, Miliband hesitantly, and then Corbyn explicitly, renounced the New Labour way of doing politics and its version of the state but found it more difficult to present a new settlement. Starmer's Labour fully broke with the Corbynista era but has not yet developed the political terrain of where they are going and what they stand for.

Could a Third Story Emerge of Labour Britain?

'Post-crash, post-Brexit, post-Covid, conditions are far less hospitable to those wishing to tell a hopeful, inclusive story about British identity. But if such a story "can" be told, in my view it should have liberal institutions at the heart of it ... Many of these institutions have been weakened in recent years, but Labour should prioritise restoring their public legitimacy as part of any project to rejuvenate British identity.'
HELEN MCCARTHY, ACADEMIC (2024)

There is no possibility of returning to the Labour Britain of 1945–75 or trying to resuscitate the New Labour nation of 1997. Yet for some these remain the primary reference points: yearning for the Britain of the post-war settlement; alongside an enduring fascination with the Blairite era and its triumphalism.

Nostalgia has always been a pillar of Labour culture, but the party's years in opposition between 1979–2024 brought this to a new level (Jobson, 2018). The 'spirit of '45' reached new levels and saw a Ken Loach film of the same name, while in the Corbyn era radicalism was mixed with a romanticism of Labour's past, particularly concerning Keir Hardie and Clement Attlee.

None of this aided Labour in the present day or offered guidance on some of the core dilemmas the party faces. Neither did it offer a new set of stories about Britain or the future. Without these, there remains under Starmer's Labour in office a void and absence where there should be a mobilising story and animating project. Creating these comes with challenges and problems, but without them the current Labour government will find that it is pushed around and defined by others and events, and that an even more virulent, illiberal and judgemental story of Britain on the right may find traction.

In such an environment, can the aims and prospects of a convincing Labour story be outlined? In order to do so, Labour must address each of the following.

First, the legacy and endurance of Britain as an empire state needs facing up to. This is not just about past events, histories and coming to terms with the actions of the empire and what it did in the name of Britain. Rather, it is about understanding the nature of how the British state came into being – how it became defined by empire, imperialism and colonialism – and the UK's record as a warfare state, engaging in serial military expeditions and wars and apportioning a significant part of its cutting-edge technologies, science, design and research and development to military activities to the detriment of the wider domestic economy (Edgerton, 2005).

Second, the changing nature of Britain's geopolitical footprint saw the shrinkage of 'Greater Britain' and 'Global Britain', seen at the height of empire. This was not a smooth process but one of imperial retreat and even humiliation, while the UK reacted domestically by altering its formal nationality acts, which restricted immigration.

A common response among observers is to see the end of the empire as a domino theory of Britishness falling apart, which led to other traditional reference points declining – the military, churches, the royal family. Ian Jack encapsulated this when he wrote, 'First the Empire went …' (Jack, 2009, p. xii). Sometimes this is offered as liberation, other times as a lament, but this is too simplistic. The empire was never just out there overseas; it existed domestically too, providing a way by which the British saw themselves and the world. Its continuing influence can be seen in the swagger of Brexit and the latest version of 'Global Britain' (see Schofield, 2013).

Third, the importance of the UK's partial democracy in underpinning the forces of small- and large-C conservatism needs recognition. The UK is a country where its population are not citizens but subjects, where there is no such thing as any fundamental rights (with every right contingent on Acts of Parliament and therefore liable to be taken away by Parliament) and there is no such thing as fundamental law (as happens in countries with written, codified constitutions).

Fourth, the nature of the British state and its truncated democracy has aided the transformation of the state into a post-democratic entity. The state post-Thatcherism has evolved into an administrative and technocratic entity with numerous hands-off agencies and regulatory bodies restricting accountability and the political realm. This has concluded with the state embodying the values of post-democracy and an insider class politics of government, business and elites that is a closed system run by and for these groups.

Fifth, the salience of 'England as Britain' has become increasingly problematic as the UK has become more divided and polarised in its politics, while Scotland, Wales and Northern Ireland have become increasingly assertive in presenting different political environments and territories from Westminster politics.

'England as Britain' operates on several levels. It provides one of the central pillars of how Westminster sees the UK and governs it, diminishing the devolved nations, subsuming England and restricting its ability to speak and act as a nation and political community. A consequence is that large parts of the left and liberals still evade talking explicitly about England, leaving this terrain and territory to the right with disastrous results. For example, in the 2016 Brexit vote and its lead-up, Brexiteers and the likes of Nigel Farage claimed to speak for an English resentment and nationalism. The fact that Labour and liberals left this unchallenged helped Brexit win and has not been countered in the years since.

Former Labour minister John Denham has made observations about England's lack of voice and democracy:

Labour has denied England its own national governance – there is not even a national budget nor a civil service structure. So Labour's current story of the UK is increasingly at odds with the actual lived constitution, as evidenced symbolically by the use of the union flag for campaigning in England, but nowhere else in Britain.

(Denham, 2024)

Sixth, Labour's spatial understanding of the UK has been absent from too many analyses. Instead, much talk about Labour that influences how the party sees itself and the UK is of an abstract 'Labour Party' and 'Britain', which has missing from it a sense of space and place (see Miliband, 1961). This version of Labour and Britain, presented as one seamless entity and as homogeneous, is often reduced implicitly to the UK. Politics and power is about Westminster and a narrow caste of elite political players, with the only room for referencing communities coming from the parliamentary seats MPs represent.

Seventh, Labour's understanding of the territorial dimensions of the UK has always contributed to its politics. Even when Labour was at its peak years of stressing a homogeneous Britain, there were other traditions and perspectives in the party to draw upon, such as the Independent Labour Party's radical currents, which gave the party an alternative perspective to champion when devolution emerged as an issue from the 1960s and 1970s onward.

Labour was aware of Scotland, Wales and the north of England and the need to build institutions, autonomy and allocate resources to what were traditional Labour heartlands, but this was in the context of accommodating needs and the supremacy of Westminster power, not remaking how it was expressed across the UK.

One example of how Labour does not grasp fully the territorial politics of the UK can be seen in how the establishment of the NHS is portrayed. This is continually presented as one piece of legislation in nearly all the literature, including accounts of the 1945–51 Labour government, Clement Attlee and Nye Bevan (see Morgan, 1984; Thomas-Symonds, 2010; 2015). The reality is the NHS was set up via three separate parliamentary acts for England and Wales, Scotland and Northern Ireland and now under devolution has four distinctive, autonomous systems.

A final observation is the need to address Labour's silences and evasions. Labour has historically seen itself as a force for progress, enlightenment and democratisation. Yet, over the years, it has interpreted these very pragmatically and as whatever Labour chooses to do in any given moment.

Labour came to buy into the empire state, the UK's partial democracy and evolution into post-democracy, being complicit with 'England as Britain' and the omissions from its spatial and territorial understanding of the UK. A major factor reinforcing all of these was the belief in a majoritarian Labour government in the Commons elected on a minority vote using the levers of the British political system to push through change.

If Labour showed a willingness to address the above, what, then, could that third story entail? It would recognise the need to have a degree of awareness about the empire state and the rise of post-democracy; it would from this recognise that a wholesale transformation is required at the political centre if the UK is to have any prospect belatedly of becoming a modern, democratic European country and state.

To do this, Labour needs a greater understanding of Britain's past: one distinct and more challenging than Panglossian accounts of conventional history. This would entail reflecting upon the role of collective memories and myths, both in the stories of Britain as well as stories Labour has told itself. This would better understand history and Labour's role, positively and less positively at times. It would comprehend the nature of the UK, not just as an empire state and something that nurtured the rise of post-democracy, as well as a state of unions and union of four distinct territories.

The long legacy of empire has increasingly come to the fore, but less known is when the legal concepts of empire were removed from law. This occurred when the British Nationality Act 1981 took the term 'colony' out of UK law on 1 January 1983, at the apex of Thatcher's popularity post-Falklands. As critical point is how the UK advanced one person one vote, which happened much later than the 1928 equal franchise between men and women. It was achieved in UK Westminster elections in 1948 with the abolition of separate university constituencies and plural voting and in Northern Ireland in 1968, under pressure from the civil rights movement campaigning against Stormont one-party rule.

Underpinning the latter is that this is an example of the success of the Labour movement in advancing democratic rights and abolishing the relics of privilege and pre-democratic rights. This was a central strand of the Labour movement in its 'forward march' period, but it says much about the party's collective amnesia that such achievements are now largely forgotten. For example, Paul Foot's comprehensive account of the struggle to win the vote and extend the franchise across 528 pages doesn't find room to mention any of these milestones (Foot, 2005).

What Chance a New Kind of British State and Britishness?

The choice before Labour is simple, albeit challenging. It can continue to be trapped in someone else's story, where it is not a creator of its history or the country. Or it can attempt, in difficult circumstances, to tell a new story. There are no easy answers, but the first option has been the path chosen for many years and plays to increasingly diminishing returns, with the party's room for manoeuvre and compromise in the name of progress more and more curtailed.

Many obituaries have been written of the UK in recent decades, starting with Tom Nairn's *The Break-Up of Britain* (1977). The 2014 Scottish independence referendum, 2016 Brexit vote and shifting contours of Northern Ireland led numerous writers to highlight the centrifugal pressures reconfiguring and loosening the UK and assess how this will lead to crisis and potentially the break-up of the union (Ward, 2023). However, a whole host of domestic, historic and geopolitical factors are at work. One taxonomy we can apply to the question of the UK is Albert O. Hirschman's *Exit, Voice and Loyalty*, where the perceived price of exit and entry (Scottish independence; Irish reunification) are factors in consideration (Hirschman, 1970, pp. 97–8).

A new set of stories for a different Britain is not some optional extra compared to the art of government and statecraft. It goes to the core of the purpose of politics. Any new stories must connect to a wider societal settlement and social contract; providing a sense of solidarity, belonging and togetherness that has been conspicuously missing in the UK for decades. This story should bring together institutional, policy and popular buy-in with a willingness to reconfigure state and government, which has to entail transforming the core qualities of the state, the values it represents and the relationships it nurtures.

A new kind of British state is about Britishness, what it stands for and represents, and the type of union the UK embodies. These sound like impossible hurdles to jump for any political project – and being set up to fail. Yet throughout British history these ideas have been in flux and changing – and they continue to be so today. A different kind of state was inherent in the plans of Macmillan, Heath and Wilson pre-Thatcher; following which Thatcher and Blair created new kinds of settlement, statecraft and state that may now have finally reached their end point. Similarly, the idea of what Britain is and stands for has gone through continual convulsions and reinvention and is likely to do so in the future.

Britishness may be seen as unproblematic and fixed by some, and a 'forged identity' by other caricaturing historians such as Linda Colley, but it has shown a degree of adaptivity and flexibility by accommodating seismic changes such as the rise of the Labour Party and organised labour, immigration and multiculturalism more successfully than many of its European neighbours (for all the endless backlashes on the right) (Colley, 1992).

Such notions of identity connect to what kind of union the UK sees itself as and whether it can convey a genuine partnership between its four nations as it has done in the past, but in a more equal, democratic and collaborative manner. This brings us to one of the major fault lines of tension – the battle between traditional Toryism, the radicalised right, conventional Labour and a more radical, decentralised approach.

The last of these would celebrate common values and difference on these isles, recognising that there is something unique in the hybrid in the UK that could (if it embraced renewal and democratisation) offer a way of organising and thinking about government that was an example of 21st-century collaborative practice; one at home with multiple identities and political power centres and relationships of respect and mutuality between them.

This set of arrangements could entail a set of self-governing nations including an England that spoke collectively for itself within the context of autonomy and interdependence. One of the challenges to advancing this will be the need to defeat what writer Bernard Crick called 'the English ideology': the absolutist tradition of indivisible power at the heart of Bagehot's 'English Constitution' (Crick, 2008).

Underpinning all this is the glaring absence of a convincing set of stories about Britain and its future. This missing strand of politics, public life and culture has profound consequences. It requires the articulation of new stories linked to a different Britain of the future, one connected to actions and policies in the here and now. If progressives do not step up and act in this arena, other voices will move into this terrain, including those of the reactionary right.

Stuart Ward, author of *Untied Kingdom: A Global History of the End of Britain* (2023) assesses that 'if anyone can tell it a viable *progressive* story of Britain, it is probably Labour as the only functionally Unionist party left with any chance of actually governing anywhere' (2024). Michael Keating, an expert in territorial politics, notes that the days of imposing collective stories from on high are long gone:

The time is long past when governments could tell stories from on high. The UK was, in many ways, mercifully free of the sort of national propaganda found in Jacobin republics and the USA. There was just the Whig history, which you could take or leave. As I have, half-seriously, argued, the post-devolution UK has the opportunity to move directly from a pre-modern to a post-modern (and post-sovereign) state form without getting stuck in the stage of the unitary nation state. Labour should just relish national pluralism. After all, the SNP have not managed to craft a hegemonic national story, so what does Labour have to worry about? (Keating, 2024)

Such stories need to be authentic; to challenge miserabilism, the status quo and prevailing sense of powerlessness, while giving voice to the politics of hope. If this were not enough, they also must respect the differing traditions of the four nations of the union. This includes the need for a new English story, acknowledging Scottish and Welsh self-determination and addressing the Irish question.

Besides this is the question of what pan-British stories can plausibly begin to sketch a route out of the present? What values do they embody? What kind of institutional framework? How do they address the unreformed nature of the political centre? Are they post-British politically; or would any arrangements of self-governing nations still involve a British dimension?

All this points toward a new kind of Britain and Britishness that has little in common with the current Westminster and political dispensation. It is also a future that Labour at the moment has little connection to or understanding of. Yet present-day Britain is broken, there can be no return to 'normalcy', things are in movement and flux, and a different future is already emerging in the here and now. Labour, the left and liberals should be part of that conversation and future and not oppose it or see it as a distraction.

The stories of any future Labour Britain need to be reinvented and reimagined to realistically have any chance of success. They need to contain new ideas of political power that inform a radically remade political centre; embodying a set of relationships across the nations and regions of the UK and creating different ideas about what 'Britain' is.

This carries risks and threats, but inaction or holding to old traditions will no longer do. Instead, it will invite the forces of reaction and populism to feel galvanised and present their own version of a future Britain that is much more punitive and harsher than the present. For too long Labour has clung to the old ways, with every generation proselytising about the merits of the latest 'New Britain' hype and not delivering; time is running out both for Labour and Britain as the stakes rise by the minute.

17

Why Patriotism Matters: How the Government Could Put an Inclusive Patriotism into Practice

Sunder Katwala

It is hard to identify any leader or party who secured the public trust to govern a major democratic society without a sense of ease with its national symbols. So it is natural that Keir Starmer would seek to adopt patriotism as a theme of his party leadership and now his government.

Previous Labour Prime Ministers have made that work when linking the symbolism of patriotism to their 'state of the nation' argument about the need for change too. Starmer recognises that tradition and has sought to place his own ambition for a decade of national renewal within it. As he told his party in opposition:

> If you think our job in 1997 was to rebuild a crumbling public realm, that in 1964 it was to modernise an economy left behind by the pace of technology, in 1945 to build a new Britain out of the trauma of collective sacrifice, in 2024 it will have to be all three. (Starmer, 2023)

Yet the politics of identity may be more complicated for this Labour government than it was for any of those predecessors. The UK is a more consciously multi-national, multi-ethnic and multi-faith polity in this century than before. The post-devolution era makes it clearer that there will be competing patriotisms across the nations of the UK – and different ideas about what each of them mean. Immigration and ethnic diversity are at higher levels than ever before. This is a more multi-faith and more secular society at the same time: all faiths are minority faiths now, with 46 per cent of the population identifying as Christian, even nominally. The challenge is to find a patriotism that alienates no one from these conflicting identities and viewpoints.

Progressive Dilemmas About Patriotism Revisited

Progressives often worry about patriotism (Katwala, 2023). The charge sheet takes different forms. The primary charge is that it can be dangerous – an atavistic appeal to animal instincts and blind loyalties that will drive war and injustice abroad and exclusion and xenophobia at home. When arguments about identity are central to the so-called 'culture wars', is that not clear evidence that arguments about patriotism are more likely to exacerbate the problem, rather than form part of the solution, in polarised times?

But those are not the only kind of counter-arguments about patriotism. Another objection places much less emphasis on the dangers of patriotism and much more on its irrationality and meaninglessness. It may be more common to hear the argument that patriotism seems to be an unnecessary and pointless distraction in times like these. That may be a particularly strong instinct among progressives – when the economy is in a state, the least well-off are suffering most, and the planet is burning, are there not much more important things to focus upon?

The serious arguments against patriotism – that the wrong kinds of nationalism are toxic and dangerous – must be taken seriously. Much ink has been spilled over how to differentiate patriotisms and nationalisms, good and bad, in every generation, from George Orwell onwards.

Progressive objections to patriotism that focus primarily on its irrationality and meaninglessness could be taken less seriously. 'How could anybody take pride in a mere accident of birth?' is often the central challenge. Those who argue this often seem to regard it as a self-evidently slam-dunk case to end any rational argument, with remarkably little curiosity as to why most people everywhere, in their millions and billions, do not agree. The main flaw in this argument is that it mishears and misunderstands the claim it is trying to counter – conflating the idea that something can be special with the idea that it must be considered superior too. Yet it is hardly irrational to have a sense of attachment and affection, belonging and pride, in relation to our family members, the place we grew up in, without needing to believe they are superior.

The argument that patriotism seems an unnecessary and pointless distraction may become more common, yet this significantly underestimates the potential importance of patriotism in fostering the sense of solidarity that can underpin and sustain effective social coalitions to address progressive priorities. It was a sense of mutual obligation and a duty of care for each other that created and sustained consent for welfare states and public services. Climate change will require global co-operation, it will depend on a sense of obligation towards each other at a local and national level too. Writing off patriotism as a distraction is a significant risk for those who have not yet identified as strong a social glue to replicate it as a source of solidarity that can encourage us to pursue a common good. Internationalists should certainly engage with national identity, since it is always being contested between various more inward- and outward-looking varieties. A commitment to internationalism – to peace, to development, or to accept refugees – does not come only from identifying as a citizen of the world. It can reflect a sense of what we believe we want our own country to be known for or to stand for, too.

The Limits of a 'Progressive Patriotism'

There is a rational case for patriotism in a democratic liberal society. Most people still think so today – in most places, most of the time. Patriotism has become more important as it has become more difficult: the individualistic, diverse and fast-changing societies that Western democracies have become today makes it all the more necessary to put in the effort to find a sense of belonging that can bridge our differences. This should matter especially to social democrats. Fundamentally, the success of social democratic politics in this century depends on increasing the sense of common purpose and reducing the social distance between different groups of citizens in an increasingly plural and diverse democracy. That will be essential to secure sufficient support at the ballot box to carry on governing; to pursue a successful social democratic policy agenda on the economy, public services or climate transition; and to have more confidence in navigating identity challenges and challenging polarisation.

In societies like ours, we need a civic and inclusive patriotism that can bind people together from different places, backgrounds, faiths and ethnicities, across social classes. But an underappreciated risk is that the quest for an inclusive, inoculative and tamed patriotism becomes excessively rational – when it needlessly concedes all of the emotional content that it might want to make use of. As Yascha Mounk has argued, the lofty ideals of an excessively civic constitutional patriotism do not fully describe what it is that citizens in diverse democracies actually love about their countries and share with each other (2022). Arguments about the complexity and difficulty of 'defining' the characteristics of national identities may underestimate the importance of each of us earlier having 'lived experience' of it from a young age while at primary and secondary school in our perception of national occasions, sporting events, national saints' days and remembrance, before we hear any of those more intellectual arguments.

Definitions have some role to play. Governments do need to be clear about the obligations of a common citizenship – particularly that the rights we enjoy depend on our willingness to respect those of others. Teaching citizenship in schools is all well and good, but what really determines whether we have an inclusive patriotism is whether students find what is taught on the curriculum more or less convincing, based on their experiences of how this talk of equal citizenship and mutual respect is lived and felt.

'Blood and soil' nationalism describes the most utterly toxic forms of expansionist and genocidal projects. This is also a dead metaphor, a cliché, that does not think through the words. Civic and cultural patriotisms cannot be based on blood – but soil is not blood. Indeed, an appeal to a shared sense of place can be one of the most important ways to at least manage and mitigate, if not necessarily transcend, deep social conflicts. It is because we live side by side that, whatever political choices are made, people across Scotland, Northern Ireland, Wales and England need to find ways that we can live well together. An inclusive and civic patriotism should have plenty to say about place, rural or urban, and from coast to coast, about the land that we share now and that we all call home.

Patriotism can take many forms. It can be angry or hopeful; it can be inclusive or exclusive. It can focus more on the past or the future. It will be more effective if it links the two to show how Britain is a product of our long history, not some kind of breach and betrayal of it. Yet a civic patriotism should have little fear of exceptionalism. There are dangers in chauvinistic or superior exceptionalisms – especially when combined with a sense of grievance and dispossession. But all societies are exceptional from the inside. What I would advocate is a new shared vision of civic and cultural patriotism – of story and song, of the places we cherish, of the land and the islands we all call home – that is as confident about making an inclusive emotional appeal to the heart as well as the head. What makes a civic patriotism inclusive is not that it should thin out our shared inheritance, but rather that it seeks to offer equal voice and status to those who join the club and to their children, so that the stories we tell about ourselves are open to challenge, across generations and across groups, and include all of the chapters and stories when we seek to understand the history of how we became us, the society and people that we are today.

Putting an Inclusive Patriotism into Practice

Keir Starmer is clearest about how he does not want to talk about identity. He hopes to lower the temperature. His offer of a politics 'that treads a little lighter on all of our lives' could have a broad resonance. 'It needs your full attention. It needs you constantly focusing on this week's common enemy. And that's exhausting, isn't it?' He tends to see the 'culture wars' largely as a politics of performance, criticising 'pointless populist gestures' from the Conservatives and contrasting the impotence of protest politics on the left with the opportunity and responsibility to make a difference in power, commenting:

> On the other hand, a politics that aspires to national unity, bringing people together, the common good, that's harder to express, less colourful, fewer clicks on social media. And, in some ways, it's more demanding of you. It asks you to moderate your political wishes out of respect for the different wishes of others. Forty-five million voters can't get everything that they want, that's democracy. (Starmer, 2024)

The 2024 general election result was a curious and complex landslide won with both the broadest and the narrowest winning electoral coalition of modern times. Labour is the first party to win both most votes and seats in England, Scotland and Wales since 2001, and the first since universal suffrage to win most seats in every region across the three nations of Great Britain, and most votes in every social class group, giving it a crushing dominance in the House of Commons with a majority of 172. Yet this unprecedentedly evenly spread support amounted to the lowest share of the vote for any winning post-war government. This gives Keir Starmer a clear interest in bridging divides, rather than amplifying them, if he can find the tools to do so.

Yet there are doubts too about how far the government has a substantive or coherent agenda on the politics of identity. Labour's embrace of patriotism is often viewed cynically as largely a performative exercise in political optics. In opposition, the symbolism of patriotism was deployed to communicate that the party had changed. In government, this may be seen as too intangible and diffuse an agenda to invest much political capital in. The five public missions of the Labour government – economic growth, the NHS, energy policy, crime and opportunity – reflect an appetite to rebalance the agenda – from an age of identity to an age of economics. Yet any government must navigate a wide series of identity issues, including migration and asylum, community cohesion and interfaith relations security, terrorism and extremism from Islamism and the far right. The riots and disorder that the government faced within its first month in office demonstrated the power of external events to reset the agenda of British politics. So what might an attempt to give content to the politics of an inclusive patriotism look like?

1. Bridging social divides should be an overarching cause for a mission-led government
Bringing people together and bridging our divides should be a core

aim of a decade of national renewal – showing how this can be a practical agenda, not merely a rhetorical aspiration. Rather than hoping to avoid tensions over identity, we need effective strategies to engage with and defuse them. Yet we have never before had a proactive or sustained strategy for integration in this country. Strengthening social connection across our society cannot be the work of government alone but a stronger civic response. The government should set out how and why social connection – reducing the sense of social distance between people from different groups and backgrounds – is something we can pursue in practice, challenging civic institutions and citizens to play our part in bringing that about.

2. The fairness test: integrate class, gender and ethnicity into the vision and practice of inclusion

If mission-led government has given Starmer his framework for tracking progress, it is the mission to break down barriers to opportunity – a story about social class – that most reflects his own identity and motives. This is the mission with the potential to give a social democratic heart to the Starmer project. Yet one of the main risks to social democratic politics in the 21st-century is the question of how to prevent the politics of opportunity descending into a politics of competing grievances.

A social democratic mission of building broad coalitions for mutual solidarity is derailed if disadvantages facing those from minority or majority groups are set up as causes we must choose between. Indeed, the centre-left may have most to lose, since everybody may start to feel that the party is on somebody else's side – where, for example, ethnic minority voters feel ignored and taken for granted even as some white working-class British voters perceive Labour as a party that looks out for minorities first.

So a 'fair chances for all' agenda must commit to tackling unfair barriers of all kinds. In practice, this should mean championing a model of equality, diversity and inclusion – within the public sector and beyond it – that integrates social class, ethnicity and sex with other protected characteristics. A more rigorous approach to auditing progress and gaps would also legitimise specific interventions for specific groups that risk being left out or left behind, where the evidence demands it.

3. Tackling the causes of prejudice and extremisms

The first responsibility of government is to keep citizens safe. That requires intelligence and policing to be directed proportionately to shifting threats. Three-quarters of terrorism threats come from extreme Islamist networks, but the growing far-right threat fostered in diffuse hateful online networks broke out in the riots and disorder in the summer of 2024. As historian David Olusoga notes, attacks on asylum seekers, mosques and ethnic minorities amounted to the most concerted effort at organised racist violence for decades.

The disorder seen in the summer of 2024 was opposed by 85 per cent of the public. But up to a tenth of people approved of it, with around one in fifty people elated by it. The paradox of racism in Britain in 2024 is that this is a society with fewer and fewer racists – decade by decade – yet with a wider experience and fear of racist abuse today than at the turn of the century. There is a profound, positive attitudinal shift across generations: the result of more meaningful contact from an earlier age making the lived experience of ethnic contact an everyday norm. Yet even as the recruitment rate into racism falls across generations, a shrinking toxic group has become more virulent and violent.

It is sadly necessary for government to provide funding to protect places of worship including synagogues, mosques and community centres. Protecting people from the consequences of hatred and promoting ways to report hate crime when it happens must be underpinned by effective strategies to address the causes of extremism, hatred and prejudice too.

Yet social contact between different groups – and the confidence and resilience that it can build – is unevenly spread across our society, across areas of lower and higher diversity. Nobody should go to school in 2020s Britain without significant, meaningful contact across ethnic, faith and social class lines. Every school governing body can consider their contribution to achieving that – and to consider how meaningful contact between pupils can engage parents and grandparents too.

The government must do more to bring together work across different strands of hatred and prejudice to help to promote solidarity. A 'levelling up' of approaches to racism and prejudice is needed for the aspiration to a 'zero tolerance' approach to be rooted in active strategies. Experiences from tackling antisemitism can inform efforts to put in place some of the missing foundations for tackling anti-Muslim prejudice, where government has lacked a working definition, a lead independent adviser or a sustained forum for policy and civic society engagement. Tackling the causes of violent disorder requires a stronger effort to unpack the causes of fear, hatred and prejudice in order to underpin a sustained effort to tackle it.

4. Immigration: how do people become us?

The most vocal arguments against immigration are invariably a story about 'them' and 'us' – that there are too many people coming in; that they are taking jobs, houses or resources; that they are not like us and do not like us; but that the domestic population are not even allowed to talk about this for fear of being called a racist.

The underlying weakness of a progressive response that makes an appeal to think rationally, weigh up the pros and cons and understand that 'they' are good for 'us' is its transactional nature. While more benign in intent, 'they are good for us' is another kind of 'them' and 'us' argument. It leaves the immigration debate as polarised as before, in part because these arguments about 'them' and 'us' talk past each other – an exercise in mutual incomprehension. Open or closed. Control or compassion. Anywheres or somewheres.

The Starmer government is under immediate pressure over the chaos in the asylum system. Having scrapped the Rwanda scheme and committed to processing the asylum cases of tens of thousands of people stuck in limbo, it needs also to show how serious negotiations with European neighbours could restore order to the English Channel, with a deal to determine whose claims get heard where.

The government also wants to reduce overall levels of immigration – seeing exceptional levels of net migration at 680,000 a year as unsustainable. That number is likely to halve in its first year, though Labour does not have a target level of its own. It does not know either the economic domestic conditions or the geopolitical picture abroad at the end of the parliament. The sensible alternative to a numerical target is to introduce more visible democratic accountability on immigration. The Home Secretary presenting a Budget-style annual immigration report on the flows and impacts of the previous year – and the government's projections, targets and proposals for the next one – would be one rational step to show how we could approach immigration as a normal policy issue, considering choices and trade-off as we might overspending and taxation, rather than always an existential one.

The phrase 'legitimate concerns' may have become a political cliché, yet unpacking the principles underlying it is crucial to ensuring we have the democratic debate about immigration policy and integration that gives no space to racism, threats and violence. It is not possible to engage with legitimate concerns, legitimately expressed, without being clear about what is illegitimate in a democratic society.

Yet immigration and integration are existential issues too. So the most important way to increase public confidence in immigration would be to proactively strengthen the links between those who come to settle in Britain and the communities they join. The new government should do that proactively. It should champion universal English fluency by 2030 for all of those settling in the UK and pioneer efforts to make civic welcoming a sustained social norm, from community sponsorship of refugees to promoting English language conversation clubs as a forum for mixing between migrants and 'welcomers'. It should review the citizenship rules and processes to encourage those who settle in Britain to become British and to celebrate it when they do.

A 'they are good for us' is a much narrower and more limited case than one where we approach immigration and integration in a way that expands, over time, who we think the 'greater us' can be.

5. Make national moments matter – to bring an inclusive patriotism to life
Major national occasions can be the moments when an inclusive patriotism can come to life. Prime Ministers and governments need to be careful about how to engage with them. The long shadow of the Dome shows how overt political control can backfire. Major events could easily become lightning rods for cultural conflict too. But, when we get them right, these events can help us to strengthen what we share, especially if they help to create bridging social contact across divides as well as bonding contact with those we already know.

The 80th anniversary of VE Day may be the focal point of the first year of the new parliament. It will be a poignant occasion, honouring the remaining frail veterans of a conflict that will have drifted beyond living memory by its centenary in 2039–45. It is an opportunity too to grow public awareness of the contribution, service and sacrifice of those from every colour and creed.

The Euro 2028 football tournament – co-hosted across the UK and Ireland – will have wider geographic reach than past major sporting events. Since up to five host nations will compete in national colours, so Euro 2028 could become a showcase for inclusive patriotism within each nation and for sport's power to connect. For example, in England, the tournament year coincides with the fiftieth anniversary of Viv Anderson becoming the first black English international footballer in 1978 – a key moment in social history that exemplifies how much sport broadened who we understand to be English.

As it is the first major UK-wide multi-national event of the post-devolution era, beyond Royal occasions, Euro 2028 will doubtless provide a backdrop for competing visions, aspirations and arguments about the future of the UK, and relationships within and across Ireland, and perhaps for new leadership to seek to set out how we can be a society that chooses to take pride in what we can do together to make our unusual multi-national patriotism work.

18

Rethinking 'Multiculturalism' and What Unites People

Savitri Hensman

Multiculturalism has stirred up strong feelings in Britain, positive and negative, for over half a century. The concept has been promoted or attacked in public policy and debate, while being understood in widely varying and sometimes contradictory ways. This is further complicated by the difference between England (marked by ongoing debates over 'Englishness') and Scotland and Wales, where responses to English political, linguistic and economic domination add an extra dimension. In Northern Ireland, the situation is even more complex.

A 'Multicultural' Britain

Education should equip young people for life in a 'multicultural' Britain, Liberal peer Donald Wade urged in the House of Lords in 1971. He emphasised the value of pre-school activities bringing children together, warned of the risk of discrimination, even if unintended, and rejected an approach based on 'self-development for each community.'

Instead he suggested that

a multi-cultural society implies an understanding of, a respect for and a desire to learn about each other's culture and history. It means much more than just teaching Asians English. It means that our children should know more about the religion and culture of their classmates. It is not enough just to teach in the sixth form something about the Hindu religion, Sikhism and the Muslim faith, because many youngsters never reach the sixth form.

(House of Lords, 1971)

This built perhaps on a call a half-decade earlier by Roy Jenkins, then Labour Home Secretary, not for 'the loss, by immigrants, of their own national characteristics and culture' but instead for 'integration' defined 'not as a flattening process of assimilation but as equal opportunity, accompanied by cultural diversity, in an atmosphere of mutual tolerance'.

While there had been people of Caribbean, Asian or African descent in Britain for centuries, greater numbers had settled since the Second World War, amidst labour shortages in the UK, and had made a valuable contribution to the economy and public services. Not all politicians had as positive a view of ethnic and cultural diversity, however. There was a long history of racism that had not disappeared after the days since the British Empire covered much of the globe. Black and minority ethnic people were especially affected by an Immigration Act passed that year, further limiting the right to enter and stay even for UK citizens. They were seldom found in leadership positions and media portrayals were often stereotypical. In wider society too, attitudes were frequently patronising or hostile.

Yet popular music, and the arts more widely, reflected and assisted a shift in thinking about the value, as well as complexity, of interpersonal and social relationships across communities, if prejudice, discrimination and fear were countered. So did the work of 'public intellectuals' such as renowned academics with a high media profile. This was linked in part to how technology had made it easier to share sounds and images within countries and internationally. While artists and thinkers in the USA and beyond exploring such themes captured the imagination of some in Britain, work also emerged from a specifically British context. Meanwhile, the UK was moving towards joining the EEC, further expanding opportunities for cross-cultural contact, including educational and job opportunities abroad.

Multiculturalism is a 'misguided dogma', Conservative Home Secretary Suella Braverman claimed in 2023. 'It has failed because it allowed people to come to our society and live parallel lives in it … And, in extreme cases, they could pursue lives aimed at undermining the stability and threatening the security of society.'

The then Prime Minister Rishi Sunak, also of Indian descent, distanced himself from her comments. The country was 'a fantastic multi-ethnic democracy', in his view, where 'we have done an incredible job of integrating people into society'. To him that 'speaks to the progress we've made over the years' and 'something we should all collectively be incredibly proud about'. It was important though 'that everybody subscribes to British values. That's the thing that unites us and binds us together.'

In a Good Friday post on X/Twitter in March 2024, he elaborated on what 'British values' might mean, mentioning Jesus: 'Let us reflect on the values of compassion, charity and selflessness he embodied,' he wrote. 'These values are at the heart of British values, inspiring us to build a society based on respect, tolerance and dignity for all.' While many people might wish to see such values widely reflected in Britain and beyond, some might have been sceptical that this was what his government's policies actually encouraged (Sunak, 2024).

Hostile Environment Britain

Much has indeed changed since the early 1970s. Depictions of people of colour in the media have become more common and varied, and even taking account of higher numbers in the overall population, musicians and writers from diverse backgrounds had sizeable followings outside their own communities. Representation in leadership positions became less exceptional. Yet ethnic inequalities in some aspects of health, for instance, were stark, while changes in the law had left increasing numbers of British people of Commonwealth descent who had long been settled, or even born, in the UK at risk of expulsion.

Overall, aided by Brexit and curtailing of aspects of human rights, the environment was in some ways becoming more hostile to those regarded as outsiders. In the face of 'culture wars' that stirred up suspicion and resentment of Muslims and sometimes other minorities, including disabled people, more moderate politicians were sometimes pushed out or reinvented themselves to appear enthusiastic about exclusionary policies.

Laws on staying in the UK had continued to get tighter, affecting even family reunion for people long settled in Britain, though sections of the British public continued to believe the myth that immigration was 'uncontrolled'. A 'Windrush scandal' had come to light a few years earlier, when in some instances older people who had arrived from the Caribbean many decades earlier as children or young adults had their entry papers destroyed by the state, which then demanded that they prove they were in the UK legally. Those who did not satisfy the authorities, despite a lifetime of service for instance through working for the NHS, were deported, destroying their lives and tearing their families apart. While the government backed down when this was exposed, it was slow to compensate the victims – and changed the law to make it even easier to remove people of colour long settled here and with no other home, for instance for comparatively minor offences or at the Home Secretary's discretion.

Parties competed on how tough they intended to be towards migrants and refugees trying to enter the UK on boats from France or by other irregular channels, the usual ways having been largely blocked off. Asylum seekers who did reach the country were often detained in horrific conditions that worsened trauma, though in many instances they were able to demonstrate even to sceptical officials that they had a well-founded fear of persecution. Over the centuries, successive generations of refugees had navigated suspicion and hostility and they and their descendants had contributed hugely to cultural, scientific and wider life in the country, yet what newcomers had to offer was played down and fear promoted. Even actively recruited overseas students paying massive fees that funded university expansion, and workers plugging skills gaps, entering through regulated routes, as well as their dependants, were repeatedly referred to as if posing a major threat to society's well-being.

Reactions to conflict in the Middle East further deepened tensions. The murder of civilians and hostage-taking by Hamas in October 2023 was horrific and indefensible; at the same time the Israeli government's massive violence against defenceless Palestinians met with outrage and large peaceful demonstrations in Britain, where the authorities helped to resource Israel's military action. Though some protesters were Jewish, certain government ministers tried to make out that anger at what was happening was necessarily antisemitic, as if no decent person would be bothered by children of colour being driven from their homes, starved or killed in their thousands, unless motivated by hate for someone else. While Muslims were especially affected, and targeted, more generally divisions deepened.

Amidst the decline of many areas due to deindustrialisation and other economic and social change, made worse by austerity amidst soaring costs, discontent grew, though often channelled against neighbours whose plight was similar or worse rather than those wielding power. In England, the Labour Party leadership, aspiring to regain office, focused more on practical measures to improve the economy, public services and the environment than their Conservative rivals, for whom 'culture wars' had become central. Yet these too, in attempting to emphasise their business-friendly credentials and reduce expectations of speedy improvements for those who felt alienated and overlooked, also emphasised the supposedly key importance of reducing the presence of those from supposedly alien cultural backgrounds, whose presence might undermine cohesion.

Undoubtedly friction did occur at times, sometimes exacerbated by blunders in policy and practice by decision-makers. Yet many of the problems that existed cut across communities: even if minorities targeted for verbal attack had vanished overnight, shortages of secure and reasonably paid jobs, the housing crisis, serious under-provision of support to children and families in need, knife and gun crime and drug misuse would have continued to take a devastating toll.

Clearly some interpretations of 'multiculturalism' regard friendliness and mutual respect among people from different ethnic and faith backgrounds – without eradicating difference – as an essential aspect, or at least shared commitment to values such as compassion, tolerance and dignity for all. Others emphasise separation. Scholars have examined and debated some of the varied ways the word has been used over the past half-century and potential implications. However, some influential figures became increasingly vocal about their hostility to the concept, however understood.

In this climate, in April 2024, ex-Labour MP turned ex-Tory party deputy chairman Lee Anderson, by then in Reform UK, outspokenly attacked 'multiculturalism', lamenting how the presence of ethnic minorities had supposedly left Blackpool streets dirty and uncared for. An area that, fifty or sixty years ago, had probably been 'full of traditional British families,' with washing lines and kids playing outdoors, had been 'flooded with migrants', he claimed. A woman had told him how 'the Romany community started to move in' and 'the British' moved out (reflecting a view of national identity in which nobody could be both). 'I want my country back!' he demanded (Smiles, 2024).

In late July, horrific stabbings in Southport left three small girls attending a yoga and dance workshop dead. The seventeen-year-old suspect charged was born and raised in Britain (though with parents from Rwanda), in a Christian household. Yet misinformation and innuendo rapidly spread through social media and the far right exploited the tragedy to mobilise angry crowds in many towns and cities. This echoed ways in which mainstream politicians and media in the USA and other parts of the world had helped to create a narrative that justified hate, on which online 'influencers' and 'cyber-warriors' could build, with horrific consequences.

Mosques were attacked, hotels housing asylum seekers set ablaze, a library and food bank destroyed and police injured as they struggled to contain the violence. People of African or Asian descent were met with verbal abuse and worse. Yet large numbers of people also gathered in solidarity to defend their neighbours. 'There are many, many more of us than you,' some sang, as they rallied against the far right. Others were understandably more cautious but gathered to help clean up afterwards and strengthen community ties. Days later, when providers of legal advice on immigration across England were threatened, thousands of anti-racists and anti-fascists from diverse backgrounds thronged the streets in a massive display of care and solidarity. There were also large numbers of police and in many areas the hardliners did not show up, though there were a few largely muted incidents.

Nevertheless the impact of events in late July and early August has been devastating not only to people in Southport, already shocked and grieving, and to black and minority ethnic people feeling afraid and marginalised, but also to those white majority ethnic people facing deprivation and overstretched public services whose interests the far-right attackers were supposedly championing. Health and care workers who came from overseas to fill vacancies, some of whom narrowly escaped serious harm, are in some instances planning to leave the UK, which will result in even more severe understaffing, with grave consequences. The ability of the higher-education sector to attract students and staff from abroad has been further undermined, alongside tourism, further damaging the economy and learning and social opportunities especially in already run-down areas.

Against this background, countering the far right and promoting healing includes offering a vision of the future that goes beyond co-existing to flourishing together across difference. I believe that certain aspects of the concept of multiculturalism that captured the imaginations of many half a century ago or so can be helpful – but firstly it is important to address some of the shortcomings which have become apparent in certain notions of what it might mean to live in a multi-cultural Britain.

Culture, Difference and Change

To begin with, a thriving multicultural society cannot be achieved without tackling the thorny problem of racism. While Donald Wade, for instance, was active in this cause in the 1960s and 1970s, some versions of multiculturalism play down the impact, offering instead an unrealistic picture of harmony without addressing a key obstacle.

Ideally, the new Labour government would dial down the rhetoric on migrants and refugees and more generally address policies that perpetuate racism, having learned that reinforcing aspects of far-right untruths and harmful ideology can bolster its appeal, as well as opening the door to grave social and economic damage. However, this is unlikely to happen without sustained pressure. Meanwhile, grassroots action is critically important.

Addressing racism effectively is not about disparaging most UK cultural heritage or requiring white individuals to engage in self-abasement. Instead, it involves recognising the multiple ways in which at least some attitudes and practices that perpetuate inequity have been absorbed by most of us (including at times being internalised by people of global majority heritage), though we can make efforts to break free – and, most importantly, join in challenging structural and systemic discrimination. Attempts at celebrating cultural diversity without seeking justice could lead, at worst, to a treatment of the other as merely entertaining or 'exotic', as at best to an evasion of uncomfortable realities that might break through the pretence that all is broadly well. Or blame could be heaped on minorities for not wanting to mix even if they lack chances to do so, for instance affordable opportunities to learn English if not yet fluent, or to move into an area without white families moving out in large numbers.

Nor should people of the same broad or specific ethnic or religious background be treated as uniform blocs that can be represented by 'community leaders' (whatever type of community or leadership is considered), though there may be figures who are influential or have a key role in communication. For instance, contacts among a handful of prominent men and occasionally women, aimed at promoting cross-cultural exchange and mutual understanding, have their place. But others with a similar range of racial and faith-based identities may differ from these in multiple ways and interact with one another in all kinds of other settings, positive or negative (even if such encounters, friendships and rivalries may go largely unnoticed because they are informal and involve, say, 'only girls' or cleaners working the same shift rather than organisational chairs, businessmen or clergy). Experience, opinion, power and status vary, along with personal and family preference, which may mean that an apparently shared culture may take on different nuances.

Also, culture is continually changing amidst economic, technological, social, political and environmental upheaval and contact with different people and practices, while traditions may take on fresh meanings or be misremembered. While people, especially those who feel unmoored amidst aspects of today's world, may understandably feel nostalgic at times, it is impossible simply to roll back the clock – and unhelpful to direct frustration against people who did not bring about the change but are soft targets.

Nor do all aspects of 'tradition' deserve to be romanticised, in any cultural group. At times, certain men in minority ethnic communities tried to make the case that they should be allowed to abuse their wives because it was part of their culture and certain white professionals swallowed this argument. Yet, not so long ago, blatant sexism was endemic in multiple cultures across the world (for example, in Britain, marital rape was legal) – and equally wrong. Multiple inequalities are still common in both majority and minority groups, often with attempts to justify these on grounds of 'culture', even if this results in inconsistencies. For instance, not discriminating against people on grounds of being lesbian, gay, bisexual or transgender (LGBT+) may be condemned at different times for either undermining Western culture or imposing this on others.

Cultures, as well as being constantly changing, can be based on factors other than ethnicity and religion; and may overlap. So people may talk of a school, workplace or professional culture, youth or pub culture, the culture of trade unionism and so forth, also shifting with time; and one or another aspect of someone's cultural identity may be most apparent when moving from one setting to another. Regional cultures have often been disparaged in England, especially if northern or Midlands-based and associated with working-class people. Within Scotland and Wales too there are marked differences that may influence status as well as cultural expression.

If the term 'multiculturalism' is used in a way that glides over complexities, it may conjure up images of well-defined separate groups of people, each with a fixed culture and identifiable representatives, equally able to choose whether to relate to one another positively. Other obstacles to a culturally diverse and caring society in which all thrive include broader social trends and human weakness.

In a neoliberal society, in which long-standing ties have in many instances been weakened or dissolved, affecting human relationships as well as material security, discontent can fester. Frustration may be channelled inwards or against immediate neighbours rather than broader social forces, or wild accusations or conspiracy theories can swiftly take hold and spread. Aspects of culture may also be commodified and neatly packaged for consumers, or cross-cultural relationships seen primarily as a way to extract more from workers or pitch more skilfully to customers rather than valued because these promote human flourishing. In such a setting, cynicism or despair can take hold.

Some of the ideals that influenced earlier generations of minority and anti-racist activists, linked to a broader vision of peace and well-being for everyone facing marginalisation (however imperfectly realised), probably faded in the latter half of the twentieth century, though were not totally lost. Cultural differences then took on an enhanced significance, less balanced with other forces bringing people together.

Human fallibility too remained an issue, including being prone to prejudice of various kinds, judging others' failings more harshly than one's own, being tempted to compete in unhealthy ways, for instance as to which cultural group (or who, within such a group) was superior, most authentic or most downtrodden and so forth.

At international level, a surge in xenophobia and open prejudice of many kinds has created further challenges, while progressive movements have not always proved good at reaching out to others rather than being obsessed with ideological purity. Yet sometimes people have been able to mobilise effectively against forces that divide and the use of notions of piety and patriotism in destructive ways. Perhaps, while crises such as the rise of the far right and catastrophic climate change have sometimes led to greater fragmentation and the worst kinds of behaviour, they have also at times reawakened awareness of the importance of mutual care and courage in seeking to do what is right.

What Can Unite Us

Drawing on the work of certain researchers, I think certain concepts (if understood in sufficiently nuanced ways) may help in making sense of multicultural Britain today and identifying sources of hope (Neal et al., 2019). Shared spaces and activities may offer moments of closeness and interdependence with longer-term effects. Conviviality can go beyond describing pleasant encounters between culturally different others, important as these may be, to take in contradictions and conflict as well as openness. And community can be seen as something continually created, rather than fixed. Creating more spaces to bring together academic thinking and experience on the ground may be fruitful.

There may be various strands in work to promote greater unity amidst difference, involving action as well as openness to learning and development. Some people may be better suited to some types of action than others. Fact-sharing can be important, especially in response to online disinformation campaigns. Yet the far right plays on engaging people emotionally, for instance feeding fears and insecurities or countering concerns about one's own status by downgrading others. In addition, even noble sentiments, such as wishing to protect the vulnerable, may be harnessed for negative purposes. It is important for those seeking to tackle the spread of untruths that turn people against one another to relate to, not just inform, the people they seek to reach.

This may include creating spaces for dialogue and exchange of stories based on experience, which may build empathy. The arts too can be ways to reach out across divisions and explore deeper kinds of truth. Shared activities which may be mutually enjoyable or achieve common goals, such as beautifying a particular neighbourhood, can be of value. These may open the door to talking about, and maybe taking action on, trickier issues. For instance, the fatal stabbings in Southport touched on fears widespread in many urban areas among people of diverse cultural backgrounds: that a child one cares for may be seriously harmed or, even harder to contemplate, may seriously harm others. Or, if a child oneself, there may be continual fears about one's safety or in some instances one's capability to do something dreadful. Yet the protests did nothing to address such issues; quite the opposite. Greater co-operation in addressing such painful problems may strengthen mutual bonds.

Identifying shared values and aspirations may also offer a source of unity amidst cultural difference, for instance, common commitment to universal human rights and international humanitarian law or visions of a more just, loving and sustainable world. People from, and informed by, many cultural backgrounds have played an important part in developing such frameworks and dreams, which will no doubt continue to be refined through ideas and actions based on diverse experiences.

I am not sure whether the term 'multiculturalism' carries too much baggage, or too many contradictory meanings, to be as useful as it might; yet it is still widely used. Either way, despite challenges and setbacks, the hope of a just and thriving multicultural Britain in which everyone is cherished persists. Yet whatever terms and labels we use, the realities of how the UK addresses the needs of different communities and pressure points over immigration and fragile communities, and doing so in a culture of solidarity, anti-racism and compassion, needs championing by government, public agencies, civic groups and campaigners.

19

Beyond Belief? Re-grounding a Public Politics of Hope

Simon Barrow and Fiona Brocklesby

What does 'hope' mean for life in the constituent parts of modern Britain and the wider world of which we are part? What does it mean in a political context, in particular? The authors sat down to talk personally about this in the immediate aftermath of the UK general election in July 2024 and in the context of the coming to power at Westminster of the first Labour government since 2010. Our outlooks, politics, commitments and beliefs have many points of connection, convergence and overlap. But we also have different backgrounds, engagements and locations, bringing a diversity and richness to this exchange, alongside a willingness (indeed, an eagerness) to move beyond parochialisms and to search for unifying possibilities in the context of working towards the things we both believe in: equality, inclusion, social and economic justice, environmental sustainability and peace for the nations of these islands, the continent we inhabit and the planet that houses and nurtures us.

Because our conviction is that hope is personal and relational as well as political, and to give some context for the origins and fabric of this exchange, here is a little bit about us, aside from the professional details at the end of this book. We have both travelled widely, but presently live in different parts of the UK – Fiona in London, and Simon in Edinburgh. We have both been shaped by, and participant in, Christian communities: Catholic and Anglican (with strong ecumenical and 'peace church' links), respectively. We have both spent much of our working lives in secular occupation, though Fiona has been a governor at a Catholic foundation school, and Simon has also worked at senior level for the churches across Britain and Ireland.

We have both been immersed in politics and identify broadly with democratic socialist aspirations, but Fiona has been and remains active in the Labour Party, while Simon joined the SNP ten years ago alongside active involvement in trade unionism. We both have wide interests in art, literature and music. We have worked in different forensic and specialist professions (law, public policy, education, philosophy and theology), but we have also spent time as part of, and in close proximity to, communities where people live on the edge. We own our privilege but cite backgrounds and experiences that are far removed from, and in contention with, much of what gets labelled 'elite' in society at large.

Differentiating Hope from Optimism and Pessimism

So where did our conversation begin? With the nature of hope itself. We agreed that hope is different from both optimism and pessimism. Optimism in the predisposition to believe that things will work out well. Pessimism is the fear that they will turn out badly. Hope is an investment in life that seeks for the good, the true, the beautiful, the just and the loving (interpersonally and corporately), but does not suppose that this arrives gift-wrapped. It is a practice, not a wish. We were aware as we talked that for the two of us, and for many people in this world – an overwhelming number globally, and a much smaller number across the UK – hope is also what could be called a religious or spiritual virtue; something residing in a belief about God and/or about the very nature of things, whatever one believes about ontology and destiny.

'The arc of the moral universe is long,' Martin Luther King Jr famously declared, 'but it bends towards justice.' Hope, in those terms, is the conviction that justice becomes believable when we make it so by investing our lives; but also that in a certain, perhaps finally undeterminable sense, we are working with the grain of reality when we work for the values of dignity, justice, humanity and sustainability for all. The issue is how we put flesh on those bones, what keeps us going when things seem to be moving in a wrong direction, how we develop collective resources, virtues and skills to 'keep hope alive' (as the popular slogan has it), and how the practices and commitments of hope translate into political action in a divided and wounded world, starting with the very local.

Hope as a Common, Everyday Experience

That last point is important to both of us. Fiona, in particular, wishes to ground hope (including political hope) in something very rooted, everyday, tangible and practical. She is struck, she said, by the extraordinary resilience people have in their lives – especially those who live at the rough end, coping with problems of poverty, addiction, homelessness, family breakdown, mental health problems and much more. Of course, in the day-by-day world, some are crushed, some survive, some transcend, and some find ways of doing more than surviving 'despite it all'. But in the midst of circumstances deeply shaped by upbringing, kinship (or lack of it), class location, personal psychology, resources and much more, there seems to be a broad inflection towards bouncing back, believing that things can improve, determination to find a way out or forward.

This is closely related, Fiona said, to her observations about what people hope for in life, if you ask them and listen well. What many, if not most, people want is something that is quite ordinary yet for a number of us, and in different circumstances, also feels extraordinary. Good health, a means of earning a reliable income, a warm and liveable home, education, companionship, the opportunity to progress in life, a sense of being heard and responded to, affordable transport, leisure time, family and friends. The list could go on. A number of these things are about survival. Others are about flourishing. All are deeply personal, yet they also depend upon public infrastructure and services, a well-functioning economy and many other things that suggest the ways in which we depend upon one another as human beings, in our relationship with the earth, and in our relationship to the biosphere.

The Erosion of Hope in the Political

That vital connectivity is easy to lose at the core of 'modern life', however. People hope for decent and secure sources of income, but in spite of a dramatic overall growth in national and private wealth in recent decades, life in Britain today is uncertain and precarious for too many. The gig economy, seasonal work, the rise of automation, austerity, the withdrawal of services, government crackdowns on benefits and other forms of social support – all of these things make the everyday hopes for a better life of ordinary people difficult and frustrating. Then we are also drowning in forms of consumption that whet our appetites while often denying the ability to satisfy them through lack of money, education, access or resources.

At the same time, everything from public spaces and the natural world is being commodified and monetised. Inequality also breeds dislocation, dissatisfaction and resentment. Hope for the individual cannot really subsist and be fulfilled without a social hope, a hope for the group, for the many. Yet again, returning to politics, the tendency in recent years has been away from the political realm as a sphere where the possibilities and hope for 'better' can be met. Disenchantment with politics and politicians is manifested in the fact that turnout at the 2024 election was just 59.9 per cent, the second lowest since 1885, with only 2001 being lower at 59.4 per cent. Correspondingly, the share of the vote of the two largest parties, Labour and the Conservatives, was 57.4 per cent, the lowest since the 1918 general election.

What this tells us is that increasing numbers of people are giving up on politics, and among those who are not, there is a search for something different – a search that, in electoral terms, the First Past the Post system makes difficult (for many, nigh on impossible) to bring to fruition. This is fertile ground for Nigel Farage, for Reform and for the wider far right in many parts of Britain and across Europe. These are the forces that wish to capitalise on dissatisfaction by sewing further seeds of division and scapegoating migrants, ethnic minorities, claimants and others who are 'different' for our woes – rather than looking at the monopoly control of wealth and power that exists everywhere from the City of London outwards. We shall return to this danger later.

Connecting Smaller and Larger Hopes

The key thing for both of us at this stage in the exchange was to recognise that, while our own sources of hope might sometimes be painted on a grand tapestry, for a significant majority of people the canvas is much smaller. As we have said, life very much revolves around the everyday, and binding ideas like religions and ideologies have been losing traction since the 1960s in particular, despite the arrival of new faiths and philosophies through the movement and influx of people from around the world. This led us to a twofold observation. On the one hand, what we call 'hope' loses contact with reality if it loses contact with what it is that is most important to people in the deep and interpersonal fabric of their lives. On the other hand, losing the aspiration to build better and bigger together, to be able to confront things like the existential threat of global warming, means that individual or small hopes will be lost, swamped or distorted.

Somehow, we felt through our conversation, we need a way of both affirming and recognising hope in what could be termed (in a non-pejorative sense) the mundane, without losing the desire to awaken hope in politics, hope in collective action, hope in systemic change, hope in forms of spirituality that reach beyond the self-therapy of 'mindfulness', and hope in beliefs and ideas that can look back to the riches of tradition and the nurturing of community (in churches, mosques, synagogues, temples, gurdwaras, humanist assemblies and other places) without closing themselves off to the future, or to a deep need for 'the other' as a companion and teacher, rather than a threat.

For both of us, what could be called 'smaller hopes' and what could be called 'larger hopes' need each other and can feed off each other. But not unless they are nourished, resourced, encouraged and affirmed in particular ways. That got us into the part of our conversation where we talked about understanding the changing nature of the UK and its different constituent parts, nations and regions; and also about what sort of 'belief frameworks' were operating in what is often dubbed 'a secular society', and how those can be accessed and operationalised in a positive way for a plural context.

Regarding the former, we noticed different cultures, aspirations, ideas and senses of community in different parts of the UK. Fiona talked about her own neighbourhood and the work of community organisations and networks within it. Being in London, she is part of a community of communities (some wealthy, some deprived, some both), but also in the place with some of the largest global financial operators in the world. A place where the money economy and the social fabric economy sometimes feel worlds apart. Part of what it is to hope therefore rests on doing everything possible to grow and sustain community and neighbourhood action and to make its voice and influence far greater within institutional politics.

For Fiona, that meant practical things like getting the council to engage, listen and respond better. People have hope when they are heard, when they can see even small things changing, when they feel that they have some genuine influence. Representational and elective politics is not sufficient for that. We agreed that much more investment is needed in (genuinely) consultative, deliberative and participatory democracy, starting at the grassroots. Citizens' juries, civic assemblies, events for crowdsourcing proposals and policies, local participatory budgeting, town hall accountability meetings – these are among mechanisms for building the kind of collaborative endeavour out of which social hope and new ways of seeing and doing politics can emerge, we believe. But there is a long way to go, and there are forces pushing in the opposite direction.

The Need to Bring Power Back to the People

The centralisation of government (in Scotland, where Simon lives, the proportion of citizens to elected representatives in local council is among the worst in Europe), obscene concentrations of wealth and the worsening pressure of work and family on people's lives all make participation challenging. So do different educational and class backgrounds and limitations. Not everyone has the time, inclination and skills needed to engage. Lifelong learning, arts and culture could make much more possible, but these too are being cut back. We need major cultural investment, not culture wars. This is also a way of strengthening social solidarities, out of which hope and aspiration grow. Simon noted that, in his experience, the sense of communal solidarity felt stronger in many parts of Scotland than in parts of England (where the far right has been most active), but this too is being eroded as pressure on public services rises.

Likewise, Scotland has its own distinct and historically rooted challenges, such as sectarianism on the west coast and elsewhere, and also its opportunities. In the latter area, the challenge for Scotland throughout its recent history has been net emigration. The global Scottish diaspora is much larger than the domestic population, and to thrive economically and in other ways, the nation needs more people. This, together with a political culture that leans left (Scotland has not given the Conservatives a majority there for nearly seventy years) and politicians from most parties who abhor the anti-immigration rhetoric flying around in Westminster, means that the nature of the migration debate in Scotland is different, and in many respects healthier. That offers hope for the building of a diverse society, though the difficulties of reception, integration and transmission require careful handling and resourcing. Pressure on local government spending is a serious issue in this regard.

At this point in the conversation, we acknowledged the issue of Scottish independence as both a source of real hope for many but also despair and anger for others. What some see as Scotland rejoining a world the UK abandoned with Brexit in a spirit of self-determination linked to internationalism, others see as separation, isolation and abandonment. What we hope for, and where we invest our hopefulness, depends to a large extent on how we view the world, how we universalise our experience, and how we frame our visions of the future.

The Thorny Question: Politics, Religion and Hope

On the issue of religion and its connections with politics in terms of both fusion and division, again we found concurrence on the basis of different but overlapping belief backgrounds. Broadly speaking, we agreed that the best way to characterise the variegated situation across the UK is that we live in localities and societies that are 'mixed belief' – with 'belief' in this context meaning both various shades of religious opinion, predominantly Christian in some areas, less so in others, and also different shades of syncretism or non-belief: 'spiritual but not religious', Humanists, agnostics, atheists, and those who in US research are referred to as 'nones' (people who respond 'nothing in particular' when asked about religion).

The role of religion in sparking hope is significant, but the role of religion in politics is controversial. Some want to keep the two apart completely. Simon is strongly in favour of the separation of church and state and the disestablishment of the Church of England. It is democratically inappropriate (and, many would argue, an abuse of the subversive message of Christ towards governing authority and 'the religion of power') to have unelected representatives of one denomination from one religion in one country in a legislature for the whole of the UK. But the churches and other faith organisations, we both agree, have a really important role to play within civil society, through NGOs and in campaigns for peace, justice and equality. These are places where hope is very much kept alive, nurtured and developed – and also spaces where people of faith and people of 'good faith' (but no religion) can work together fruitfully and learn from one another.

The issue of faith and politics comes down to the question of 'what *kind* of religion, and what *kind* of politics?' A religion that wishes to take power and rule over others is a threat to plural democracy – and probably to itself, too. We are seeing this in the way the religious right have occupied Republican politics and the MAGA (Make America Great Again) ultra-nationalist movement in the USA, with some angling overtly for an authoritarian, theocratic-style order. Such moves are also rigorously opposed by other persons of faith. On the other hand, when people talk about 'keeping religion out of politics' they are usually not talking about restricting religious voices in civil society or prohibiting lobbying, just separating organised religion from dominating within the institutions of democratic government, where all voices should be heard but none privileged. Likewise, few non-believers would criticise or resent the intervention and example of people like the late Archbishop Desmond Tutu or Martin Luther King Jr, whose voices and actions within the political arena were powerful in their advocacy of rights and justice for all, not just for their own religious bodies, or at the expense of others.

Pioneering Partnership in Belief and Hope

In this regard, though she has been a governor at a Catholic-foundation school, Fiona is clear that publicly-funded education should be open to all, and should not discriminate on the basis of religion in selection, admissions, staffing and curriculum. Simon, who is also acting chair and a co-founder of the Accord Coalition for In-clusive Education (which brings religious and non-religious people together to advocate for reform of faith schools in England and Wales) very much agrees with this.

The model we advocate instead is one of partnership between the religious and non-religious in public life, a plural form of secularity that seeks to create an open dialogue around beliefs and ethics, and a more intentional discussion about different sources of hope and pos-sibility among people of all faiths and none, looking specifically at how particular traditions can invest in political and social pluralism for their own benefit and for the benefit of 'the common good'. This is a notion that, along with subsidiarity, is a key component of Catholic Social Teaching (CST), we both observe. But crucially, it has found acceptance among those of different convictions and can be advocated and defended on grounds other than what might be seen as restrictive-ly 'religious' ones.

Inter alia, it is noteworthy for us that figures on the political right who often talk about 'Christian values' seem either ignorant of, or dis-missive towards, CST and the deep traditions of the churches and other faiths in relation to social thought, peace-making and social justice, as well as the more radical movements known collectively as liberation theologies.

An Encouragement and a Warning: The Weaponisation of Religion

In summary, and acknowledging the powerful voices of ethical and secular humanists, we believe that faith and belief in the broadest, most conversational sense can play a crucial role in promoting a wide and rich conversation about hope and the future of politics. There is, however, a dark side to be acknowledged. In recent months, Nigel Farage and Reform, along with other siren voices on the far right, have been increasing the volume of rhetoric about Britain as a 'Christian country'. By this, they mean to smuggle in selective notions of belonging and toxic notions of ethnicity, weaponising religious language to justify the scapegoating and demonisation of Muslims, migrants and others they disapprove of or fear.

This is part of a populist political project (which sadly played a huge role in the Brexit campaign) to push the Overton window and institutional and party politics towards the right, and a vision of society cast in terms of what elsewhere is rightly identified as White Nationalism. These forces offer a faux and dangerous 'hope'. They must be resisted, politically, through education, and in spaces of public discourse. People of faith, and especially in this instance Christians, have a particular responsibility to push back against the hijacking of religion by those who seek to use it to buttress their own power, to divide society, and to create a false hierarchy of worth within the social, cultural and political order.

Cultivating a Public Discourse Around Political Hope

Penultimately, we asked together what a 'public politics of hope' might mean in practice. The challenges and possible answers emerge at different levels and in different contexts. First, returning to our opening theme, hope takes the shape of common purpose, investment in new possibilities and the encouragement of constructive engagement through increasing the capacity, resourcing and agency of ordinary people in relation to what effects them and their neighbours most at a community level. This can and should draw strongly on the 'ordinary' and 'mundane' day-to-day and year-by-year hopes of most citizens for a better and fairer society for themselves and future generations.

We therefore need spaces for more intentional discussions as to what a 'good society' looks like and how to work towards it together. Is this not something that faith communities could be working with secular civic organisations to sponsor and encourage? That, of course, requires an appreciation that 'we', whoever 'we' are, cannot claim a monopoly of wisdom and will need to hear and respond to those who think and see differently. But the purpose of such conversations is to encourage precisely that capacity to listen and appreciate and to be able to share the wisdom we have learned from our respective backgrounds, engagements and upbringings.

It would be particularly beneficial to involve politicians and public officials in such conversations, in the first instance as listeners rather than protagonists. Because political parties, lobbyists, civil servants, campaign groups and think tanks (the whole fabric of 'political discourse' in and around our public institutions, in fact) need to recover an explicit dialogue about values – by which we mean values-in-practice, not simply values as abstract or theoretical notions. This goes deeper than the present culture of 'mission statements', which produce tick lists of aspirations and behaviour but which are often very thin in terms of understanding the resources and changed relationships necessary to turn them into something approaching real culture-change. Again, the technocratic spirit of the age will readily compartmentalise and instrumentalise 'values', but the real hard work is synching organisational, missional and policy change with relational change, plus considerations as to what feeds and sustains the human spirit, individually and corporately (through the notion that people are always persons-in-relation, not isolated individuals, and need each other).

Culture and Learning as Hopeful Resources

Here once again, the role of arts and culture is crucial. But so is learning from other societies, where overarching commitments to creating a common good and confronting class or caste-driven divisions is rooted in shared belief frameworks that operate within and beyond particular religious, political or ideological systems. That would include, for example, the ancient African concept of *Ubuntu*, meaning 'humanity towards others'. This is often recounted as reminding us that 'I am what I am because of who you are and who we all are'. That is the very opposite of Margaret Thatcher's 'there is no such thing as society'. The practical question is how such an understanding might reshape the way we do politics. For example, how do we handle our opponents? Is forgiveness possible or necessary in political life? What about compassion in politics (around which there is now a very effective action-and-reflection network of the same name)? How do we face the realities of power, its use and misuse, including huge divisions of wealth and control, while aspiring to a shared humanity as the determining factor in shaping our lives, both interpersonally and institutionally?

Such conversations, and the creation of spaces and facilitative processes for them, can and should go alongside the more formal business of setting up citizens' juries, assemblies and events to empower people to shape the wider issues of which they are part, but too often remotely so. The organised citizens' deliberations around the referendum on abortion and reproductive freedom in Ireland is an oft-cited example of a process of bringing people on all sides of a difficult debate together in order to enable the creation of a different atmosphere to the sterile and bitter recrimination that often dominates such 'debates' (Pelese,

2018). But there are other examples, including the crowdsourcing of ideas for a constitution in Iceland. In Scotland, it was a constitutional convention that helped shift the dial on devolution in the pre-Blair era, and there are now discussions about what kind of gatherings and exchanges at a civic level could help to break the current deadlock on the constitutional question around independence.

Similarly, local 'participatory budgeting' exercises have proliferated in Britain and other parts of the world in recent years – though the challenge here is to ensure that local and national governments do not use them cynically, as a way of getting people to manage cuts for them, and that they are not dominated by people with social, economic and educational advantage. In the areas of community wealth-building, peace-building, conflict transformation, local currencies and resource-sharing there is a plethora of ideas being cultivated through grassroots groups in Britain and well beyond. The mapping, sharing, piloting, reporting and replicating of such ground-up initiatives would in itself be a real spur to hope and new approaches to traditional political and economic questions.

Investing in Citizenship Is Key
At the heart of all this is the renewal of citizenship and the development of the capacity, ability and willingness of ordinary citizens (not mere subjects) to become involved in creating their own solutions to shared problems. Here the work of Dr Simon Duffy and Citizen Network is crucial, alongside specific initiatives like the 99% Organisation, which mobilises against poverty. This is hope as tangible will, in action. For a public politics of hope is not just about reform of our parliamentary system and voting system towards proportionality (vital though that is). Nor is it just about changing the culture and procedure of political parties, encouraging them to agree to work together wherever possible, in spite of disagreement (important though that is, too). It is

about something akin to the syndicalist spirit of self-organisation and systems of networked autonomy. It is also about those who sit on the edges of institutional life, seeking to bring in the energy, critique and vision of voluntary, associational and civic groups. And it is about the 'prophets' (a word meaning forthtelling, or declaring a moral position, not foretelling, or 'predicting the future', in the Hebrew and Christian scriptures) who stand outside systems of domination calling for a new and different way, and for *shalom* or *salaam* (peace based on justice and the restoration of right relations among people, in the Jewish, Christian and Muslim traditions).

From Catastrophe to Hope via *Metanoia*, Virtue and Jubilee?

A final but important word from us. The stark truth for our world today, and for the nations and regions that make up the UK, is that we face an existential crisis. Global warming and the existent (not merely future) climate emergency threatens our very survival as a species. Biodiversity is reaching critical levels of erosion. Our 'politics as usual' and our 'economics as usual' are literally killing the planet, and our political, corporate and economic force-leaders are still struggling to act with anything like the urgency and decisiveness required. Wishing on technological solutions alone is not sufficient, as the lessons of the earlier so-called Green Revolution might warn us. We need major change in the way we organise human ecologies across the globe, which makes a new way of doing politics, economics and democracy crucial not optional.

This in turn requires a change of heart, mind and will, and a human willingness to turn around and head in a new direction: one of hope and possibility in the face of catastrophe and destruction. Again, there is a word for this: *metanoia*. In the Christian gospels, it is a Greek word usually translated 'repentance', which sounds pious or prescriptive. In fact, it simply means 'turning right around', or embarking on a new and different path. There is a connection here with various iterations of the tradition of ethical thinking known as virtue ethics, starting with Aristotle in the constrained, partial and particular circumstances of Athenian democracy. Virtue ethics begins not by asking what moral rules we should follow or be compelled towards, or what utilitarian decisions we can justify in the interests of the largest number of people. Rather, it asks what 'the good' is, what kind of habits and behaviours (virtues) within human community need to be cultivated to grow it, and what kind of character among human persons needs to be cultivated in order to make these virtues doable and sustainable.

What a hopeful turnaround it would be within our organisational cultures if we could talk again about the good, about character and about practices and habits that build the present and future we desire? Instead, right now, the word 'virtue' is used mainly as an insult. 'Virtue signalling' is the term employed to denote and mock something as an empty gesture of piety or public expediency. That surely needs to be reversed. We need actions instantiating aspirations, rather than the cynical dismissal of aspiration towards the good. (As the wise moral philosopher Mary Midgley once pointed out, the overlooked benefit of even hypocrisy is that it reminds us that there is something to aim at which we are falling short of.)

In addition, both Christians and Jews inherit a spiritually driven political framework for the kind of system change and change of direction our world needs to be contemplating right now. It is called 'Jubilee', and it was first used in modern times by the largely but temporarily successful Jubilee 2000 campaign (set up by Ann Pettifor and others). This was an international coalition in over forty countries that called for the cancellation of developing countries' unsustainable debt by the year 2000. Jubilee, the concept that inspired it, is the ancient Hebrew tradition of seeking the equalisation and restoration of land, property and ownership rights through seven cycles of 'sabbatical years'. It is about a complete transformation of the economic system, through radical reform rather than revolution.

This biblical Jubilee also shaped the commitment of Christ and the early Christians to stand alongside the poor and dispossessed, rather than with the representatives of empire. 'Remit our debts, as we remit the debts of others' is at the core of what the church calls 'the Lord's Prayer'. The phrase was later sanitised into 'forgive us our sins' in order to turn wrongdoing into a purely personal matter removed from the harsh realities of economic and political injustice. That switch, as much as the burying of the subversive demands of the Torah, which set out the original demands for a Jubilee of sharing in the Hebrew tradition, suited those who wanted to turn Christianity (and, indeed, all religion) into a tool of the establishment and the status quo.

In historical terms, of course, there are extensive disputes about how far original Jubilee injunctions on land reform and redistribution of wealth were implemented. In ancient Israel, too, there were those whose sole business was to thwart the equalisers. But the original Jubilee is not simply obscure history, nor is it something to be dismissed under the rubric of 'religion'. Believers and non-believers alike today are still using its inspiration to turn the spotlight on tax evasion, speculative finance and unaccountable corporate capital. Maybe, in relation to the climate crisis, inequality and much else, we need a Jubilee awakening through acts of human *metanoia* (turning towards new pathways). For this to be possible, we need a larger and more expansive set of civic and public conversations, across the UK and beyond, about hope as a practical determination for change, rather than as merely a cipher for wishful thinking.

That would naturally raise profound questions about how we 'do politics' in practical and organisational terms, beyond both the dominance of powerful economic interests and the cynicism and manipulation that can all-too-readily characterise parliamentary manoeuvrings between and within party blocs. The challenges a new Labour government faces at Westminster, and within the ecology of nations across these islands, are a small subset of this much larger question – ones that have to be handled on their own terms but that also beg the much wider and broader discourse around 'political hope' we have sought to unpack here.

Section VI

Beyond Britain

20

The Island of Ireland,
Brexit and the UK

Jennifer A. Cassidy

In the realm of ancient Irish mythology, the tale of Tír na nÓg speaks of a land of eternal youth and beauty, a paradise where time stands still. This mythical narrative, much like the concept of nation-hood, embodies a vision of an ideal state, one that remains untouched by the ravages of time and change. Yet, the reality of nations, much like Tír na nÓg, is subject to the inexorable forces of change and transformation. The island of Ireland, with its rich tapestry of history, culture and political strife, has long been a land where the currents of change are deeply felt. The relationship between Ireland and the UK has been particularly tumultuous, shaped by centuries of conflict, co-operation and co-habitation.

The advent of Brexit represents a transformative event, one that has significantly impacted national identities and intergovernmental relationships on the island of Ireland and within the UK. The decision of the UK to leave the European Union (EU) has not merely been a political manoeuvre; it has struck at the very heart of what it means to belong to a nation, to be a part of a larger collective identity. As Benedict Anderson posits in his seminal work, *Imagined Communities*, nations are socially constructed communities, imagined by the people who perceive themselves to be part of that group (Anderson, 2006). Brexit has disrupted these imagined communities, challenging long-held notions of identity, belonging and sovereignty.

This chapter delves into the profound ways Brexit has reconfigured identities and governance structures on the island of Ireland, within the UK and between both entities themselves. It provides an analysis of the new political terrain that Labour now governs, finally, with the backing of the ballot box. It also explores the innovative policies and ideas necessary for a reforming, radical administration.

Brexit has fundamentally reshaped the political, socio-economic and identity landscapes of the island of Ireland and its relationship with the UK. The departure from the EU necessitates a revaluation of identities, governance and intergovernmental relations. A reforming, radical Labour government must navigate this complex terrain, addressing immediate challenges while laying the groundwork for a stable and cohesive future. This analysis illuminates how Brexit has reshaped perceptions of identity and sovereignty on the island of Ireland, and how the new political climate has altered the positions of major parties and stakeholders. By drawing on political analysts, sociologists and leading public officials, in the field of national identity, Anglo-Irish relations, and changing socio-economic state relations, we delve into the evolving notions of what it means to be Irish, British, or Northern Irish in a post-Brexit context.

The economic consequences of Brexit are profound, necessitating new economic strategies and co-operation mechanisms. This chapter will explore the economic disruptions caused by Brexit and the potential for new trade agreements, investment in cross-border infrastructure, and support for affected industries. Drawing on the work of economists like Seamus McGuinness and Adele Bergin, we analyse the economic interdependence between Northern Ireland and the

Republic of Ireland and propose new initiatives to foster economic resilience. This discussion will highlight the critical role of economic interdependence in reconfiguring national identities and ensuring sustainable growth.

Brexit has brought significant changes to governance structures, with implications for devolution and regional autonomy. This chapter examines these changes and their impact on governance and intergovernmental relations. By exploring potential changes to governance structures and intergovernmental relations, this chapter provides in-depth analyses relating to the prospects for enhanced co-operation between the UK and Irish governments and reforms to the Northern Ireland Assembly.

The social impacts of Brexit, particularly in terms of community relations and identity politics, are critical. This chapter explores how Brexit has influenced social cohesion and division within and between communities on the island of Ireland. Drawing in the prominent work of social scientists such as Claire Mitchell and Katy Hayward, we furthermore examine issues such as community integration, protection of minority rights and the role of social policies in promoting cohesion. By understanding these social dynamics, we can propose policies that foster unity and address the divisions exacerbated by Brexit.

Finally, current and potential future developments, economically, socially, democratically, and geopolitically, are also explored. This chapter considers economic trends, social changes, geopolitical considerations, and technological and environmental factors, using forward-looking analyses and weaving in insightful commentary throughout, by political science experts in the realm of 'the island of Ireland, Brexit and the United Kingdom'.

Through a detailed exploration of key themes – identity and sovereignty, economic interdependence and disruption, governance and intergovernmental relations, social cohesion and division, and future scenarios and policy responses – there is an illumination of the challenges and opportunities that lie ahead. This examination not only provides a grounded analysis of our current social, economic and political environment in late 2024 but also proposes informed, strategic directions for the new Labour government to successfully navigate the complex post-Brexit landscape.

Historical Context and the Good Friday Agreement

Pre-Brexit dynamics

The historical relationship between Ireland, Northern Ireland and the UK is a tapestry woven with threads of conflict, co-operation and profound political change. The partition of Ireland in 1921 marked a significant turning point, creating two distinct political entities: Northern Ireland, which remained part of the UK, and the Irish Free State, which would later become the Republic of Ireland. This division was not merely a political manoeuvre but a reflection of deep-seated historical, religious and cultural differences. Richard English, in his comprehensive works on Irish history, underscores the complexities of this partition, emphasising how it entrenched a dual identity dynamic that continues to shape the socio-political landscape of the region (English, 2006).

The period known as the Troubles was a time of intense sectarian conflict in Northern Ireland. This era was characterised by violent clashes between unionists, largely identified as British and Protestant, and nationalists, who identified as Irish and Catholic. The conflict claimed over 3,500 lives and left a lasting impact on the socio-political landscape of the region. The Troubles highlighted the profound challenges of reconciling these conflicting identities within the framework of the UK political system.

Amidst this backdrop of strife, the Good Friday Agreement (GFA) of 1998 emerged as a beacon of hope. The GFA was a monumental peace accord that sought to address the deep-rooted divisions by establishing a new political framework for Northern Ireland. Indeed, any analysis of this period emphasises the GFA's role in transforming the political dynamics of the region. By advocating power-sharing and creating institutions that promoted cross-community co-operation, the GFA aimed to bridge the historical chasm between unionists and nationalists. Arguably, the GFA reimagined the political landscape of Northern Ireland, offering a new path towards reconciliation and shared governance.

The Good Friday Agreement

The GFA was a seminal moment in the reconfiguration of national identities and governance on the island of Ireland. The GFA established a devolved government in Northern Ireland, where power was shared between unionists and nationalists. This devolved government was designed to ensure that both communities had a stake in the political process, thereby reducing the potential for conflict.

In his work *The New Northern Ireland Politics*, Jonathan Tonge offers an insightful perspective on the GFA, highlighting its pivotal role in reshaping identity politics in Northern Ireland. Tonge emphasises that the agreement facilitated a new era where individuals could embrace dual identities, being both British and Irish, thus fostering a more inclusive and pluralistic society. The agreement recognised the right of individuals to identify as British, Irish or both, a crucial development in a region where identity had long been a source of division. By legitimising multiple identities, the GFA promoted a more inclusive and pluralistic society.

The GFA also established several cross-border institutions aimed at fostering co-operation between Northern Ireland and the Republic of Ireland. These institutions were vital in promoting economic, social and political collaboration across the border, further integrating the two regions. The establishment of the North South Ministerial Council, for instance, created a platform for joint decision-making on issues of mutual concern, ranging from agriculture to infrastructure development. Tonge emphasises that the cross-border institutions created under the GFA were instrumental in promoting not just economic co-operation but also a sense of shared identity and mutual respect (2006).

Brexit referendum and its immediate aftermath

The Brexit referendum of 2016 was a watershed moment that introduced new uncertainties and challenges to the delicate equilibrium established by the GFA. Northern Ireland voted predominantly to remain in the EU, contrasting sharply with the overall UK decision to leave. This divergence highlighted the unique position of Northern Ireland within the UK and the complexities of its relationship with both the Republic of Ireland and the broader European context. The immediate aftermath of the Brexit vote saw heightened political tensions and economic uncertainties. The prospect of a hard border between Northern Ireland and the Republic of Ireland became a contentious issue, threatening to unravel the co-operative frameworks established by the GFA. Scholars like Brendan O'Leary have emphasised the constitutional implications of Brexit, in particular how it challenged, and arguably continues to challenge the foundations of the GFA. O'Leary in his work *A Treatise on Northern Ireland* highlights that Brexit posed, and arguably poses, a direct challenge to the Good Friday Agreement, especially in its provisions for an open border and the delicate balance of identities it sought to protect.

Politically, Brexit has strained the power-sharing arrangements in Northern Ireland. The uncertainty surrounding the border and the future relationship between Northern Ireland and the EU has exacerbated existing tensions between unionist and nationalist parties.

Socially, the Brexit vote has deepened divisions, with many in the nationalist community feeling that their European identity and rights are being eroded. Economically, the potential disruption to cross-border trade poses significant risks, particularly in sectors such as agriculture and manufacturing, which are heavily integrated across the border. O'Leary highlights that the economic consequences of Brexit, especially the disruption to cross-border trade, threaten the economic stability and interdependence that have been critical to the peace process (2019).

For all who seek to understand a post-Brexit era on the island of Ireland, the historical context and the GFA provide a crucial backdrop to understanding the transformative impact of Brexit on the island of Ireland and the UK. The partition of Ireland, the Troubles and the GFA have all played significant roles in shaping the identities and political structures of the region. The Brexit referendum and its aftermath have introduced new challenges, threatening to disrupt the delicate balance achieved by the GFA. By examining these historical dynamics, we gain a deeper insight into the reconfiguration of nations and identities in the post-Brexit era.

Political Terrain and Identity Post-Brexit

The current political climate in Northern Ireland and the Republic of Ireland post-Brexit is characterised by significant flux and uncertainty. The decision of the UK to leave the EU has had profound implications for the political dynamics on the island. In Northern Ireland, the political environment has become increasingly polarised, with major political parties such as Sinn Féin, the Democratic Unionist Party (DUP) and the Social Democratic and Labour Party (SDLP) grappling with the new realities imposed by Brexit.

Sinn Féin, which advocates for Irish unification, has viewed, and arguably continues to view, Brexit as both a challenge and an opportunity.

Post-referendum, the party quickly leveraged the Brexit vote to bolster its argument for a united Ireland, emphasising the economic and social disruptions that Brexit would cause. Mary Lou McDonald, the leader of Sinn Féin, consistently argues that Brexit has revealed the inadequacies of the British government's commitment to all people in Northern Ireland, arguably seeking to reshape how the people of Northern Ireland view nationhood, political allegiance and identity.

In contrast, the DUP, which staunchly supports Northern Ireland's union with the UK, faced significant challenges in maintaining its position in power. The party's endorsement of Brexit alienated many of its constituents who were concerned, and continued to be so, by the economic and social ramifications of leaving the EU. Arlene Foster, the DUP's leader, acknowledged this tension, emphasising the need to respect the democratic decision to leave the EU while ensuring that Northern Ireland's unique position and its integral place within the UK are protected (Foster, 2017).

Political analysts such as John Garry have pointed out that the post-Brexit political landscape in Northern Ireland is marked by deepening divisions and the entrenchment of identity politics. Garry (2019) highlights that the Brexit referendum has exacerbated existing political fault lines in Northern Ireland, making the reconciliation of unionist and nationalist aspirations the most challenging for decades.

Turning to the theme of identity and sovereignty, we see that Brexit has fundamentally reshaped perceptions of identity and sovereignty on the island of Ireland. The traditional understanding of sovereignty, rooted in political and territorial control, has been challenged by the realities of Brexit. Nationalist communities in Northern Ireland have increasingly identified with the EU, seeing it as a guarantor of their rights and an alternative to British sovereignty. Scholars like Rogers Brubaker argue that Brexit has prompted a rethinking of identity, where sovereignty is viewed as layered and shared rather than monolithic (Brubaker, 2017).

We see this argument's foundation arise from Anthony D. Smith's theories on nationalism and identity. Both are integral to this context. Smith's concept of 'ethno-symbolism' highlights how historical memories and symbols play a crucial role in the construction of national identities. The Brexit vote has reignited these historical narratives, with nationalists evoking the memory of past struggles for Irish independence and unionists emphasising their historical ties to Britain. Smith (1991) strengthens this analytical lens, illustrating that national identity is constructed and reconstructed through historical narratives that imbue the present with the weight of the past.

This reconfiguration of identities poses both challenges and opportunities for the new Labour government. Labour must navigate a complex political terrain, where the traditional boundaries of national identity and sovereignty are increasingly fluid. Policy experts and political commentators suggest that Labour's approach should focus on promoting unity and stability through inclusive policies that recognise the multifaceted nature of identity in Northern Ireland.

Labour's policy platform, as articulated by its leader, Keir Starmer, emphasises the importance of addressing the socio-economic disparities exacerbated by Brexit. Starmer has committed to ensuring that the voices of all communities in Northern Ireland are heard and respected and that the benefits of economic and social progress are shared equitably (Starmer, 2021). This approach aligns with the recommendations of a number of political analysts, including Jennifer Todd (2020), who argues that policies aimed at social inclusion and economic development are essential for bridging divides and fostering a sense of shared identity.

The political terrain in Northern Ireland and the Republic of Ireland post-Brexit is marked by significant challenges and opportunities. The reconfiguration of identities and the evolving notions of sovereignty necessitate a nuanced and inclusive approach from the new Labour government. By addressing the socio-economic impacts of Brexit and promoting policies that foster unity and stability, Labour can navigate this complex landscape and contribute to the reimagining of national identities on the island of Ireland. It is arguably possible to state that the future of national identities in a post-Brexit era will depend on the ability of political leaders to embrace complexity and foster inclusivity.

Shining a Spotlight
The Northern Ireland Protocol

The Northern Ireland Protocol emerged as a critical element of the Brexit negotiations, designed to address the complex issue of the Irish border. The protocol aimed to avoid a hard border between Northern Ireland and the Republic of Ireland, thereby preserving the integrity of the GFA. It effectively keeps Northern Ireland aligned with certain EU regulations, allowing for the seamless flow of goods across the border while creating regulatory checks between Northern Ireland and the rest of the UK. O'Leary (2019) elucidates that the protocol represents a unique solution to an intractable problem, balancing the need to maintain an open border on the island of Ireland with the UK's departure from the EU.

The impact of the Northern Ireland Protocol on trade has been profound. By keeping Northern Ireland within the EU's single market for goods, the protocol has facilitated continued cross-border trade with the Republic of Ireland. However, it has also introduced new trade barriers between Northern Ireland and Great Britain, leading to disruptions and increased costs for businesses. The dual arrangement has produced varied consequences for political stability (Hayward, 2021). In one respect, it has prevented the establishment of a hard border on the island, a critical aspect for maintaining peace and stability. On the other hand, it has fuelled unionist discontent, with regulatory checks perceived as a threat to Northern Ireland's place within the UK. As Hayward (2023) asserts, the protocol has become a lightning rod for unionist grievances, symbolising a perceived dilution of their British identity.

Current challenges surrounding the Northern Ireland Protocol are manifold. Disputes over its implementation have led to political standoffs and legal challenges. Unionist parties, notably the DUP, vehemently opposed the protocol, calling for its abolition or significant revision. This opposition strained the power-sharing arrangements in Northern Ireland and complicated efforts to restore political stability. Furthermore, the economic disruptions caused by the new trade barriers have exacerbated tensions, with businesses struggling to adapt to the new regulatory environment. Indeed, the ongoing disputes over the protocol highlighted, and continue to highlight, the fragile nature of intergovernmental relations and the complexities of managing national identities in a post-Brexit era.

The Northern Ireland Protocol offers several lessons for managing intergovernmental relations and national identities. First, it underscores the importance of nuanced, context-specific solutions in addressing complex political issues. The protocol's unique arrangements reflect an attempt to balance competing identities and sovereignties, a critical consideration in divided societies. Second, it highlights the need for ongoing dialogue and negotiation. The evolving nature of the disputes surrounding the protocol demonstrates that static solutions are insufficient in the face of dynamic political landscapes. Finally, the protocol illustrates the importance of economic considerations in political agreements. Ensuring that trade flows remain unimpeded is crucial for maintaining political and social stability. Hayward succinctly observes that economic stability is a cornerstone of political peace; disruptions in trade can quickly translate into broader societal tensions (Hayward, 2023).

The role of identity and citizenship post-Brexit

Brexit has fundamentally altered the landscape of identity and citizenship on the island of Ireland. The changes in citizenship laws and identity perceptions have resulted in profound implications for social cohesion and political engagement between all political entities and borders. The post-Brexit environment has seen a reassertion of Irish identity among nationalists, who increasingly view EU citizenship as a crucial component of their identity. Conversely, unionists grapple with the erosion of their British identity, feeling marginalised within the broader UK framework.

The alteration in citizenship laws has been impactful. The right to hold both British and Irish citizenship, enshrined in the GFA, has taken on new significance in the post-Brexit context. Many in Northern Ireland have sought Irish passports to retain their EU citizenship, a trend that underscores the fluidity and complexity of identity in the region. Rogers Brubaker's framework on the politics of belonging provides a useful lens through which to understand these shifts. Brubaker (2023) expounds that citizenship is not merely a legal status but a deeply embedded sense of belonging; the changes wrought by Brexit have compelled individuals to re-evaluate their place within the broader political and social order.

The impact on social cohesion has been consequential. The reconfiguration of identity has deepened divisions within communities, with contrasting perceptions of what it means to be British, Irish or European. This has affected political engagement, with nationalist communities feeling increasingly empowered to push for unification, while unionists face internal fragmentation. As Claire Mitchell (2023), sociologist and researcher from Belfast, posits, 'Brexit has intensified identity politics, leading to greater polarisation and a reawakening of old loyalties and divisions.'

Emerging trends in identity politics furthermore highlight the influence of demographic changes, migration and evolving social attitudes. The younger generation, more likely to identify as European, play a pivotal role in shaping the future landscape. This demographic shift, coupled with increased migration, has introduced new dynamics into the identity discourse. Michael Keating (2021) emphasises that the generational shift towards a European identity and the impact of migration are transforming the political and social fabric of Northern Ireland, creating a more diverse and complex identity landscape.

The interplay between identity, citizenship and governance provides critical lessons for future policy. Recognising the fluidity and multiplicity of identities is essential for fostering social cohesion and political stability. Policies that promote inclusivity and respect for diverse identities can help bridge divisions and build a more cohesive society. Brubaker (2023) highlights that the future of national identities in a post-Brexit era will depend on the ability of political leaders to embrace complexity and foster inclusivity.

Social Cohesion and Future Dynamics

The social impacts of Brexit on the island of Ireland have been profound, affecting community integration, minority rights and the broader societal fabric. In Northern Ireland, Brexit has exacerbated existing divisions, challenging the fragile social cohesion that was fostered by the GFA. The issue of community integration, which has always been a delicate balance between unionist and nationalist communities, has come under renewed strain. Mitchell (2018) aptly observes that Brexit has reopened old wounds, bringing historical grievances to the fore and making the task of community integration more difficult.

The protection of minority rights is another critical issue. The nationalist community, which largely identifies as Irish and European, feels particularly vulnerable post-Brexit. The removal of EU protections and the uncertainty surrounding rights have heightened anxieties. The erosion of EU safeguards has left many in the nationalist community feeling disenfranchised and marginalised. This sentiment is compounded by concerns over citizenship rights and the potential for a hard border, which would symbolise a regression to a more divided past.

Social policies play a crucial role in promoting cohesion and addressing these challenges. Effective social policies must focus on inclusivity, economic equality and cultural recognition. Policies that enhance economic opportunities and access to education and health care are vital in bridging the divides. Colfer and Diamond (2020) suggests that inclusive social policies addressing economic disparities and promoting cultural understanding are essential for fostering long-term social cohesion.

Looking ahead, the future dynamics of the island of Ireland and the UK will be shaped by a confluence of economic, social, geopolitical and technological factors. Economic trends indicate that Northern Ireland and the Republic of Ireland must adapt to new trade realities and potential shifts in global economic dynamics. The post-Brexit economic environment poses both challenges and opportunities. The disruption to established trade routes necessitates innovative economic strategies to foster resilience and growth. Irish economist Mary Murphy (2022) highlights that adaptation to new economic conditions will require strategic investments in infrastructure and cross-border collaboration to mitigate the adverse effects of Brexit.

Geopolitically, the relationship between the UK, Ireland, and the EU will continue to evolve. Brexit, however, has realigned these relationships, with Ireland now positioned as an influential EU member state and a key interlocutor between the EU and the UK. The geopolitical considerations extend beyond Europe, with potential impacts on the broader international stage, including relations with the United States. Arguably, Ireland's role within the EU and its strategic position in post-Brexit geopolitics will be crucial in navigating future challenges and opportunities.

The social impacts of Brexit on the island of Ireland underscore the need for robust social policies that promote cohesion and protect minority rights. The future dynamics will be shaped by a complex interplay of economic, social, geopolitical and technological factors. By understanding these emerging trends and their implications, policy-makers can develop strategies that foster unity, resilience and sustainable growth. Keating (2023) aptly notes that navigating the post-Brexit landscape requires a comprehensive approach that integrates economic, social, and environmental considerations to build a cohesive and prosperous future.

Recommendations and Conclusion

The myth of Tír na nÓg, a land of eternal youth and beauty, continues to serve as a fitting metaphor for the aspirations of a stable and cohesive society. In the context of Brexit, the island of Ireland and the UK, achieving this ideal requires addressing complex issues of national identity, sovereignty and intergovernmental relations. This chapter has provided an exploration of the impacts of Brexit, the creation of a new political terrain, the role of the Northern Ireland Protocol and the evolving nature of identity and citizenship, and it now turns to policy recommendations.

Policy recommendations

To address the identified issues, the new Labour government should implement a series of practical steps that align with the themes and analysis presented in this chapter. First, it is crucial to ensure the stability and effectiveness of the Northern Ireland Protocol. This involves continued negotiations with the EU to refine and adjust the protocol to minimise economic disruptions and address unionist concerns.

Hayward (2023) emphasises that ensuring economic stability is essential for maintaining political peace and fostering social cohesion.

Second, Labour should promote policies that protect and enhance the rights of all citizens in Northern Ireland. This includes safeguarding the rights enshrined in the GFA, such as the right to hold both British and Irish citizenship. Brubaker's (2019) previously discussed concept of the politics of belonging highlights the importance of inclusive policies that recognise and respect diverse identities. By ensuring that all communities feel valued and protected in this way, Labour should seek to harness this conceptual lens of the politics of belonging through their policy construction and formation. Such policies have a viable hope of mitigating the continued political, economic and social polarisation entrenched within UK society. Although, it should be noted that such divisions had been planted before the referendum was called. It was its direct outcome, and the prolonged challenging negotiations that followed, which clearly sewed these seeds. Seeds which continue to develop and multiply, further strengthening the role of polarisation in the social, economic and political landscape of both islands.

Third, Labour should invest in cross-border infrastructure and economic initiatives that strengthen ties between Northern Ireland and the Republic of Ireland. Economic interdependence has historically played a critical role in fostering peace and stability. John FitzGerald (2020) in 'Commuting across the Irish border' argues that economic collaboration is a cornerstone of social integration and political stability. Initiatives that promote joint ventures in technology, green energy and transportation can create shared economic benefits and reinforce the interconnectedness of the two regions.

Strategic directions

Long-term strategies for fostering unity and stability must emphasise flexibility and adaptability to respond to evolving dynamics. One strategic direction is to promote intergovernmental co-operation through regular dialogue and collaborative frameworks. The evolving nature of Brexit's impacts requires dynamic and responsive governance structures. O'Leary (2023) highlights that ongoing dialogue and negotiation are critical for managing the complexities of intergovernmental relations and national identities.

Another strategic direction is to engage with the younger generation, who are more likely to identify as European and embrace a more inclusive identity. Educational programmes and cultural exchanges that highlight the shared heritage and future of the island of Ireland and the UK can foster a sense of unity and common purpose. Keating (2021) points out that engaging the younger generation is key to shaping a future that embraces diversity and inclusivity.

Additionally, Labour should prioritise sustainable development and environmental policies that address the challenges of climate change. Collaborative efforts in green technology and renewable energy not only provide economic benefits but also create common ground for co-operation. In her work 'Reshaping UK/Ireland relations: Brexit's cross-border and bilateral impact', Murphy (2022) emphasises that sustainable policies are imperative for long-term stability and prosperity, as they offer both the island of Ireland and the UK novel opportunities for collaboration and innovation.

Looking forward

This chapter explored the reconfiguration of nations and identities in the context of Brexit, focusing on the island of Ireland and the UK. By examining the historical context, the GFA, the political terrain post-Brexit and empirical case studies, this chapter has directly highlighted the profound impacts on the key themes highlighted in the opening section; national identity, sovereignty and intergovernmental relations. The central thesis that Brexit has fundamentally altered these landscapes was presented and analysed, necessitating a revaluation of policies and strategies to foster stability and cohesion between both islands.

The new Labour government are the prime agents to re-evaluate these policies and strategies to foster stability and cohesion between both islands. They face a complex and dynamic environment that requires thoughtful, inclusive, and adaptive policy responses. By ensuring economic stability, protecting citizenship rights, investing in cross-border initiatives and promoting intergovernmental co-operation, Labour can navigate the challenges of the post-Brexit era. They must also accept that the reimagining of national identities and the management of intergovernmental relations are critical tasks that require innovative and inclusive approaches, if diplomatic relations are to be strengthened, respected and valued by political entities involved.

In embracing these recommendations and strategic directions, Labour can help build a future that reflects the ideals of Tír na nÓg – an enduring vision of peace, prosperity and unity. Through ongoing dialogue, co-operation and innovative policies, the island of Ireland and the UK can navigate the complexities of the post-Brexit landscape, travelling towards a more stable and cohesive future.

21

Can Labour Renew Britain?
The View from Ireland

Fintan O'Toole

Although the polls had been predicting it for many months, the result of the United Kingdom's 2024 general election was nonetheless stunning. This was the worst performance in the 190-year history of the Conservative Party. It lost almost half its share of the vote and 250 parliamentary seats. One former Prime Minister (Liz Truss), nine Cabinet Ministers (including the Secretaries of Defence, Education and Justice) and other prominent Conservative figureheads were unceremoniously ejected from the House of Commons by their constituents. This was a tidal wave of anger washing over not just out-going Prime Minister Rishi Sunak but also the past fourteen years of Tory rule, and it made landfall with a deafening roar.

Seldom in any democracy has a governing party gone so quickly from triumph – Boris Johnson won a huge majority in 2019 – to disaster. The reasons are clear: a botched exit from the European Union, stark social and economic decline, institutional decay, a revolving door of ineffective and sometimes disastrous leaders, Johnson's anarchic antics and Truss's ill-fated and short-lived experiment with extreme neoliberal economics. Over the past decade and a half, the widespread feeling that the United Kingdom was on its last legs was reflected in surging English nativism and Scottish, Welsh and Irish separatism that in different ways threatened to pull the union apart. The voters have left the world in no doubt as to whom they blame for this malaise.

On the other side of the coin, Labour leader Keir Starmer now finds his party with a 411 seats, a total that brought him close to repeating Tony Blair's historic victory of 1997. From the very low state it was in when he became leader just five years ago, Labour has not only been resurrected; it has ascended into a heaven of euphoria. It has recaptured most of the 'red wall' of working-class constituencies that, in 2019, it lost to Johnson's strange charm and his promise to Get Brexit Done. It has regained its dominance in Scotland, which had seemed over the course of this century to have become the fiefdom of the pro-independence Scottish National Party. It has also won twenty-seven of thirty-two seats in Wales.

The new Labour government can therefore claim to be a genuinely 'British' one in ways that none of its predecessors since Blair's could. In the short term, the threat of the country breaking up has undoubtedly receded. The United Kingdom under Johnson – who inaugurated an especially unruly series of chaotic Conservative governments – seemed to be under the same spell of performative, personality-driven reactionary politics as the United States under former President Donald Trump. Now, the accession of the pragmatic, charisma-free Starmer bucks the trend toward the far right in so many European democracies, from Italy and France to the Netherlands and Sweden. It holds out hope that the centre can hold after all. The sigh of relief will be heard far beyond the shores of the United Kingdom.

And yet, as overwhelming as they are, these results come with a very large caveat. Labour's overall share of the vote, at 34 per cent, was actually quite low. It rose by less than 2 per cent from the poor showing of 2019. The popular rage that has swept the Tories out of power is not matched by a surge of belief in Starmer's ability to save the country. Starmer owes his huge majority to the vagaries of the First Past the Post electoral system, which can conjure dramatic national swings in seat numbers from relatively small changes in individual constituencies. Equally, the vast sea change in the relative fortunes of the Conservatives and Labour in just five years suggests how extremely volatile the United Kingdom remains.

Even as Starmer grasps the reins of power so firmly, the road ahead remains rocky. The deeper tremors that have slowly but inexorably been eroding the social and political foundations of the country will continue to rumble just under the surface. Although it was hardly mentioned in the campaign, the Brexit debacle is a continuing reality that will severely constrain Starmer's frantic push for economic growth, without which his promise of renewal will quickly turn hollow. Living standards are in shocking decline, amplifying social divisions and widening the gap between southern England and the rest of the United Kingdom. And without vast new infusions of cash, the looming collapse of public and health services threatens to destroy some of the few remaining sources of a collective British identity.

The Weakness of Labour

None of these challenges can be met without radical reform to the basic system of government. For years now, London has shown itself to be incapable of solving large-scale problems or giving all citizens the belief that the central institutions of power belong to them. The slogan that won the Brexit referendum for the Leave side in 2016 – 'Take Back Control' – was so effective because it identified a genuine loss of faith in the promise of democracy: that the people are running the show. The wildly careening course of British politics since then has surely done nothing to restore that faith.

Nor does Keir Starmer present himself as a man who lights fires.

His public demeanour is stiff and remarkably downbeat. Despite its slogan of 'change', his party's offering to the electorate was relentlessly risk averse. Labour has accepted the very fiscal constraints laid down by the Conservatives while largely eschewing tax increases to raise the revenue it needs if it is to shore up public services and begin to make up the deficit in investment. Given the multiplying social and economic stresses facing the country, the new leadership will be tempted to avoid bolder reforms in favour of mere crisis management.

But such a cautious approach would not really be risk free. It would in fact risk squandering a parliamentary majority of historic proportions. Either the incoming administration can seize the moment to finally shake up the system and confront the core constitutional and democratic issues on which the long-term viability of the union may depend, or it can choose to muddle through and hope for the best. For such a fractured polity, this could be the last time there is such a choice.

The End of a Certain Britain

From the very start of the campaign, a sense of doom hung over the whole idea of a Conservative United Kingdom. On 23 May, the day after Sunak called the unexpectedly early election, he made a campaign stop at the Titanic Quarter in Belfast, an upscale waterfront development area named after the ill-fated ocean liner that was built in shipyards nearby. Inevitably, a reporter asked the Prime Minister if he was the captain of a sinking ship. After all, it was hard not to predict the dramatic implosion of the Conservatives, who had returned to power under Prime Minister David Cameron in 2010 and then supplied a dizzying merry-go-round of failed leaders since 2016: Theresa May, Johnson, Truss and finally Sunak. In a recent book, *The Conservative Effect 2010–2024*, the political historians Anthony Seldon and Tom Egerton have concluded that 'overall, it is hard to find a comparable period in the history of the Conservatives which achieved so little, or which left the country at its conclusion in a more troubling state' (Seldon and Egerton, 2024).

Yet the *Titanic* metaphor raised a less obvious but more profound question. What if the sinking ship is the United Kingdom itself? That the country is in deep trouble is not in dispute. Wage growth between 2010 and 2020 was the lowest over any ten-year period in peacetime since the Napoleonic Wars. The country's annual growth rate in productivity since 2007 has been a minuscule 0.4 per cent, its lowest over an equivalent period since 1826. It is perhaps apt that one of the country's most popular cultural exports of recent times, the Netflix historical fantasy *Bridgerton*, is set in a version of the early nineteenth century – the last time the British economy was performing so sluggishly.

GDP per capita has grown by a mere 4.3 per cent over the past sixteen years, compared with 46 per cent in the previous sixteen years. Moreover, GDP growth over the past few years has been driven almost exclusively by increases in the overall size of the population – in other words, by the immigration that both main parties say they want to limit severely. Conservative governments, theoretically tax averse, have been forced to increase overall taxes to a level not seen since 1950, when the United Kingdom was still recovering from the Second World War. The average annual real wage has fallen about $14,000 below its level before the financial crisis of 2008. These economic trends will not simply disappear with a change in government.

Two-Nation Britain

Measures of social well-being are no more encouraging. The National Health Service, a source of justifiable British pride since its inception in 1948, is in crisis: in June, the nonpartisan Institute for Government described its current state as 'dismal' and found that 'hospital performance is arguably the worst in the NHS's history'. There are three-quarters of a million more British children living in poverty than when the Conservatives came to power in 2010, and 4.3 million children are going hungry. Many local agencies have gone bankrupt, leading to deep cuts in basic services such as waste collection, social care and libraries. In 2022, the Commission on the UK's Future, an independent body chaired by former Labour Prime Minister Gordon Brown, found that on the simple measure of GDP per capita, 'half the British population' – more than 30 million people – 'live in areas no wealthier than the poorer parts of the former East Germany, poorer than parts of central and eastern Europe, and poorer than the U.S. states of Mississippi and West Virginia.'

A sense of decline flows through and around the land in the form of rivers and shores polluted with sewage. In March, one of the great English public rituals – the annual Oxford–Cambridge boat race on the River Thames – was for the first time preceded by warnings to the rowers that because of the concentration of *E. coli* bacteria in the water, they should cover cuts and grazes with waterproof dressings and take care not to swallow any splashes from what used to be called the 'Sweet Thames'. The British Environment Agency has found that in 2023, the companies managing the national water supply – water service was privatised by Prime Minister Margaret Thatcher's Conservative government in the late 1980s – spilled more raw, untreated human effluent into the country's rivers and seas than in any previous year on record.

Indeed, the electoral revolt against the Tories in many of their rural bastions was partly driven by the feeling even among traditional Conservative voters that what the poet William Blake called 'England's green and pleasant land' had been blighted. For many of those voters, such concerns are made worse by the awareness that they were, after all, supposed to be entering an era of uplift and optimism. Just five years ago, in his first speech in the House of Commons after he swept to power as Prime Minister, Johnson insisted that the years of 'managed decline' were over and hailed 'the beginning of a new golden age'.

Of course, the fulcrum of this transformation was supposed to be the United Kingdom's exit from the European Union. The narrative spun by Johnson and his allies was that the country's natural exuberance had been stifled for half a century by bureaucrats in Brussels and that, freed from these encumbrances, the union would now flourish. The cold reality is that Brexit has merely shown that the United Kingdom has no one to blame for its problems but itself. And those home-grown problems have been made worse by the folly of erecting new barriers between British exporters and their primary markets in Europe.

The Sounds of Silence and Labour

Among the more striking features of Starmer and Labour's campaign this spring was the utter absence of Brexit from party talking points. This silence may, in purely electoral terms, have been wise: polling now suggests that just 13 per cent of voters see relations with the EU as one of the most important issues facing the country. Anand Menon, the director of the think tank UK in a Changing Europe, noted during the campaign that 'if you do focus groups and mention Brexit, the biggest reaction you get from voters is a yawn and an eye-roll'. Yet it is nonetheless remarkable for the opposition to decline to attack the ruling party for its single greatest policy fiasco and for voters to seem bored and irritated by their country's most momentous political change of the past half-century.

In the 2016 Brexit referendum, Johnson and his fellow advocates had persuaded a small majority of voters that breaking with Brussels would restore 'Global Britain' to its natural place at the summit of prosperity and achievement. In fact, this vision was more a narrowing than an expansion of the horizons of Britishness. It was driven by an inchoate but resurgent English nationalism. It had little appeal in multicultural London, in Scotland, or in Northern Ireland, all of which voted heavily to stay in the EU, as did Welsh-speaking Wales.

But enough of Johnson's English compatriots were persuaded of this proposition to give him a massive parliamentary majority in the election of December 2019, just seven weeks before the Brexit deal was consummated.

It is hard to think of a successful political project whose lustre has faded as quickly as Brexit. In June 2024, in a report titled 'Life in the Slow Lane', the nonpartisan Resolution Foundation found that 'since 2019, Britain's relative performance in goods exports has tanked', noting that it has grown at just 1.1 per cent annually, a mere fifth of the average for members of the Organisation for Economic Cooperation and Development (Fry et al., 2024). The reasons for this kind of collapse are not mysterious: choosing to leave the world's largest single market has consequences. As the report boils it down in hard cash, had the United Kingdom preserved its pre-Brexit market share, its exports would have grown by $64 billion instead of shrinking by $4 billion between 2019 and 2022.

Increasingly, the British economy is kept afloat by its export of financial, legal, technical and advertising services, much of it driven by US companies outsourcing this kind of work to British firms and notably by private equity outfits. This is very good for bankers, lawyers, ad executives and management consultants – but far less so for farmers, manufacturing workers and ordinary consumers. There are many more losers than winners: in March 2024, the Office for Budgetary Responsibility found that its prediction that Brexit would lead to a long-term 4 per cent drop in productivity is being borne out, one of many factors contributing to the worst decline in living standards since the 1950s.

Amidst these disastrous effects, few in the British political class seem willing to say the 'B-word'. Given that just 18 per cent of those who voted Leave in 2016 now think Brexit is going well, Sunak, an enthusiastic Brexiteer, declined to even mention it on the campaign trail.

But consider Nigel Farage, the veteran anti-immigrant and anti-EU campaigner who now leads the far-right Reform Party. If Farage can reasonably be said to be the progenitor of Brexit, he now seems able to do no more than shake his head in disappointment at the way his child has turned out and issue vague admonitions that it must do better.

Keir Starmer and Labour's omerta may be far more telling. In the weeks before the election, he hardly uttered a word about Europe; as the new Prime Minister, he will have a strong temptation to ignore not just Brexit itself but all the unresolved questions of British identity that were wrapped up in it. In part, this may be a matter of sheer expediency. Almost all the country's public services – from health and social care to policing and prisons to water and sewage to schools and libraries and even to basic nutrition for large parts of the population – are struggling. The country urgently needs massive amounts of public investment. But Labour has accepted the fiscal restraints it has inherited from the Conservatives – government borrowing is to be limited to 3 per cent of GDP and overall government debt is targeted to keep falling – and it has promised not to raise taxes for 'working people'. Squaring that circle will be so hard that Starmer may well feel that large-scale political reforms are a luxury he cannot afford.

The Lingering Legacy of Empire
But Starmer will soon confront the inescapable truth that he cannot address the country's economic failure without also confronting the profound problems of the union itself. First, Labour will need growth to fund those urgent public services improvements it has to deliver to its newly expanded electorate. Ironically, because its trade with the rest of the world has shrunk, the United Kingdom has actually become more dependent on European markets since 2019. The solution is obvious: the government has to undo at least some of the damage it has

done to its trade with the EU. Starmer has gestured broadly in this direction but has ruled out the only moves that would actually make a difference – seeking to rejoin the EU's single market or its customs union.

Something has to give, and when it does, all the big questions that were raised by Brexit – sovereignty, the United Kingdom's post-imperial place in the world, the antiquated nature of the country's democracy, the tensions between its individual nations – will be back on the table. It would make sense, therefore, for Starmer to address these large existential issues while his government still has the air of novelty and while the British electorate is so clearly crying out for a fresh start.

The second reason why Keir Starmer cannot ignore the parlous state of the union is the strong connection between power and prosperity. The parts of the country with the least political power – roughly speaking, the northern region of England, Scotland, Wales and Northern Ireland – are also the ones that are the most impoverished. Feelings of national and regional resentment have been channelled into different forms of separatism – independence movements in the so-called Celtic fringes; 'independence' from the EU in England – but they have common roots in the realities of the country's chasmic geographical inequalities.

According to the economist Philip McCann, the United Kingdom is 'almost certainly the most inter-regionally unequal large high-income country' in the world (2019). And those gaps have expanded in recent decades. In 2019, GDP per capita in London was $73,000 – almost 90 per cent higher than in Scotland and eastern England, where it was just $38,000. Brexit, which has depressed manufacturing exports while allowing the service economy to continue to thrive, has only exacerbated these regional inequalities; just within England itself, the wealth gap between the south-east and the languishing north is expected to reach $290,000 per person by 2030.

The Big Questions and Brexit

Even Boris Johnson recognised this. His signature domestic policy was 'levelling up' – bringing all regions up to the standards of the richer southern areas. But neither he nor his successors managed to do much to achieve that goal. In March, a report by the all-party parliamentary Public Accounts Committee found that only 10 per cent of funding for the 'levelling up agenda' had been spent and that Conservative ministers were unable to furnish 'any compelling examples' of what the funding had accomplished. These failures are not merely the products of incompetence; they highlight the inability of a top-down post-imperial state to devolve real power to its member nations and its neglected regions.

As an opposition party, Labour was hardly blind to these issues. In 2022, it published the findings of the Brown Commission on the UK's Future, which made precisely this connection between the United Kingdom's economic stagnation and its forms of government: 'At the root of this failure' is 'an unreformed, over-centralised way of governing that leaves millions of people complaining they are neglected, ignored, and invisible' – people who, as the commission put it, increasingly see themselves 'treated as second class citizens in their own country'.

It was with this democratic deficit in mind that the Brown Commission proposed radical constitutional changes, among them the abolition of the 'indefensible' House of Lords and its replacement with an elected 'chamber of the nations and regions' and greatly enhanced status and powers for the devolved Scottish, Welsh and Northern Irish assemblies, as well as for cities and regions in England. It also recommended at least the beginnings of a written constitution, with a 'constitutional statute guiding how political power should be shared' as well as 'constitutionally protected social rights – such as the right to health care for all based on need, not ability to pay' (Commission on the UK's Future, 2022).

At the time, Brown's ideas were driven by his sense that this may be the last chance for the United Kingdom to right itself. Polling showed that the proposed reforms had significant voter support; they also were endorsed by Starmer. At the launch, the Labour leader predicted that people would someday look back at the report and view it as 'the turning point between an old economy that was not working and a new economy that has worked for the whole of the United Kingdom' (Starmer, 2022). Yet none of Brown's proposals were featured in Labour's hypercautious election campaign, and Starmer seems disinclined to spend his new stock of political capital on overcoming resistance to such a fundamental rethinking of the union.

Can Britain Reform Itself?

What the incoming government needs to recognise is that the United Kingdom has already changed irreversibly. It was created and held together by huge historical forces: the development of the British Empire, the forging of a Protestant (and explicitly anti-Catholic) identity, the Industrial Revolution, the apparent invincibility of British arms in the nineteenth and twentieth centuries, the successful invention of a 'relatable' monarchy, and the building of a post-war social democracy. All these stabilisers have been kicked away. The empire is no more; the United Kingdom is no longer a majority Christian, let alone Protestant, country; its industrial base was abandoned under Thatcher; its days of military might are long gone; the monarchy, with the death of Queen Elizabeth, has lost its anchor in history; and many of the achievements of British social democracy have been destroyed by the Conservatives.

It is still, just about, possible to imagine a whole new kind of union, one that revels in the diversity of a place that has many different national, regional and ethnic identities and plays to its potential economic strengths by reopening itself to trade and human capital from

Europe and further afield. But Starmer and his government would have to begin by acknowledging that what was holding the country back was not, after all, an unaccountable Eurocracy in Brussels but rather an overcentralised government in London – one that was created to rule a far-flung empire of largely voiceless subjects and still rules over a smallish island with citizens who want to feel in control of their own lives.

Starmer will certainly try, however hesitantly at first, to rebuild the social democracy that buttressed the union in the decades when the empire was vanishing and gave ordinary people in every part of the country a tangible sense of common belonging. He seems, at least in principle, to understand that the only viable future for the United Kingdom is, in effect, as a federal democracy in which power flows to and from the nations and regions – and the people who inhabit them. He is, moreover, rather good at reinvention, having reinvented himself from his early persona as a radical left-wing human rights lawyer to a stolid technocrat and having given his party a similarly drastic makeover.

Can Keir Starmer go further and reinvent the union? It is not at all clear that he wants to take on that task. He seems inclined to see his own triumph across so many different parts of the country as proof that the kingdom is indeed still united and intact; that a restoration of decency, competence and coherence to government will also serve as a restoration of pride in Britishness itself.

In the immediate term, he may well be right. Feelings of relief and renewal will certainly be widespread. But they won't last unless communities start to see improvements in public services, reductions in poverty and rises in productivity and wages. Those things in turn will not happen without far-reaching changes in the way the country functions, both internally and in its relations with Europe. The same political systems that got the country into such a deep hole will not suffice to get it out. They are not for the purposes they have to accomplish: bringing the United Kingdom, gradually, back to where it belongs in the EU; restoring pride in institutions such as the National Health Service; convincing people across the union that they have an equal stake in the country's future.

Starmer has to create a virtuous circle in which a radical renewal of the United Kingdom's sclerotic democracy feeds into and is in turn fed by an energetic revival of its flaccid economy. But if there is no virtuous circle, there will be a vicious one. Political disillusionment will quickly take hold again. Over four million people voted for Farage's far-right Reform Party, giving it 14 per cent of overall party support. Although the workings of the electoral system translated this into just four Commons seats (including one for Farage himself), it gives him a solid base from which he can seek to capitalise on the Conservatives' disarray.

If Keir Starmer fails to turn public anger into a more long-term optimism, the sour English nationalism that Farage taps into will thrive on that hopelessness. With traditional conservatism in such deep disarray, there is the potential for the right wing of English politics to end in a Make America Great Again-style takeover. Not the least of its consequences will be the blocking of any moves toward taking the country back into Europe. That in turn will renew the drives toward separation in Scotland, Northern Ireland and Wales.

Labour's victory has given the United Kingdom a chance to save itself by remaking itself. It has sprung from a very deep pool of disenchantment with the way things work in the country – and the multiple ways in which they patently do not. If Starmer grasps the truth that his triumph is a function of the United Kingdom's brokenness, he will have the courage to begin to fix it. If not, it will remain dangerously unfixed. And it may indeed become unfixable. The party that has dominated it for 200 years has imploded. It would be foolish to imagine that the same thing could not happen to the country.

22

The Anglosphere, Brexit and Trump

Andrew Gamble

Foreign policy figured little in the 2024 UK election, which as usual was dominated by domestic issues. The opposition parties focused on the idea that Britain was 'broken' because nothing worked any more. The cost of living, the state of the national health service, housing and immigration were the most salient issues. There was relatively little focus on the Ukraine war, the renewed fighting between Israelis and Palestinians in the Middle East or the increasing tensions between the US and China in the Indo-Pacific.

Still more striking was that neither party seemed willing to discuss how Britain should navigate an increasingly uncertain and threatening international environment or what new assumptions about Britain's place in the world should guide policy after the twin shocks of Brexit and Trump. Neither party wanted to recognise that Britain was 'broken' not just domestically but internationally, because the assumptions that had guided British foreign policy since the 1960s – hugging the Americans close and pooling sovereignty with Europe – no longer held. Brexit and Trump had left Britain rudderless.

The subject of Brexit was studiously avoided by both the largest parties. Labour announced that it would seek a closer relationship with the EU but ruled out most of the things that might actually make the relationship closer, such as a return to the single market, the customs union or free movement. The parties pledged themselves to increase defence spending to counter the threat from Russia and promised to support Ukraine and strengthen NATO. But there was little public discussion of the isolationist and protectionist turn in US politics or the consequences for the Western alliance if Donald Trump were to win a second term and went ahead with his threat to weaken the US commitment to NATO, or even withdraw from it altogether. It will be imperative to address such global developments if Britain under the Labour Party is to find its new place in the world.

Britain's Place in the World Post-1945

Since 1945, Britain's foreign and defence policies have given priority to the Atlantic alliance and the cultivation of a special relationship with the world's leading power, the United States. The British have some-times disagreed with the United States, but since the Suez invasion of 1956 the British have never acted independently of the United States in pursuing their interests around the world. They have positioned them-selves as the United States most loyal ally. The UK's nuclear deterrent has been supplied by the US since the 1960s, and in return Britain has supported the US within NATO and the UN Security Council.

The US encouraged successive British governments to join the Eu-ropean Community, to help ensure solidity in the Western alliance and to make it less likely that Europe would diverge too far from US interests or become a rival superpower. When the new British Prime Minister, Keir Starmer, met Joe Biden in Washington in July 2024, he made the customary declaration of faith in the special relationship between Britain and the United States. 'The special relationship is so important. It was forged in difficult circumstances, [has] endured for so long, and [is] stronger now than ever.' Joe Biden reciprocated. 'I kind of see you guys as the knot tying the transatlantic alliance together, the closer you are with Europe' (Hughes, 2024).

Winston Churchill first articulated the idea of a special relationship when he suggested that Britain after the Second World War stood at the centre of three overlapping circles – the British Empire, Europe and Anglo-America. By being a central actor in all three, Britain could compensate for its clear inferiority to the two superpowers of the postwar era, the United States and the Soviet Union. But Churchill's framing of Britain's place in the world, though an artful political device, was built on sand.

The British Empire could not survive for long in the new circumstances created by the war, and over the next twenty years it was rapidly dismantled. With its disappearance went Britain's claim to be a global power of the first rank. The two circles that remained, Europe and Anglo-America, both implied British dependency rather than British leadership. It took a while for Britain's governing class to accept the implications of Britain's new international status.

Labour and Conservative governments refused to engage with the negotiations which led to the first steps towards European integration and the signing of the Treaty of Rome in 1957, despite being urged by the United States to do so. Even as they dragged their feet on Europe, the British were aware that they could no longer relate to the United States as equals. The special relationship between the two countries was always more special for Britain than it was for the United States.

The dilemma that emerged for Britain after Suez and the withdrawal from empire was whether it should prioritise its relationships with the United States or with Europe. This choice between Europe and America has divided British political parties ever since (Gamble, 2003). Many in the governing class had concluded by the 1960s that Britain's future lay with pulling sovereignty with a European Community that was increasingly integrated both economically and politically. But others resisted, either because they were not reconciled to Britain's loss of its empire and great power status or because, like Enoch Powell and Tony Benn, they championed national sovereignty and the right of the British people to order their affairs in their own way.

Britain and Europe

The Conservatives became the European party and eventually secured entry in 1973. The majority of the Labour movement and the party in Parliament opposed entry, but a Labour government in 1975 presided over a referendum that produced a two-thirds majority in favour of staying in. This did not settle the issue. Labour campaigned in the 1983 election on a promise to withdraw from Europe, but by the end of the 1980s the two parties had changed places, with Labour now enthusiastic about European membership and the Conservatives increasingly sceptical or actively opposed.

From the 1990s onwards, the opponents of British membership of the European Union began to raise the possibility of Britain's withdrawal. British ministers continued to favour membership, although in deference to domestic anti-European opinion they resisted new measures of integration. The exception was the single market, which Margaret Thatcher enthusiastically championed. But on many other issues, particularly monetary union, the British demanded opt-outs and came to be seen as reluctant Europeans, sceptical about the benefits of closer integration. For many on the right of British politics the issue came to be posed as a choice between Europe and America to determine Britain's future. They wanted Britain to break away from Europe and align itself much more closely with the United States. Europe and America for them represented different economic, legal, social, cultural and political values. This binary made the choice for one or the other mutually exclusive.

British ministers were less eager to see the world in this abstract black-and-white way. Reluctant to commit fully to European integration, they were nevertheless keenly aware of the economic benefits of EU membership and had no wish to surrender them. They believed that there was no need to choose between Europe and America. They could ride both horses at once, maintaining a close security relationship with Washington while remaining at the centre of the EU despite not participating in the eurozone.

Tony Blair's image of the UK as a bridge between the US and EU, which suggested a Britain moored somewhere in the mid-Atlantic, summed up a widely held view in the British governing class. Washington was happy with this role Britain had assumed, but in many European capitals it led to suspicions that Britain was semi-detached and not fully committed to Europe. It reawakened old fears voiced by Charles de Gaulle when he vetoed Britain's application to join the Common Market in 1963. Britain in his view would always be insufficiently European. It would always give priority to its global interests and its relationship with the United States rather than to Europe. Blair, the most pro-European of British leaders since Edward Heath, confirmed this diagnosis when he supported the US invasion of Iraq.

The idea of Britain as a bridge between Europe and America lost its meaning when Britain voted to leave the EU. Leavers argued that Britain had no need of its European circle and could rely just on the American one. The Anglo-American relationship has a long and complex history and a variety of terms have been used to characterise it. They include the Anglo-world, the English-speaking world, Anglo-America and most recently the Anglosphere (Kenny and Pearce, 2018).

Anglo-America and the Rise of the Anglosphere
Anglo-America is the broadest term, denoting that (dwindling) part of America that feels a particular empathy to things British, the

transnational political space of the English-speaking peoples, as well as a variety of political myths and political projects. The Anglosphere is a very good instance of the last of these. Anglo-America is, however, more than a political project, it is an 'imagined community' (Anderson, 1991), encompassing both ideals and interests, which is constructed and sustained through various narratives and embodied in particular institutions. Such transnational political spaces are a key feature of our world, although less studied than either nation states or the global economy. Such spaces and the communities of interest and ideals to which they give rise can be a potent source of political identity and political projects.

This notion of Anglo-America as a transnational political space embracing the English-speaking world is particularly important for understanding the relationship between Britain and the United States, and in particular for understanding the Anglo-American worldview and the project for Anglo-American hegemony that arose in the final decades of the nineteenth century and the early decades of the twentieth and has assumed many forms – Greater Britain, the Grand Area, the Atlantic Partnership and, most recently, the Anglosphere (Bell, 2007; Watt, 2008; Bennett 2004; Vucetic, 2011). The vote in the 2016 UK referendum to leave the UK has breathed new life into it. The idea of Global Britain was popular among Leavers because it denoted close ties with the US and the wider Anglosphere as an alternative to ties with Europe.

The notion of an Anglo-American worldview does not depend on whether Presidents and Prime Ministers happen to agree with one another and form a strong bond. It is about whether the UK and US despite at times having conflicting interests have nevertheless collaborated in the creation and sustaining of a particular form of world order. For many external observers, the UK and US successfully established an Anglo-American hegemony in which first Britain and later the US took the leading role. It has endured for most of the past 200 years since the defeat of Napoleon at Waterloo, and it has promoted a particular kind of world order, and in recent times a particular form of globalisation.

The Anglosphere is the latest narrative of Anglo-American hegemony, developed primarily by neoconservative circles in the US in the period since the end of the Cold War, although with some important British contributions. The idea behind the Anglosphere is that the United States should recognise the special contribution which the English-speaking nations make to US hegemony. They provide an inner ring, a line of first defence, a coalition of the willing. They are states that are closest to the United States because they share its values, its language and its worldview.

The claims go further than this. For some time now, there has been a current of writing that has celebrated the contribution of the Anglosphere to the modern world, providing the institutions that made the breakthrough to modernity possible (Macfarlane, 2000). The countries of the Anglosphere are regarded as pathfinder societies, the shock troops of modernity, which gave the world the first modern nation state, the first liberal democratic state, the first large secular republic, the first industrial society and most recently the first information economy (Bennett, 2004). The Anglosphere has been more successful, it is argued, than other industrial societies in the past and will continue to be so in the future because English-speaking societies are high-trust civil societies, naturally enterprising and innovative and open and receptive to other cultures. This is what makes them economically dynamic (Veliz, 1994; Mead, 2008).

Proponents of the Anglosphere do not share the older ideas of some form of federal union to link the English-speaking states. They favour instead the creation of a network Commonwealth, or association of English-speaking states (Conquest, 1999), which could foster a range of coalitions of the willing on security, on trade, and on science. Countries of the Anglosphere need to recognise that their primary loyalty and identity is to their fellow members in the Anglosphere, rather than to any other grouping, such as the EU. They would identify as Anglosphere countries with a special relationship to Europe, rather than European countries with a special relationship to the United States.

Looked at from the point of view of the United States, the Anglosphere appears as one of many strategies by which the United States seeks to maintain its hegemony over its allies (Cafruny and Ryner, 2007; Pijl, 1984) and prevent any serious rival emerging. From Britain's standpoint, the Anglosphere shows how the dream of a 'Greater Britain' remains potent despite everything. The British governing class is still attracted to the idea of playing a role in a larger space than a national territory can afford. With the empire gone, the link to the United States and the hegemony that the Americans have established is still a favoured option.

The Consequences of a More Isolationist USA

The pull of Anglo-America remains strong in British politics. Every US President from Kennedy to Obama encouraged Britain to be a full member of the EU, seeing advantages in having a country as closely in step with the US as Britain was, and sharing the same perspective on world order and the need for US leadership, at the heart of the EU, which from the US perspective was a key pillar of that order and the wider Western alliance. But the election of Donald Trump in 2016 has threatened all that. Trump openly supported Brexit, declared the EU a 'foe', identified himself with the forces of populist and Christian nationalism around the world and sought to divide and weaken the Western alliance by dismantling multilateral institutions and pursuing an aggressive America First strategy.

Trump's defeat by Joe Biden in 2020 meant a return to many of the familiar policies and assumptions of US post-war foreign policy. NATO was reaffirmed as a key alliance to which the US was committed, demonstrated by the strong support the US and NATO gave to Ukraine when Russia invaded in 2022. But some differences remained, notably a more protectionist economic policy and the priority given to containing China. The future of US policy remains in doubt because bipartisanship has been severely weakened following the rise of Trump and the grip of his kind of populist nationalism on the Republican Party in Congress and in the country.

Trump's challenge for a second term in the White House raised the possibility that British governments might soon have to confront a very changed world. In the worst-case scenario, NATO might disappear following the US decision to withdraw and suspend its security guarantees for the continent and end its support for Ukraine or any other European state threatened by Russia. Even in the best-case scenario, where the US stays in NATO, US support and concern for Europe are likely to weaken in the future whenever the Republicans control the presidency and Congress.

One of the United States' two main parties is increasingly repudiating the global role in upholding a liberal world order that the US has performed for the last eighty years. J. D. Vance, the Republican candidate for Vice President in 2024, has called NATO a tax on the American people and argues that US foreign policy should be realist, prioritising America's interests ruthlessly by discarding old alliances and ideals. The most important part of American foreign policy according to Vance, speaking at the Quincy Conference in May 2024, is to ensure the strength of the US domestic economy and the strength of its domestic population (Vance, 2024).

British Choices and Dilemmas

Britain withdrew from its European circle in 2016 by ending the forty-year project to pool sovereignty with its European neighbours. The isolationism endorsed by Trump and his Republican allies now threaten the American circle as well. The foundations on which British foreign policy have been based for much of the post-war era are under threat as never before. Signing up to a regional bloc dominated by a protectionist and illiberal US is very different from the post-war commitment to a liberal, rules-based international world order and a Western alliance led by the United States. Some British political leaders on the right, such as Nigel Farage and Liz Truss, are happy to complete the severance of ties with Europe and align with Trumpian America. But most are not.

The dilemma facing the new Labour government is acute. It hopes to continue and build upon the policies established by its predecessor in the field of defence and security. But there is no firm ground any more. At the summit in Washington in July 2024 to commemorate NATO's seventy-fifth anniversary and at the European Political Community meeting held shortly afterwards, Keir Starmer reaffirmed support both for the special relationship with the United States and a new relationship with the EU. But Britain had spent the previous eight years disengaging from Europe, and the special relationship with the US depended on US Presidents continuing to support the transatlantic alliance, which the rise of Trump and the Make America Great Again movement in the United States have put in doubt.

The uncertainty about future policy in Washington goes further than security and defence. The first Trump administration pulled out of the UN Climate Change Conference, refusing to commit to its targets, and showed a more general hostility to all multilateral institutions such as the World Trade Organization, preferring bilateral deals between countries. In doing so, it threatened the institutional architecture that had been an important foundation of US hegemony for the past eight decades. When coupled with a new aggressive economic protectionism to safeguard American jobs and prosperity, aimed primarily at China but also including the EU and the UK, the prospects of the UK concluding a free trade agreement with the United States, which might help compensate the loss of access to the EU after Brexit, appeared bleak. The hope of many Brexiters that Britain could thrive again after Brexit as a free-trading entrepreneurial economy depended heavily on the maintenance of a liberal world order underpinned by the United States, which could encourage all major economic players, including rising powers like China and India, to participate in it. But in the years since Brexit, our world transformed into one of economic and military blocs, and prospects for the kind of growth in world trade experienced when globalisation was at its height in the 1990s and early 2000s has receded.

A sensible strategy for the UK might therefore be to pivot strongly towards the EU, rebuilding links and establishing new forms of co-operation, if only to provide some insurance against the implosion of the Anglo-American relationship. The US is travelling towards protectionism under both the Democrats and Republicans, but so far only the Republicans under Donald Trump are threatening to undermine the transatlantic alliance. Britain might gain economic security by seeking an associate relationship with the EU, agreeing at some stage to rejoin the single market. Military security in the absence of the Americans will be much harder. The Starmer government has announced a major defence review and is keen to encourage greater security co-operation with its European counterparts, preparing for the possibility that Europe may need to defend itself against an expansionist Russia without US help. The ending of bipartisanship in US foreign policy makes the US an unreliable partner and destroys the basis for the special relationship.

Choosing Europe rather than America has its own problems. The legacy of Brexit is still strong. If Britain was still a member, it would be in a much stronger position to promote military co-operation, climate co-operation and economic co-operation with its European counterparts. Being outside the bloc is a huge disadvantage. The simple answer would be to rejoin, but the new government has ruled that out. It would need another referendum, which would be bitterly divisive.

Polls indicate that such is the disillusion with what Brexit has achieved, a vote to rejoin is probable. But like the 2016 result, it is likely it would be narrow, nothing like the two-thirds majority achieved in the referendum in 1975. It might also not be won at all, because the EU would not offer Britain the preferential terms it previously enjoyed arising from its various opt-outs from EU policies and institutions. It is understandable that the British government does not want to reopen the bitter divides of the years after Brexit. But if it does not rejoin at least the single market and the customs union and become an associate member like Norway, then securing meaningful co-operation is going to be hard. It would probably involve Britain becoming a rule-taker, aligning itself with changing EU rules and programmes without any say over their design. In the security field, where EU co-operation is much less developed, Britain might be able to achieve more, especially if the Trump threat to withdraw from NATO is realised. But there will still be difficulties, not least that not all members of the EU are members of NATO, and even some of those that are, like Hungary and Slovakia, are pursuing pro-Russian policies and will oppose the EU developing a new anti-Russian security policy.

The future cohesion of the EU is a more general concern. Increasing support for populist nationalists threatens the cohesion of the bloc in developing common policies on security, climate, migration and the economy. Like the United States, the European Union has in the past been reassuringly dependable. But in the future, it might be much more fragmented or united around policies that the current government in Britain would reject. Making common cause with its

European counterparts and deepening co-operation with them on all aspects of security might seem Britain's best choice. But Brexit cannot be undone quickly, if at all, and Britain now starts from a much weaker position in securing its place in the world.

23

The US and the UK: Lessons from Both Sides of the Atlantic

D. D. Guttenplan and Anand Menon

Don (D. D.):

After Joe Biden's disastrous debate with Donald Trump, many of us in America cast a wistful eye across the Atlantic and thought, 'If only we had the kind of parliamentary system where the party deciding that its leader is going to drag it down to defeat is capable of staging a rebellion and replacing that party leader.' But, of course, everyone knows that can't happen in American politics, because it's a personal system, not a party system. Then Biden was persuaded to withdraw. But the problem remains. The parties are hollowed shells, and they never have anything like the kind of power to do that: except that's exactly what happened.

I think it's worth noting that even as British politics comes in some ways to resemble American politics more and more, particularly in lamentable things like the role of money, the role of consultants and access for cash (which have long been the norm in American politics but are still scandals in Britain) this traffic is not entirely one way. We've just seen what in British terms would be a party coup in America, and that has changed the political landscape here.

Anand:

Regarding the degree to which we're coming to resemble you – I'm sceptical about that in some profound ways. But first, the immediate past. We spent the best part of fourteen years of Tory misrule casting envious glances around the world. Remember Jeremy Corbyn? The vast majority of his MPs were desperate to get rid of him. They tried a couple of times, failed, and we ended up with Keir Starmer, who declared during the recent election, 'Yes, I campaigned for the leader, but I knew that Jeremy Corbyn couldn't win, so it was OK.' They were stuck with a leader that they profoundly didn't like, and who I think most MPs thought couldn't possibly win. And they found there was no easy way of getting rid of him. Therefore, it's not as simple here as some might think.

Don:

I was in Britain when Corbyn became Labour leader. But the part you left out of your account is that he came much closer to winning in 2017 than anyone expected, and that created a problem, too. Because, if he'd gone down to disastrous defeat in his first election campaign, the case for replacing him would have been simple. Instead, you had a party that was split between 'one more heave for Jeremy' and 'let's clean the slate and start again'.

Anand:

Absolutely. If we come on to foreign affairs, it was Russia that was quite central to the way he plummeted in approval ratings for the second election in 2019. But regarding the parallel between the two systems, one of the big differences is that in British politics nowadays we talk about volatility. We talk about the fact that those enduring ties between voters and parties which used to structure politics have gone. A huge proportion of people change the party they vote for from one election to the next. A large number of seats changed hands at the 2024 election. That's a fascinating contrast with the US, where, as far as I can tell from this side of the Atlantic, the vast majority of people have made up their minds. They know who they're going to vote for and wouldn't consider voting for the other lot. Those are two very different trajectories, despite the shared dysfunctions.

Don:

I think that's true on the surface. Except that you have to realise that the American system is really a two-party one where, over time, other things being equal, the parties are supposed to resemble one another more and more, because they're competing for the centre. But in fact, what we've seen since 2016 (and I would argue before 2016) is this hyper-polarisation, so your tribal party loyalty remains fixed. 'My parents were Democrat, I'm a Democrat, my children will be Democrats.' Or we are Republican, depending on where you live, and in part your ethnicity. Donald Trump's campaign really reshuffled that and gave a whole bunch of voters who had been weakly aligned Democrats a reason to leave their party – particularly, I would argue, because he was running against Hillary Clinton. Which is to say America as a sort of Bill Clinton/North American Free Trade Area (NAFTA) had transformed its economy from one of industrial production with relatively well-off, prosperous industrial workers to an internationally competitive workforce, where if you weren't internationally competitive, you were left out and *felt* left out.

All Hillary Clinton offered voters in the US was the elimination of even more jobs, because they're dirty jobs related to coal and oil, which we are phasing out. Suddenly, you had this large working-class block that had been neglected by both Bill Clinton and Barack Obama, and then became unmoored from the Democrats, and for which only Donald Trump was making a serious play in 2016. That was a realignment election, except that Trump only delivered symbolic gains for those people. But symbolic gains are, for many, better than nothing. 'If your offer is symbolic gains or nothing, we'll take symbolic gains'.

Now Biden began to deliver economic alternatives. Trump says that that he's going to end the green transition and the electric vehicle mandates. He's going to drill, drill, drill. Statistical prosperity isn't giving the Democrats the bump they might have expected. And some people have recognised that these green jobs are good union jobs. They pay high wages. They're going to be around for a while. The chips plants are in parts of the country that the Democrats have lost but are now getting back.

People had the sense that they were being seen by Trump. But was he giving them anything? This allowed Biden, with some clever investments and smart politics, to win back some swing voters in some of those swing states in 2020. The Democrats were making a very different offer under Biden than they'd been making under Hillary Clinton. But will it continue, and will it be enough?

Anand:

There are so many parallels here with what Keir Starmer's government is thinking of doing in terms of the green transition. Most of their investment plans are in the north of England and in Scotland, which isn't a coincidence. It's basically trying to secure the good jobs of the future in places where Labour needs to secure a stronger foothold or win back voters. Actually a lot of what he was saying reminded me of one of my favourite books, Thomas Frank's *Listen, Liberal*, where he talks about how the Democrats lost blue-collar voters.

During the 2017 UK election, Frank wrote a piece for *The Guardian* about Wakefield, which is the town in West Yorkshire I come from. He compared what was going on there to the towns he'd written about in his book, and the parallels were absolutely remarkable. The way in which the Labour Party had alienated its traditional base, the way in which blue-collar workers had increasingly got fed up with being patronised and ignored. Eventually, a lot of those voters voted for Boris Johnson in 2019. The left is having to deal with its own failures at the moment and try to learn from these mistakes of the past.

Don:

I'd like to think that was the case. I share Frank's view that, absent a populism of the left, a populism of the right (if that's the only offer for change) will be taken by large numbers of desperate people. But there's one huge issue in Britain that cuts through this, and which was in some ways a harbinger to Trump. That, of course, is Brexit. That involved workers who feel that what we in America call the coastal elites, and what in Britain you'd call the Westminster elite, regarded them with contempt. I was in Britain when Brexit passed. I got a phone call from Lord Glasman, the architect of Blue Labour. He was jubilant, but he also said, 'This means that Trump is going to win.' Because, in his view, there was a zeitgeist factor from this revolt against elites that was not just confined to Brexit and Britain. He was quite prescient in that.

Anand:

That's true. Brexit allowed Boris Johnson to remake the political map of Britain in 2019. In many ways, the Brexit coalition was like Trump's coalition. It was the same unholy alliance, in the sense that it was an alliance that could agree when it comes to their hostility to governing elites (even though Trump and Johnson are both elite in a different way) but couldn't agree on a single thing when it came to the practicalities of economic policy.

Don:

How much do you feel that racism or 'racial resentment' is essential to understanding the politics of the right in both our countries? And what might have happened in Britain had Dominic Cummings been allowed to deliver an essentially populist economic programme, which he and Michael Gove seemed to be arguing for within the Johnson administration? Except that Johnson was, of course, far too feckless to deliver.

Interestingly, when Trump was inaugurated in 2017, he summoned the heads of all the major auto companies in the US. He told them that they were going to have to make more cars in the US. That was a great photo opportunity. It sent a message to auto workers in swing states: 'He sees us.' But of course, they didn't really deliver on it. I went to Lordstown in Ohio on the day that the most storied General Motors plant in America shut down, making its last Chevy. Now it's empty. They didn't deliver. In the same way, the Tories didn't deliver on economic populism. But would things have changed if they had?

Anand:

Boris Johnson's unique political skill lay in his ability to say contradictory things to different groups of people and get away with it. He managed to tell one bunch of Conservative voters that he was a traditional, tax-cutting Conservative and another group of largely new Conservative voters that he was going to invest in the north and transform their lives. My assumption was that Johnson would win a second term, because, as you said, he might not have delivered, but he gave a sense to some of those places that they were being thought about in government for the first time. By the end of a second Johnson term, it would have fallen apart because the contradictions in the economic project were just so glaring.

Don:

In a way, that's a fundamental question for rightist politics. Can those contradictions ever be resolved? Can you really deliver tax cuts and smaller government but also lift up the working class? One answer that might differentiate America from Britain is that you could if you weren't spending so much on the Pentagon!

Anand:

But you have a miraculous economy, don't you? It just keeps growing, almost regardless of who's in charge.

Don:

From the outside it looks that way, because we're the world's reserve currency. But the real growth has been in China.

Anand:

The adoption of self-imposed fiscal rules by both the Tories and Labour is another massive constraint. There is an unwillingness to move in a Keynesian direction and invest properly. But that's to anticipate what we are coming on to. Then there is the 'false elites' dimension. Johnson and Farage talk about elites, but they are the elite. Trump, too. He has given $4.5 trillion worth of tax cuts to billionaires.

What we don't talk about is the fact that Brexit itself was a very powerful symbol of failure. It was a failure of an entire neoliberal political and economic model to deliver to people. Reflect on the fact that 52 per cent of this country were willing to vote against a status quo in favour of they didn't know what, simply to register a protest against that status quo. That's quite a compelling critique of what had gone before. A powerful message. It doesn't mean class in terms of what sort of accent you have. It means, 'That lot haven't delivered for you for so long.' You still see it in the record lack of trust in politicians. And it is still the case that trust in politics decreases in lockstep with distance from London. The further you are from London, the less you trust politics.

Now is very tempting, on the progressive left, to slightly rewrite history and say that this is all down to the right, to Johnson and company wrecking things. But the problems long predate that. They go back before 2010. It's as much about a failed model as anything. And the fiscal rules are precisely a symbol of that failure.

Don:

I would agree with almost all that. But I'd add a few things. One, as the vulgar materialist in the conversation, I would point to the salience of C. Wright Mills's great phrase: 'The power elite.' Johnson counts as elite, however you slice it in Britain. He's an Etonian. He grew up in a house looking out on Primrose Hill. It's true that his parents were not ultra-wealthy, but by the time he got his newspaper career underway, he had plenty of money. Whereas Donald Trump was always despised by the New York cultural elite, and he still has a chip on his shoulder about that. He still has a chip on his shoulder about his relative smallness in the context of New York real estate. He had a lot of resentment stewing, in a way that Johnson probably didn't.

But crucially, in both countries, the leading parties are subservient to corporate interests. That perception is felt, albeit too rarely, when you're on the sharp end of corporate interests and the further you are from the comfortable economic bubble. But in terms of the fiscal rules, that's a little different, because the pound is not the world's reserve currency. That's why the magic doesn't work for you in the UK. You can try to sprinkle the fairy dust on yourselves, but if you try to fly... well, Liz Truss found out what happens then. You come down pretty hard and fast.

Anand:

That fiscal conservatism argument can and has been used fraudulently, most obviously by George Osborne and David Cameron. Because, even at the time, it seemed absurd to suggest that, when interest rates were zero, if the British state borrowed to invest, we would face the bankruptcy fate of Greece. That was palpably not true.

Don:

But you know who also made that argument? Gordon Brown. When you had a Labour government that was theoretically committed to expanding the common good, expanding the public sector, rehabilitating the economy and providing high quality public goods, Brown decided to do it through Public Private Partnerships, rather than extending the state. It didn't work because the private sector turned out to be very poor stewards of public goods. Plus, it seemed to foreclose any real choice.

Anand:

One of the problems with the Blair–Brown era was that they practised social democracy surreptitiously. They spoke the language of markets and corporate interests. But they actually did a whole load of good, too. However, they utterly failed to win the argument. During their period in power, they didn't say, 'We're doing this stuff because it's good for the country; it's not just good for the people we're helping. It helps us to mobilise human capital by giving more people opportunity. Having a better-educated population is good for the country as a whole.' They didn't make the argument for social democracy and embed it in the minds of the British public. That meant it was very easy for their legacy to be unpicked by subsequent Conservative governments. One of my hopes about Keir Starmer (though I'm not that hopeful) is that they try to win the argument as well. Because it's not enough doing things in government. You've got to embed your argument, as Margaret Thatcher did, so that subsequent leaders are bound by your legacy.

Don:

I couldn't agree with that more. Blair and Brown got the taste for stealth social democracy from their friend, Bill Clinton. He did the same thing, except that Clinton was also remaking the economy to be more responsive to Wall Street and was an enormous beneficiary of Wall Street donors to his campaign. But the person who was the biggest beneficiary of Wall Street donors in American politics in recent years was not Bill Clinton and it was not Donald Trump. It was Barack Obama. Maybe, for that reason, Obama comes much closer to your description of Blair and Brown, because he had lots of good programmes but talked about almost none of them.

In other words, it was redistribution by stealth. There was no sense that, in a prosperous society, nobody should go bankrupt because of a medical bill. That in order to mobilise the human capital of a 50 per cent female workforce, the government needed to provide childcare for people. Bernie Sanders made that argument. He made all the arguments for social democracy, and that was part of the huge wave of enthusiasm that greeted his campaign. You had a sense that here was somebody finally making the argument. But of course, the Democratic Party and its corporate donors hated it. They didn't want that argument to be made.

Anand:

Labour are always on the back foot, aren't they? Ridiculously, even with a massive parliamentary majority, they have to rationalise and justify, rather than going out aggressively and making the case for doing things differently. Now, obviously there are limits on what the government can do and spend. That being said, you could do things differently to how they have been contemplating at the moment. Re-banding council tax. Breaking out of the restrictive framework of talking about debt falling at the end of a five-year period, a rule which is just there to be gamed, as everyone knows.

I was struck during the UK election campaign that Liberal Democrat leader Ed Davey was asked in one of the television debates, 'How would you pay for it?' He said, 'Well, I would make it absolutely clear that borrowing for investment is clearly labelled as such, and so does not fall within the rule.' That markets are not going to have an absolute panic if a government decides to start borrowing to invest, because this country desperately needs better infrastructure and better public services. That is the path to growth. But Labour are cautious because they aren't in power very often. I just hope that with experience of power, a greater degree of boldness will intrude into their thinking.

Don:

Instead of seizing the initiative when you've got it, you miss the opportunity. I never understood why they couldn't decide to issue bonds for capital projects, particularly capital projects that over the long-term would be self-funding. A high-speed rail link to the north, for example; if you say you will dedicate a certain percentage of fares on this rail line to repaying the same bonds we're going to issue to pay for it with, investors would flock to those bonds, because they'd be backed by the faith and credit of the government. And there's no reason to carry something that's self-funding on your long-term balance sheet.

Anand:

The problem is that politics always takes priority over good policy. The trick is to make the two coincide. But our politics over the past fourteen years has become criminally short-term in nature. One obvious and sad example of the way this works is social care. When Andy Burnham unveiled his plan for social care in 2010, it was perfectly sensible. It didn't solve all the problems, but it would have been a damn sight better than the situation we're in now. The Tories basically shot it down by calling it a death tax. Seven years later, Theresa May brought forward a plan that wasn't massively dissimilar to Andy Burnham's in her manifesto. Labour killed it by calling it a dementia tax. In the intervening years, both parties went out saying, 'We desperately need a cross-party approach to social care.' But here we are now with a massive social care crisis, no plan to deal with it and social care being responsible for the productivity crisis in the NHS to a significant extent – because people can't be discharged from hospital when we've got nowhere to send them. That's a depressing parable of modern British politics.

Don:

I would say that we in America suffer from the same debility, although it affects different policies. That said, an American can only look at the discussion about social care in Britain with envy. Our social care is, 'You're on your own.' Now, to illustrate my point, look at the forces at work on immigration policy here, where everybody who's sane understands that we need immigration to continue to grow our economy. It needs to be managed, to avoid the kind of right-wing resentment that's very easy to stoke. The rules need to be clear and enforced, so Trump can't get away with lying about it. But we need it. Essentially, the Democrats have moved sufficiently to the right to embrace the corporate Republican programme for managing immigration, because big employers are pro-immigration. Possibly for nefarious reasons, but they are pro. Then Trump vetoed the bipartisan Congress bill because he didn't want to give Biden a win, and the Republican Party fell in line immediately, because politics trumps policy.

Anand:

On immigration in the UK, I am a little bit optimistic for several reasons. Firstly, because we've got a weird moment coming up when immigration is going to fall quite dramatically for a while, because some of the schemes that we've run for Hong Kongers and Ukrainians no longer apply. Those numbers will go down. Not letting people applying for care work visas to bring dependents with them has resulted in an enormous decrease in the number of applications for these visas. We're going to see the numbers come down, while at the same time, certain sectors of our economy are going to go into crisis as a direct result of this. The trade-offs that politicians have shied away from talking about are going to become very clear. This might become clear in the university sector as well, if we see a big drop off in the numbers of foreign students. We're going to be forced to have that discussion. This Labour government is the first government I can remember that has been elected to power on the back of an electorate that doesn't really care about immigration among Labour voters. It wasn't in the top five issues of concern prior to the election, and that gives them a little bit of space.

Don:

How should the left respond to all this? I'm afraid I think of someone who isn't really famous as a left thinker, and that's Ronald Reagan. He said, 'Trust, but verify.' We are entitled to have some hope with the emergence of Kamala Harris and Starmer, whatever the limits. I thought that Starmer's election might be a kind of reverse harbinger, in the same way that Brexit was a harbinger. You know, a harbinger that not everything is moving right. The pink tide in Latin America seems to be both receding and renewing at the same time. It's more ambiguous overall. But in the northern Atlantic countries, maybe things are not always going to the right. But I think in both cases, you have to be leery of corporate capture.

One bellwether for me in the US, and this is very 'inside baseball', is whether Harris keeps Lina Khan as the head of the Federal Trade

Commission. She's the leading anti-monopolist, a law review analyst and professor. She's taken on Google, Apple and Silicon Valley. Because, to return to an earlier theme, here are different elites. The Democratic Party's elite is essentially a sector of Wall Street, but also Silicon Valley and Hollywood. The Republican Party's elite are manufacturing and heavy industry, but also car dealers represent the bone and sinew of the GOP. They're the big donors or big activists in almost all state parties. And, of course, the car dealers are not lining up to transition to green energy. They are not even keen on selling electric vehicles. They want to sell trucks that guzzle gas and have huge profit margins.

Part of it is that the two parties are responsive to different elites in the US. It is also true that the Democratic Party elite doesn't really love Lina Khan any more than the Republican Party elite does. It will be interesting to see whether Harris buckles. If she buckles, that will be a very bad sign. I don't know whether the electorate is watching it, but certainly people like me are watching it very carefully.

Anand:
One concern I have about politics on both sides of the Atlantic is that we need a laser focus on the real lives of real people. If there's one lesson we should take from the past ten years, it's the failure of the spreadsheet politics of GDP. It doesn't tell you anything. I think that's true in the US as well as the UK, with its amazing aggregate economic numbers. They need to translate into real progress for real people. One of the problems Starmer has, given that his majority is a bit like a sandcastle (quite fragile), is that the electorate won't be that patient. You need to have real clarity on making sure that people see some change. It might not be much change, but if things need to be seen to be moving in the right direction, if government simply says, 'Don't worry, things are getting better,' that goes really badly.

The other thing that concerns me about Western politics in general is the number of people in our electoral systems who now vote against things rather than for things. You saw that in France in the second round of the 2024 legislative elections. There was a lot of it in our UK election. Much of the vote was anti-Tory rather than pro-Labour or pro-Lib Dem. I'm conflicted on this. Sometimes I think it doesn't matter. If you get the vote, you get the vote. Who cares why you've got the vote? But sometimes, in my darker moments, I think this is potentially quite dangerous if people can't find something to vote for. That is a sad reflection on the state of democracy. Plus, it allows people to fall prey to the siren calls of the far right.

Don:

The fact that people were rejecting the fecklessness of the Tories was at least a sign that they are paying attention. It is a terrible reflection on our system in the US that until Harris emerged, the choice it offered people was four more years of Trump or four more years of Biden. The problem with voting against things is that it doesn't give you a mandate to do anything. When Blair came into government, Andrew Adonis came up with a checklist of things they were going to do about education, and they did them. Or at least they did a lot of them, and they felt they had a mandate to do that. It also means you are not connecting with people's real lives. Some months ago, I spent time driving around Pennsylvania talking to grassroot activists. They have this phrase that I kept hearing, and I think reflects where they're at politically. It's 'block and build'. That's how they see their task. They're trying to build grassroot organisations, but they also feel that they have to organise to block things getting worse. If they can bring people together to block, then they have the potential to build. But if they just concentrate on building, they're going to get out-manoeuvred.

Anand:

I very much appreciated what Keir Starmer said about politics treading less heavily on our lives. Because let's face it, for the last decade since the Scottish independence referendum in 2014, politics has been stomping on our faces. It's just all been a bit too much. A period of calm would be welcomed, I think. On the other hand, if that presages a return to calm, cold managerialism, that's a worry. The fundamental difference between now and 1997, when Blair brought in his managerialism, was that growth in 1997 was around 4.6 per cent. You had a healthy economy, which gave you a degree of freedom to bring about improvements in public services without doing anything too radical and scaring the horses.

Now we're in a very different macroeconomic situation, fiscally, both in terms of public services and in terms of the economy as a whole. I do wonder whether calm managerialism is enough. Perhaps you need it with a hint of radicalism thrown in to get things done in today's circumstances.

Don:

Yes, I would say, in both cases. Our two countries operate under different economic constraints, but in terms of what one would like to see, I keep going back to the 1930s and the bold, persistent experimentation of an economy that (at least in the US) was in very deep decline and appeared to be stuck. A really gifted politician should be able both to summon the constituency for change and attend to the policy and managerial details of delivering it so that it really makes a difference in people's lives. One of the things that you see if you travel around the US, outside the coastal areas, is that it is the vast expansion of the commons and of public institutions that took place in the 1930s that we're still living on. Those were all built partly to stimulate the economy and give people work, but they also delivered public services at a micro-level to people across the country. These things still endure and that's what we need in both countries: leaders with that degree of vision.

Anand:

I think the key to that here in the UK is going to be the green transition. To simplify, this is Ed Miliband versus Rachel Reeves. Investing for the future, investing to give ourselves a leadership position in the green transition, or getting stuck on austerity. I think the house building plan is great, and I hope they follow through with it, but it's not enough. A lot is going to hinge on Miliband's success in driving his agenda forward, to be honest.

Don:

I'd be happy to end on that positively challenging note. But let's not forget the right, which in your case is Reform. I think the risk is of what I would call Mitterrandism, which is where you fail to deliver on politics, and then you just turn people off it for a generation. The stakes are much higher now, because the alternatives are much worse.

Afterword: Rediscovering a Politics of Hope and Possibility

Simon Barrow and Gerry Hassan

'Things Can Only Get Better'
LABOUR PARTY CAMPAIGN SONG, BY D:REAM (1997)

'Things will get worse before they get better.'
KEIR STARMER (2024)

The aim of this book has been to take a careful look at the political terrain that the Labour government at Westminster inhabits (both domestically and internationally), as well as the inheritance, shape and trajectory of that new administration insofar as it has manifested itself first in opposition, then in the 2024 general election campaign and more recently in the earlier stages of operation and decision-making.

'New', of course, is a relative term in politics. Following fourteen years of Tory government and what seemed a never-ending Brexit (now in its submergence and denial phase), Keir Starmer's arrival at Downing Street does indeed seem new. But just as an event-driven week can sometimes encompass what feels like a decade's worth of change in the corridors of power, so the alleged 'honeymoon period' for incoming governments shrinks, and they become tarnished and stale remarkably quickly. There are definite signs of that already. The purpose of this afterword is therefore to look unshrinkingly at the constraints and challenges facing a kingdom that sometimes feels more divided than united, in myriad ways, and on that basis to chart the possibilities of hope, recovery and progress.

Relief, Contrast and Constraint

During its election campaign, Starmer's Labour promised two things. The main framing was 'Change'. But when weaving, ducking and diving through the policy minefield, the most common promise (at once emotional and political) was 'stability'. After the extraordinary buffeting of the Johnson/Truss/Sunak years, following on from Cameron–Osborne austerity and the unexpected (but, with hindsight, entirely predictable) rupture with the European Union, almost anything would feel stable. So the first sense that many had in the wake of a sweeping – but, as John Curtice points out, actually rather fragile – Labour election win was one of relief. What a contrast there would be in the tone, feel and approach of Labour after years of faction, fraction and friction under the Tories. At last, it seemed, post the 4 July result, we have some adults in the room. We were now being ruled by a party in government that, having ruthlessly suppressed, ejected or offended away most of the Corbynite left, including its figurehead, seemed mostly united and desperate to please: or at least to appear mature, sensible and relatively caring. That includes 'being willing to spell out hard truths'. That overall impression gave way to severe cracks almost as soon as Labour took to office, with criticisms around gifts and influence, internal squabbling, and arguments about policy promises grabbing headlines across the first 100 days of office. The 'honeymoon period' has been as short as any administration in recent memory, though as of the end of 2024 and beginning of 2025, it is still 'early days'.

So, what is the truth about Labour, the fabric of the UK and the genuine prospects of change and hope that lie ahead? This is a question that requires us to push through the clichés, the headlines and the initial impressions. It asks us to look beyond present fixations and priorities, to question the shibboleths and to critique the constraints of conservatism with a small c, and of the outdated ideological assumptions that have characterised too much of politics in the UK in recent years.

This is difficult to do, because many of these constraints remain buried in the increasingly technocratic 'normalcy' of modern, professional politics as a whole, and the alleged 'common sense' that this sharp-suited, algorithmised and sound-bite coded 'adulting' shrouds by its very nature, instincts, PR defensiveness and day-to-day existence. But you can begin to tell what is really going on underneath the surface by probing the language and looking behind the policy curtain to see more precisely what has changed and what hasn't, what is being confronted and what is being avoided, where willingness begins and where it ends.

That is what section three (*Rethinking the Economy*) and key parts of section four (*Restoring Public Life and the Public Sphere*) and section five (*Reconfiguring Nations and Identities*) in this book have been very much about. There we find searching questions about the framing economic and political narrative ('there is no magic money tree', 'we can only do what we can afford') from Aditya Chakrabortty and Adam Tooze, plus the environmentally embedded challenge to a fiscally driven and almost neo-monetarist approach to addressing the tasks of investing in the UK's social fabric and our technological, productive and financial future (Ann Pettifor). We also read about the opportunity for a new and bold approach to industrial strategy, rooted in a mission-oriented methodology set out in Keir Starmer's rhetoric (Mariana Mazzucato), and the opportunity to humanise the world of work, keeping it flexible yet at the same time enhancing the networks that sustain it (Julia Hobsbawm).

Party, System, or Both?

Probing further, we have looked at the impact on the operation of a politics of anger, bile and revenge across social media, the corrosion of public spheres of conversation and unhealthy relationships between politicians and press and broadcasting (Gavin Esler), along with the issue of culture wars and the struggle for the past (Alan Lester). Crucial too are assumptions and demands in relation to the meaning of social security and the welfare state in the twenty-first century (Hilary Cottam), the possibilities of a properly inclusive patriotism (Sunder Katwala), and the reframing of negative or simplistically optimistic tropes about multiculturalism (Savitri Hensman).

In each of these areas, we can see a certain strain emerging inside the Labour government and the party. This is a tension between aspiration and limitation, innovation and conservatism, at the heart of the Starmer project – if we can refer to it as such. (There is also the issue, both the lurking and explicit addressed, of hope and possibility in parts four and five, to which we will turn shortly.) Whether it is dealing with economy, environment, health and social fabric, culture, identity or belonging, there is clear evidence of the constraining and damaging forces that seem inherent in our present outdated and unreformed political and parliamentary system. These include, particularly, the predominance of short-term thinking and policy-making – that is, the tendency to look for the immediate, 'cost effective' and expedient route to tackling presenting problems, at the expense of piloting and engineering deeper or more fundamental change that addresses their underlying causes and conditions.

The constraints here are often electoral and optics-based. After two or at most three years, governments in the UK seem to be thinking primarily about how to hold on to and regain power. Indeed, the new Labour government seems to have switched into that mode almost immediately, perhaps looking back rather nervously at the overall dominance of the Conservative Party in the modern era. They are equally aware that the distortions of the First Past the Post system have made an emphatic landslide out of a thin majority in specific regions and demographics. The decision by the Prime Minister to order the suspension of seven backbenchers from the parliamentary whip over a minor rebellion concerning the two-child cap policy signalled an early, ruthless determination to quell dissent.

These are concerning signs. While discipline is necessary to govern, so is the ability to respond to different voices and to encourage a climate of debate and creativity. It was the Blair governments that introduced iron-clad 'messaging', fault-free obedience and all-embracing political spin as core virtues in the machinery of its political operation. But these came at great cost when in the hands of Gordon Brown, who as a Chancellor benefitted from his controlling attention to detail and ability to say 'no' but as Prime Minister suffered from the consequent fracturing of relations and reluctance to say 'yes'. In other words, culture and sociality matter in government, as does the ability to adapt, change and vary – which only comes with a culture of debate and the capacity to make difference work effectively for the common good. In part, then, we can say that constraints arise from the very nature of the system. That means hope for a better future partly lies in reforming it. But it also lies in the culture of party politics, and the particular nature and history of the party that comes into government. These elements cannot ultimately be separated, but they can be examined and considered for reconfiguration in the path to something more workable, more engaging and more capable of improved outcomes and relations for the largest number.

Beginning to Fix Broken Politics

What we see in the early days of a UK Labour administration set on governing with commendable core values are symptoms of what happens in a democracy whose institutions are creaking at the very time it is confronted with increased internal fragmentation, the spectre of reactionary populism, the increasingly cross-border and cross-boundary nature of the threats and opportunities that lie ahead, the problem of corporate capture and an 'owned' (more than 'free') media, and serious questions about the identity and trajectory of its constituent nations in a wider geopolitical context. Here, we will say a little more about creaking institutions and fragmentation, before moving on to look at each of those concerns in terms of both the problems and the possibility of prospecting for hopeful solutions. Then we will conclude with some observations about the nature of political hope and possibility, pointing back to the observations of Chapter 14 on art and culture (Dave O'Brien and Orian Brook), and Chapter 19 on belief, rootedness and hopeful experimentation (Simon Barrow and Fiona Brocklesby).

First, it is important to note that it is not just politics that feels fractured, and at times broken. But that is a good place to start. Low levels of trust, fading interest or information fatigue, lack of attention and learning, and reduced or reluctant participation. All these are observable features in the political arena defined in terms of elected institutions and the parliamentary or local franchise. Such trends undermine the effectiveness and authority of representative democracy. As Barrow and Brocklesby point out, the need here is to forge genuine listening partnerships between communities and the politicians and assemblies they elect to decide and oversee key aspects of public infrastructure. That requires time, effort and resourcing.

Equally, when many votes do not count (under a disproportional, winner-takes-all voting system), when the House of Commons intentionally cannot even house all the representatives people vote for at the same time, when Westminster fritters countless hours on an archaic queuing system for voting instead of electronic registration of votes, and when one of the two houses in a bicameral Parliament remains wholly populated by patronage rather suffrage, you know you are looking at a system that has ended up paying mere lip-service to the will of the people.

Gordon Brown's commission advocating reform of the Lords is the latest in a long line of ditched wishes over the years, stretching back more than a century (Commission on the UK's Future, 2022). Labour's conference has backed the democratic necessity of proportional representation, but Keir Starmer rejects it outright. Local authorities are on the brink of bankruptcy or beyond. Aspirations for more genuine power going to Scotland and Wales (and the English regions), or for a sustainable, overarching framework, look to be in a stalemate. Scotland has been offered no pathway to decide its constitutional future by Westminster, whatever the democratic will there. There are no positive moves towards a written constitution at the centre of power. Yet without fundamental reform in these and other parts of the basic fabric, democracy risks further serious decay, and the lure of the populist, authoritarian right will grow stronger. The challenge to Labour and the centre-left is to come up with a major reset in this area.

Then there is the increasing drift away from political parties. The surge of membership to Labour under Jeremy Corbyn and his left populism is now in serious reversal with the arrival of a more technocratic, managerial, centralist and some would say authoritarian style under Keir Starmer. Similarly, the progressive nationalist surge of the SNP has ended, and its membership will soon have halved since 2015 on current trends. These two 'success stories' of recent years proved to be outliers in the end. As several contributors to this volume have pointed out, fewer people voted for the Westminster duopoly than at any time in modern history in the 2024 general election, and the turnout was also a historic low. The culture of parties, as well as the system, needs to change, both internally and in relation to the wider public. In fact, reform of those two features is inseparable.

In short, humanity, dignity and transparency needs to be restored to politics, and the easy reward of exclusion and bully-pulpit tactics needs to be marginalised and discouraged. Such changes are unlikely to come from inside the system, though newly elected independent and Green MPs at Westminster, shocked by some of what they have seen, are lobbying hard. It requires recognition and pressure from outside too, from those whose interests and votes are not being properly heard or represented. In terms of a more associational and synergistic politics within, across and beyond parties, Molly Scott Cato (Chapter 5) has much to offer by way of putative alternatives to a simple 'progressive alliance' approach, given the realities of tribalism and factionalism and the limits of the current electoral system. Sue Goss (Chapter 15) likewise explores the renovation of the fabric creatively and in some depth. It is no coincidence that it is the experience of women, politically and socially/culturally, that is posing the sharpest questions towards 'what is' and inviting the winds of change to reshape it into something truly fit for decision-making towards a liveable future.

All this requires big vision. Is that possible in a somewhat-fractured UK still shell-shocked from Tory chaos, pandemic, Brexit, the cost-of-living crisis and the provocations of far-right groups on the streets of England? The overall atmosphere often feels shrunken, if not febrile. In the US, where personalities more than policies seem to reign (for good and ill), Kamala Harris initially showed how an entirely fresh optimism and vibrancy can be injected into what seemed a deadening political confrontation. While some of this may seem to be superficial – politics as image and spectacle – and while 'fixes' cannot simply be transported from one culture to another, the conversation between D. D. Guttenplan and Anand Menon (Chapter 23) shows that lessons can indeed be learned, pondered and shared for the revival of more hopeful possibilities on both sides of the Atlantic, even when the doom clouds loom large.

Challenging the Corrosion of Corporate Capture

The submission of governing parties to corporate agendas and the interests of the super wealthy is another deeply worrying trend. In some respects, this started with Tony Blair and Gordon Brown appearing to be mesmerised by the rich and powerful. It translated into subservience to the Murdoch media empire and morphed into Private Public Partnership (PPP) and Private Finance Initiative (PFI) schemes, which ultimately drained billions from the public purse. It then continued under the institutionally corrupt Tory years with 'money for access', with the lobbying dominance of fossil fuel adjacent industries, with unaccountable and barely scrutinised contracts worth millions for PPE during the COVID-19 pandemic and with the ever-revolving door of huge individual and company donors.

For Labour, too, private donations now outweigh the contributions of trade unions, who founded the party as a means of furthering workers' rights. The early signs from Labour in government are that there is no discernible sea-change in attitudes or expectations in relation to corporate dominance – something also seen right across the think tank and policy industry, as well as in the media. Mariana Mazzucato's forensic and ground-shaking analysis of the high-level consultancy industry and what is wrong with it (Chapter 9) – especially from the perspective of the need for an entrepreneurial state geared towards public good – is also extremely important in this regard.

Money does not guarantee political success (especially in a dysfunctional voting system), but without it there is little chance of getting a real voice and representation that makes a difference. Public funding for political parties and restrictions on corporate donations over a certain amount are among the possible solutions that definitely need to be taken seriously. Likewise, a marked imbalance in the press (secured through the ownership of most national and regional titles by a handful of companies and individuals), the increasing political and financial pressure on the BBC and the tilting of social media towards the right by tech billionaires are corrosive factors for democratic renewal, for public information (the truth economy) and for civic education. An owned press – either by the state or by transnational companies and individuals – is not a truly free one insofar as it represents the interests of the few over the many and restricts rather than broadens a plurality of voices and perspectives.

In Scotland, following the example of other European countries, there are attempts to establish a Scottish Public Interest Journalism Institute (SPIJI). Its aim would be to use a 'blind trust' with a variety of sources of money to invest in investigative and public interest journalism of the kind that is being lost as media companies prioritise shareholder income over professional reporting and commentary in a rapidly reshaping and resizing industry where free digital content has been a game changer and AI will potentially make matters worse as well as better.

Again, boldness and vision is needed to chart a better future, with strong voices supporting a 'global commons' for social media ownership, rather than a few super-wealthy monopolists. This taps into the complex issues of transnational law, global regulation and international institutions, but it is something governments, including this new Labour one, can influence.

The Changing Nature of Britain

The nature of the 'Britain' that Labour speaks for, sees and aspires to encourage into being – the future, progressive Britain that has often been tantalisingly out of reach down the years – has been one of the defining facets of the party's fortunes. Labour has on occasion spoken as a force that feels it can shape the future and the future Britain – 1945, 1964 and 1997. But even on these occasions it has not managed to be persuasive for long.

More commonly, Labour has long had an ambivalent relationship with the idea of Britishness, readily ceding ground to the Tories and the right on patriotism, 'the national interest', defence and security and the Union Jack. Sunder Katwala (Chapter 17) lays out the case and potential for a progressive patriotism and a Britain that embraces its diversity; terrain that until now, Labour have been wary of. It has also had an ambiguous relationship with some of the key pillars that contribute to the idea of Britain. One of these is the England–Britain relationship. As examined in Gerry Hassan's contribution (Chapter 16), the peak of 'Labour Britain' was between 1945 and 1975, and even in this era, its contours revealed its weaknesses.

Two pillars of this era were the clear visions of 'Labour Scotland' and 'Labour Wales', which underpinned the party's dominance in each and went way beyond the party's electoral appeal, giving it an institutional ballast in each. The former was defeated by the SNP's victories in 2007 and 2011, but the latter is still ongoing – the most successful electoral Labour Party in the UK (Hassan and Shaw, 2012). A missing pillar has been, and still is, that of 'Labour England' as a political community, nation, set of institutions and symbols that Labour historically have subsumed in the wider idea of 'Labour Britain'. This evasion and silence has had major consequences, allowing the populist right to claim that they alone speak for an England they say has been ignored by mainstream politics, Labour and Tory.

A Labour idea of Britain for the twenty-first century must address a host of issues. These include the missing English pillar; remaking the political centre; and creating a convincing idea of what Britain is, the values it embodies and the kind of relationships it wants to build between government and citizens, and centre, nations and regions. It needs to comprehend what would be appropriate for a modern, outward-looking, democratic country placing itself geopolitically beyond the illusions of Great British powerism, which have disfigured Britain for so long. This is a tough ask, but trying to maintain the existing political status quo will only result in increasingly diminished returns, cynicism and a potentially reactionary backlash.

The Crunch: Facing Serious Existential Threats

It has been important that the expert observers, commentators, actors and influencers who have contributed to this book have been prepared to engage the granular detail of many of the most important challenges facing the new UK government, the particular issues that occur at national, regional and local levels, and the wider architecture of both formal and movement-based or non-governmental politics. They have also looked at who really speaks for whom, how the weight of history applies to the incoming government, the turmoil on the right and the issues of identity and culture at the core of factors encouraging or blocking progressive change. In doing so, there has been a widespread recognition of the need for fundamental reform, not mere tinkering, in a range of areas – from fiscal policy, social security and public services right through to the political and constitutional fabric itself. It is popularly said that 'the devil is in the detail'. Politics in all its forms ravels and unravels around particulars.

This is an appropriate metaphor for averting the one issue that has not been as prominent in this collection as we would have liked. 'The environment' is not a special interest issue; it is our very home world, and it is on the brink of disintegration, deformation and collapse (both in relation to shrinking biodiversity and the climate emergency brought on by global heating) on a scale that is almost unimaginable. Climate scientists and eco-futurists have seen deep into the crisis and touched the void. But governments, corporations and the military are still substantially in denial. Labour at Westminster retrenched on its environmental commitments even before elected.

So it is perhaps not surprising that the environment, though much talked about, and acted upon by brave and often vilified groups of activists, does not register seriously on the barometer of representative democracy at the moment. People mostly vote for their pockets, not the survival of the species. The issues involved in global heating are large, complex and unwieldy for many. Yet they are fundamental, not just to 'environmental policy' but to every aspect of policy-making at one level or another. We often hear that said, but less often see it acted upon amidst those prose-laden details of legislation and policy. The climate emergency also poses huge and fundamental questions to the operation of both the free-market global economy (can it really self-reform away from rapacious production and consumption?) and the capacity of democracy, politics and leadership.

The vision and determination required to tackle the existential threat to the planet is something that seems to dwarf the day-to-day concerns of present politics and present economics. Something seismic has to shift. The role of civic mobilisation, protest movements, trade unions and yes, civil disobeyers, could well be crucial in changing the agenda on a global as well as local scale. This is another reason why we need a new politics and a deep recasting of our understanding and vision of society and the global order.

But it is also important to realise that we cannot address the climate crisis without also addressing the inequality crisis. Humanity as well as the planet is out of synch, out of balance and (increasingly, unless we act) out of time. So a central, twofold challenge for any government of a globally connected nation is to start as soon as possible to take environmental as well as human well-being as fundamental to everything it does and to act in such a way as to refuse and resist the bigotry, xenophobia, anti-'foreigner' threats and toxic control tactics of the far right in all its guises. Some kind of progressive populism, unapologetic pluralism, patriotism-for-the-good (see Savitri Hensman in Chapter 18) is surely part of that mix. Labour in power is yet to demonstrate itself on such fronts.

Recovering Politics as More Than Politics

It has often been said that while everything is politics, politics is not everything. That is a very important insight. The use and abuse of power is intrinsic to every area of life we could possibly mention, and so decisions about it within the *polis* (the state or city characterised as a place of community) are unavoidable. But, at the same time, the form and style of politics does not have to be singular, the 'political perspective' is but one lens with which to look at the world, and there is much of life which in terms of its affect and proximity benefits humanly from the tentacles of organised political culture being kept at a distance. Family life, art, sport and culture might be mentioned – though they too have to be funded and managed and cannot escape moral and political claim in situations of manifest injustice. The point, however, is that a healthy politics knows its limits, accepts them and seeks to give priority to the human, the creative, the imaginative, the spiritual and other facets of being alive that are about cherishing the world rather than just instrumentalising it, arguing about it and competing for it.

If this is so, then the recovery of politics is about more than politics, the recovery of Britain is about more than Britain (as Fintan O'Toole infers in Chapter 21), and the recovery or recasting of our institutions is about more than the merely institutional, and so on. It is all about something that the Edinburgh International Festival, when it was founded in 1947–48 in the aftermath of the Second World War, talked about in terms of 'the recovery of the human spirit'. By this was meant something we search for and work at together (especially through the arts and culture) that transcends religion, party and ideology, and which can hold us together even in the face of catastrophe and trauma. Something inspirational that is capable of unleashing the resources needed to revision, reconceive, reorganise and rebuild.

Importantly, none of that detracts from the need to face the realities of power and the confrontations of class around the generation, management and sharing of wealth (as Marx and others recognised, in different ways). Rather, it suggests and recognises that, in spite of all constraints, we can still see beyond those distortions and be captured by the idea of a locality, a region, a nation, a federation, a global connectivity and above all a planet as a common home for all – something that can be seen equally in what William Blake termed 'the minute particulars' of life, and also in his visionary anticipation of 'a world transformed', and in some continual negotiation and renegotiation between the two.

This harks back to what Simon Barrow and Fiona Brocklesby talk about (Chapter 19): hope rooted in the everyday, but also much more than the everyday. The renewal of possibility happens inside-out (starting with our immediate lives and moving outwards) and outside-in (being impacted by the world around us such that we need to reconsider our own perspectives and priorities). How often in talking about 'a new politics' do we think about renewing the interiority (the inner life and well-being) of the politician, for example? What space and resourcing is there for that?

In conclusion, to end with the theme of political hope, and as we mentioned earlier, the need for root and branch change does not just apply to the current political order. In the years of his retirement, before the sad onset of dementia, the late and often controversial Bishop of Durham David E. Jenkins, who was foresighted enough to see the true environmental and human cost of mining even as he gave support to the miners in the 1984–85 strike, planned to write a book. He never completed it, but it was to have been called *The Dark Night of Our*

Institutions. His purpose was to diagnose the loss of public faith and trust in government, the law, the media, the police, the churches and other parts of what had previously been seen as the institutional fabric of state and nation in Britain, in conjunction with two other phenomena. First, 'the dark night of capital' (the crisis in economics and its evacuation of a human and environmental habitus) and secondly 'the dark night of the soul' (a period of confusion, helplessness, stagnation of the will and a sense of the withdrawal of hope that actually turns out to be a process of purification from false hope and destructive paths).

Knowing Jenkins, it would have been a thoughtful, searing, awkward and challenging read. But the point of mentioning it is not to speculate on what he might have said but instead to focus on the methodology. What he wanted to do was to bring together an understanding of the fault lines of institutional life with, on the one hand, a message about re-rooting economic activity in human and environmental benefit, and on the other, a consideration of the possibility that what is falling apart could be enabling us to see what we need to let go of as well as what we are being invited to recover in a personal but also communal sense.

If that seems an observation far removed from dissection of the immediate prospects and hopes of a Labour government at Westminster, that is precisely because it is. But if 'changing Britain' and a 'politics of hope' is to gain any traction, perhaps the deepest message of this book is that while the devil will always remain in the detail, and the detail will always matter, redemption (to the extent that it proves possible) will only be found by having our eyes opened, our wills restored and our minds transformed. And for that, despite our differences, we the people need one another. Shared, popular sovereignty still matters, but it has to be built rather than pulled off the shelf. That is where real political hope lies.

A Final Appeal: Against 'Miserabilism'

But to return finally to 'the challenge to Labour' again: in the introduction we talked of the corrosive effect of a certain kind of left-wing miserabilism, which has the potential to aid powerlessness, distrust and cynicism and thus do the opposite of helping the left and a progressive case for change. However, this does not mean that complete acquiescence in all the things that Labour does is the appropriate stance. Therein lies a similar road to encouraging a lack of power and agency, distrust and disenchantment with politics as a vehicle for changing lives for the better.

There is another pernicious pessimism that needs to be taken on and defeated. This is the official pessimism at the heart of the current Starmer project – which can be seen as an accentuated version of what was at the core of the Blair New Labour project – and which needs to be called out and challenged. 1997's 'things can only get better' was filled with boosterism and triumphalism, but there was doubt and anxiety at its core. In 2024, Starmer said in his first major post-election Downing Street address the exact opposite – that 'things will get worse before they get better' (Labour Party, 1997; Starmer, 2024). Both are false premises based on the narrowing of politics and political debate, the miniaturisation of politicians and their ambitions, and a sense of fear and foreboding about the challenges of the future.

There are many positive aspects of this Labour government, as there have been of every period of post-war Labour administration. However, the present incarnation and direction of the Starmer–Reeves political project in how it conducts itself in government, and how it negotiates decisions about public spending, taxation, the economy, and the relation between advanced capitalism and democracy seems to have little capacity or space to think big and long-term – or to make the case for fundamental change. As we note, this is a difficult exercise everywhere in the developed capitalist world on the left and centre-left. That does not mean that the questions should not be asked, or that we should give up in resignation and embrace the allure of miserabilism and with it our collective powerlessness. Britain and the world is changing and so too must the radical politics of egalitarianism, democracy and the desire for a just, sustainable planet. This book and its content is a contribution to that ongoing debate.

References

Introduction

Bacon, R. and Eltis, W. A. (1976), *Britain's Economic Problems: Too Few Producers*, London: Macmillan.

Benn, T. (1983), 'Spirit of Labour reborn', *The Guardian*, 20 June.

Bosanquet, N. (1983), *After the New Right*, London: Heinemann.

Chakrabortty, A. (2024), 'The cynical spectre of Osbornomics is haunting the Labour Party', *The Guardian*, 1 August, https://www.theguardian.com/commentisfree/article/2024/aug/01/george-osborne-osbornomics-labour-party-public-sector-cuts-rachel-reeves

Conner, J. (2024), 'How popular are the parties' 2024 manifesto policies', YouGov, 10 June, https://yougov.co.uk/politics/articles/49655-general-election-2024-which-new-policies-do-people-support

Cooper, M. (2024), *Counterrevolution: Extravagance and Austerity in Public Finances*, New York: Zone Books.

Cracknell, R., Baker, C. and Pollock, L. (2018), 'General Election 2024 Results, House of Commons Library', https://commonslibrary.parliament.uk/research-briefings/cbp-10009/

Crick, B. (1984), *Socialist Values and Time*, London: Fabian Society.

Crockett, R. (1994), *Thinking the Unthinkable: Think-Tanks and the Economic Counter-Revolution, 1931–1983*, London: HarperCollins.

Crosland, C. A. R. (1952), 'The transition from capitalism', in R. H. S. Crossman (ed.), *New Fabian Essays*, London: Turnstile Press.

Crouch, C. (2004), *Post-Democracy*, Cambridge: Polity Press.

Davies, S. (2024), Personal communication, 5 August.

Drucker, H. (1979), *Doctrine and Ethos in the Labour Party*, London: George Allen & Unwin.

Edgerton, D. (2018), *The Rise and Fall of the British Nation: A Twentieth Century History*, London: Allen Lane.

Edgerton, D. (2024), 'Labour is telling Britain it is now a conservative party – and we should believe it', *The Guardian*, 28 June, https://www.theguardian.com/commentisfree/article/2024/jun/28/keir-starmer-labour-britain-conservative-party

Geoghegan, P. (2024), 'Labour and the Lobbyists', London Review of Books, 15 August, https://www.lrb.co.uk/the-paper/v46/n16/peter-geoghegan/labour-and-the-lobbyists

Glasgow University Media Group (1976), *Bad News*, London: Routledge, Kegan and Paul.

Glasgow University Media Group (1980), *More Bad News*, London: Routledge, Kegan and Paul.

Gray, J. (2024), 'The Tory centre will not hold', *New Statesman*, 10 July, https://www.newstatesman.com/politics/conservatives/2024/07/tory-centre-will-not-hold-john-gray

Greenleaf, W. H. (1983), *The British Political Tradition, Volume Two: The Ideological Heritage*, London: Methuen.

Hancock, S. (2024), 'Long life: We little people are fed up with being mistreated by political elites', *Prospect*, July, https://www.prospectmagazine.co.uk/views/lives/67102/long-life-were-fed-up-with-being-mistreated

Harvey, D. (2005), *A Brief History of Neoliberalism*, Oxford: Oxford University Press.

Hennessy, P. (2000), *The Prime Minister: The Office and Its Holders Since 1945*, London: Allen Lane.

Hobsbawm, E. (1978), 'The Forward March of Labour Halted?', *Marxism Today*, September.

Hutton, W. (1995), *The State We're In: Why Britain Is in Crisis and How to Overcome It*, London: Jonathan Cape.

Hutton, W. (2024), Personal communication, 5 August.

Joseph, K. (1976), 'Stranded on the Middle Ground? Reflections on Circumstances and Policies', London: Centre for Policy Studies.

Kay, J. (2024), *The Corporation in the 21st Century: Why (Almost) Everything We Are Told About Business Is Wrong*, London: Profile Books.

Klein, N. (2007), *The Shock Doctrine: The Rise of Disaster Capitalism*, London: Metropolitan Books.

Labour Party (1976), 'Annual Conference Report', London: Labour Party.

Meadway, J. (2024), Personal communication, 7 August.

Mills, T. (2016), *The BBC: Myth of a Public Service*, London: Verso.

Monbiot, G. and Hutchison, P. (2024), *The Invisible Doctrine: The Secret History of Neoliberalism (& How It Came to Control Your Life)*, London: Allen Lane.

Moore, C. and Colvile, R. (2024), 'Margaret Thatcher and the Centre for Policy Studies', in Williams, K. and Colvile, R. (eds), *Conservative Revolution: The Centre for Policy Studies at 50*, London: Centre for Policy Studies.

Rallings, C. and Thrasher, M. (2012), *British Electoral Facts 1832–2012*, London: Biteback.

Saunders, R. (2024), comment on X, 12 August.

Simpson, I. (2023), 'Electoral Commission estimate 8 million missing from electoral roll', Electoral Commission, 21 September, https://www.electoral-reform.org.uk/electoral-commission-estimate-8-million-missing-from-electoral-roll/

Smith, M. (2024), 'Support for nationalising utilities and public transport has grown significantly in last seven years', YouGov, 18 July, https://yougov.co.uk/politics/articles/50098-support-for-nationalising-utilities-and-public-transport-has-grown-significantly-in-last-seven-years

Thompson, M. (2005), 'Review of A Brief History of Neoliberalism', *Dissent*, https://www.dissentmagazine.org/wp-content/files_mf/1390342754d3Thompson1.pdf

Toynbee, P. and Walker, D. (2024), *The Only Way Is Up: How to Take Britain from Austerity to Prosperity*, London: Atlantic Books.

Williams, K. (2024), Personal communication, 7 August.

Williams, K. and Colvile, R. (eds) (2024), *Conservative Revolution: The Centre for Policy Studies at 50*, London: Centre for Policy Studies.

1

Chrisp, J. and Pearce, N. (2021), *The Age Divide in UK Politics*, Bath and London: University of Bath and Institute for Public Policy Research, https://www.bath.ac.uk/publications/the-age-divide-in-uk-politics/attachments/the-age-divide-in-uk-politics.pdf

Curtice, J. (2017), 'Why Leave Won the UK's EU Referendum', *Journal of Common Market Studies*, 55 (Annual Review), pp. 19–37.

Mattinson, D. (2020), *Beyond the Red Wall: Why Labour Lost, How the Conservatives Won and What Will Happen Next?*, London: Biteback.

More in Common and UCL Policy Lab (2024), *Change Pending: The Path to the 2024 General Election and Beyond*, London: More in Common and UCL Policy Lab, https://www.moreincommon.org.uk/media/e3in12zd/change-pending.pdf

Rallings, C. and Thrasher, M. (2024), 'The Electoral Impact of the New Parliamentary Constituency Boundaries', https://downloads.bbc.co.uk/news/nol/shared/bsp/hi/pdfs/bounds_explainer.pdf

Starmer, K. (2020), Labour Party Conference Speech, https://www.spectator.co.uk/article/full-text-keir-starmer-s-conference-speech/

2

Cruddas, J. (2024), *A Century of Labour*, London: Polity Press.

Hutton, W. (2024), *This Time No Mistakes: How to Remake Britain*, London: Head of Zeus.

3

Anderson, P. (1964), 'Critique of Wilsonism', *New Left Review*, 1:27, pp. 3–27.

Artis, J. et al., (1992), 'Social Democracy in Hard Times: The Economic Record of the Labour Government 1974–79', *Twentieth Century British History*, 3:1, pp. 32–58.

Bew, J. (2016), *Citizen Clem: A Biography of Attlee*, London: Riverrun.

Bogdanor, V. (2007), 'Social Democracy' in Seldon, A. (ed.), *Blair's Britain: 1997–2007*, Cambridge: Cambridge University Press.

Cairncross, A. (1985), *Years of Recovery: British Economic Policy 1945–51*, London: Methuen.

Clarke, M. (2007), 'Foreign Policy' in Seldon, A. (ed.), *Blair's Britain: 1997–2007*, Cambridge: Cambridge University Press.

Davies, H. (2022), *The Chancellors: Steering the British Economy in Crisis Times*, Cambridge: Polity Press.

Davis, J. and Rentoul, J. (2019), *Heroes or Villains? The Blair Government Reconsidered*, Oxford: Oxford University Press.

Donoghue, B. (2018), *Harold Wilson: A Flawed Political Genius?*, Lord Speaker's Lectures.

Egerton, T. (2024), 'External Shocks' in Seldon, A. and Egerton, T. (eds), *The Conservative Effect: 14 Wasted Years?*, Cambridge: Cambridge University Press.

Hay, C. (1996), 'Narrating Crisis: The Discursive Construction of the Winter of Discontent', *Sociology*, 30:2, pp. 253–77.

Hennessy, P. (1987), 'The Attlee Government', in Seldon, A and Hennessy, P. (eds), *Ruling Performance: British Governments from Attlee to Thatcher*, Oxford: Blackwell.

Hennessy, P. (2001), *The Prime Minister: The Office and its Holders Since 1945*, London: Penguin.

Holmes, M, (1985), *The Labour Government, 1974–79: Political Aims and Economic Reality*, London: Macmillan.

Hutton, W. (2024), *This Time No Mistakes: How to Remake Britain*, London: Apollo.

Institute for Fiscal Studies (2024), Living standards, poverty and inequality in the UK, https://ifs.org.uk/living-standards-poverty-and-inequality-uk#incomes-over-time

Jay, D. (1985), *Sterling: A Plea for Moderation*, London: Sidgwick & Jackson.

Morgan, K. (1997), *Callaghan: A Life*, Oxford: Oxford University Press.

O'Hara, G. (2006), 'Dynamic, Exciting, Thrilling Change: The Wilson Government's Economic Policies, 1964–70', in O'Hara, G. and Parr, H. (eds.), *The Wilson Governments 1964–1970 Reconsidered*, Oxford: Taylor & Francis.

O'Hara, G. (2018), 'New Labour's Domestic Policies: Neoliberal, Social Democratic or a Unique Blend?', Tony Blair Institute for Global Change.

Office for National Statistics (2015), International Migration: A Recent History, https://www.ons.gov.uk/peoplepopulationandcommunity/populationandmigration/internationalmigration/articles/internationalmigrationarecenthistory/2015-01-15

Pimlott, B. (1992), *Harold Wilson*, London: HarperCollins.

Ponting, C. (1990), *Breach of Promise: Labour in Power: 1964–1970*, London: Penguin.

Rawnsley, A. (2010), *The End of the Party: The Rise and Fall of New Labour*, London: Penguin Viking.

Sandbrook, D. (2013), *Seasons in the Sun: Britain 1974–79*, London: Penguin.

Seldon A., Meakin, J. and Thoms, I. (2024), *The Impossible Office?: The History of the British Prime Minister*, 2 edn, Cambridge: Cambridge University Press.

Seldon, A. and Lodge, G. (2011), *Brown At 10*, London: Biteback.

Thorpe, A. (2015), *A History of the British Labour Party*, London: Red Globe Press.

Tomlinson, J. (2004), *The Labour Governments 1964–70: Volume 3 Economic Policy*, Manchester: Manchester University Press.

Tooze, A. (2019), *Crashed: How a Decade of Financial Crises Changed the World*, London: Penguin.

Toynbee, P. (2020), 'How James Callaghan Sowed the Seeds of His own Downfall', in Hickson, K. and Miles, J. (eds), *James Callaghan: An Underrated Prime Minister?*, London: Biteback.

5

Climate Assembly UK (2020), 'The Path to Net Zero', London: House of Commons.

Conner, J. (2024), 'How popular are the parties' 2024 manifesto policies?', YouGov blog, 10 June.

Deacon, D., Kay, J., Lawson, B., Ritchie, N., Smith, D. and Wring, D. (2024), *Report 5: 30 May – 3 July 2024*, University of Loughborough: Centre for Research in Communication and Culture.

House of Lords (2023), 'The Ties that Bind: Citizenship and Civic Engagement in the 21st Century', Select Committee on Citizenship and Civic Engagement, Report of Session 2017–19, HL Paper 118, London: House of Lords.

Shoben, C. (2022), 'New poll: Public strongly backing public ownership of energy and key utilities', Survation blog, 15 August.

Smith, M. (2024), 'One in five voters say they are voting tactically at the 2024 general election', YouGov blog, 1 July.

6

Adu, A., Elgot, J. and Courea, E. (2024), 'Labour candidates penalised for not campaigning enough in battleground seats', *The Guardian*, 21 June 2024, www.theguardian.com/politics/article/2024/jun/21/labour-candidates-penalised-for-not-campaigning-enough-in-battleground-seats

Ashcroft, Lord (2024), 'How Britain voted and why: My 2024 post-vote poll', Lord Ashcroft Polls, 5 July, www.lordashcroftpolls.com/2024/07/how-britain-voted-and-why-my-post-vote-poll/

Badenoch, K. (2024), 'People won't vote for us if we don't know what we want to be', *The Times*, 28 July 2024, www.thetimes.com/uk/politics/article/kemi-badenoch-people-wont-vote-for-us-if-we-dont-know-what-we-want-to-be-btfpbf95m

Ford, R. (2024), X, 5 July.

Guido Fawkes (2024), 'Guide to the Tory "Five Families"', Guido Fawkes, 14 December 2023, www.order-order.com/2023/12/14/guide-to-the-tory-five-families/

Hay, C. (2024), 'The "New Orleans effect": The future of the welfare state as collective insurance against uninsurable risk', *Renewal*, 31:3, www.journals.lwbooks.co.uk/renewal/vol-31-issue-3/article-9780/

Hazell, W. (2024), 'Tory candidate ridiculed for pretending to stand for other parties', *Daily Telegraph*, 1 June 2024, www.telegraph.co.uk/politics/2024/06/01/conservative-mp-appears-to-stand-for-other-parties/

House of Commons Library (2024), 'General Election 2024 Results', *Commons Library*, 26 July 2024, www.commonslibrary.parliament.uk/research-briefings/cbp-10009/

Inman, P. and Elliott, L. (2024), 'Head of OBR says lack of budget details led to "work of fiction" forecasts last year', *The Guardian*, 23 January 2024, www.theguardian.com/politics/2024/jan/23/head-of-obr-says-lack-of-budget-details-led-to-work-of-fiction-forecasts-last-year

IPSOS (2024), 'How Britain voted in the 2024 election', IPSOS, 26 July 2024, www.ipsos.com/en-uk/how-britain-voted-in-the-2024-election

Jacobs, B. (2024), 'Bewildered Conservatives Greet a Fallen British Prime Minister', *Politico*, 22 February 2024, www.politico.com/news/magazine/2024/02/22/truss-at-cpac-00142807

Mortimer, J. (2024), 'Conservative Campaign Takes Surreal Turn as Party Appears to Ditch Its Own Colour, Logo and Name in "Fake Newspapers"', *Byline Times*, 23 April 2024, www.bylinetimes.com/2024/04/23/conservative-campaign-takes-surreal-turn-as-party-appears-to-ditch-its-own-colour-logo-and-name-in-fake-newspapers/

Redfield and Wilton (2024), 'Who Watches GB News?', Redfield & Wilton Strategies, 30 April 2024, www.redfieldandwiltonstrategies.com/who-watches-gb-news

Saunders, R. (2012), '"Crisis? What Crisis?" Thatcherism and the seventies', in B. Jackson and R. Saunders (eds), *Making Thatcher's Britain*, Cambridge: Cambridge University Press.

Saunders, R. (2019), 'The closing of the conservative mind', *New Statesman*, 12 June 2019, www.newstatesman.com/politics/2019/06/the-closing-of-the-conservative-mind

Sloman, P. (2020), 'Squeezed Out? The Liberal Democrats and the 2019 General Election', *Political Quarterly*, 91:1, pp. 36–7, www.onlinelibrary.wiley.com/doi/abs/10.1111/1467-923X.12816

8

Baldwin, H. (2024), 'Bank of England's quantitative tightening is a leap in the dark', *Financial Times*, 7 February, https://www.ft.com/content/d65ccaa7-e12b-4d9a-a132-1180d39f891

Bank of England Act 1998, Section 11, https://www.legislation.gov.uk/ukpga/1998/11/section/11

Borio, C. (2019), *On Money, Debt, Trust and Central Banking*, Bank for International Settlements, BIS Working Papers, No. 763, https://www.bis.org/publ/work763.htm

Dyer, N. (2025), *Ricardo's Dream: How Economists Forgot the Real World and Led Us Astray*, Bristol: Bristol University Press, forthcoming.

Eich, S. (2022), *The Currency of Politics: The Political Theory of Money from Aristotle to Keynes*, Princeton: Princeton University Press.

Elliott, L. (2024), 'Developing countries face worst debt crisis in history, study shows', *The Guardian*, 21 July, https://www.theguardian.com/world/article/2024/jul/21/developing-countries-face-worst-debt-crisis-in-history-study-shows

Financial Stability Board (2023), 'Global monitoring report on non-bank financial intermediation 2023', https://www.fsb.org/2023/12/global-monitoring-report-on-non-bank-financial-intermediation-2023/

Gabor, D. (2024), 'The Bank of England is misusing its fiscal powers: Unwinding QE must not be allowed to tie the hands of the Government', *Financial Times*, 29 February, https://www.ft.com/content/5209be99-3f6b-4ba3-b3f3-49b544f71c28

Gaspar, V., Medas, P. and Perrelli, R. (2021), 'Global Debt Reaches a Record $226 Trillion', IMF Blog, 15 December, https://www.imf.org/en/Blogs/Articles/2021/12/15/blog-global-debt-reaches-a-record-226-trillion

Haldane, A. (2014), 'The Age of Asset Management?', Bank of England, 4 April, https://www.bankofengland.co.uk/speech/2014/the-age-of-asset-management

IMF Staff, (2024), 'Global Financial Stability Report', Washington: International Monetary Fund, https://www.elibrary.imf.org/display/book/9798400257704/CH002.xml

Klein, M. and Pettis, M. (2020), *Trade Wars Are Class Wars*, New Haven: Yale University Press.

Law, J. (1705), *Money and Trade Considered*, Glasgow: R. & A. Foulis.

Lund, S., Mehta, A., Manyika, J. and Goldshtein, D. (2024), 'A decade after the global financial crisis: What has (and hasn't) changed?', McKinsey Global Monitor, 29 August, https://www.mckinsey.com/industries/financial-services/our-insights/a-decade-after-the-global-financial-crisis-what-has-and-hasnt-changed

Martin, M. (2023), 'The Worst Ever Global Debt Crisis', Development Finance International, 28 November, https://development-finance.org/en/news/831-11-october-the-worst-debt-crisis-ever-shocking-new-debt-service-numbers

Schumpeter, J. A. (1954), *History of Economic Analysis*, London: Allen and Unwin.

Smialek, J. (2021), 'The Financial Crisis the World Forgot', *New York Times*, 16 March, https://www.nytimes.com/2021/03/16/business/economy/fed-2020-financial-crisis-covid.html

Tiftik, E., Mahmood, K., Aycock, R. and Gibbs, S. (2024), 'Navigating the New Normal', Global Debt Monitor, 7 May, Institute of International Finance, https://www.iif.com/portals/0/Files/content/Global%20Debt%20Monitor_May2024_vf.pdf

Tily, G. (2023), 'From the Doom Loop to An Economy for Work not Wealth', Trades Union Congress, https://www.tuc.org.uk/research-analysis/reports/doom-loop-economy-work-not-wealth

9

Deleidi, M., de Lipsis, V., Mazzucato, M., Ryan-Collins, J. and Agnolucci, P. (2019), 'The macroeconomic impact of government innovation policies: A quantitative assessment', UCL Institute for Innovation and Public Purpose, Policy Report (IIPP 2019-06), https://www.ucl.ac.uk/bartlett/public-purpose/wp2019-06

Kattel, R. and Mazzucato, M. (2018), 'Mission-oriented innovation policy and dynamic capabilities in the public sector', *Industrial and Corporate Change*, 27:5, 787–801, https://doi.org/10.1093/icc/dty032

Mazzucato, M. (2013), *The Entrepreneurial State: Debunking Public vs. Private Sector Myths*, London: Anthem Press.

Mazzucato, M. (2018), 'Mission oriented innovation policies: challenges and opportunities', *Industrial and Corporate Change*, 27:5, 803–15, https://doi.org/10.1093/icc/dty034

Mazzucato, M. (2021), *Mission Economy: A Moonshot Guide to Changing Capitalism*, London: Allen Lane.

Mazzucato, M. (2023a), 'Governing the economics of the common good: from correcting market failures to shaping collective goals', *Journal of Economic Policy Reform*. https://doi.org/10.1080/17487870.2023.2280969

Mazzucato, M. (2023b), 'Transformational Change in Latin America and the Caribbean: A mission-oriented approach', *Economic Commission for Latin America and the Caribbean (ECLAC)*. (LC/TS.2022/150/Rev.1), Santiago, https://repositorio.cepal.org/bitstream/handle/11362/48299/4/S2201308_en.pdf

Mazzucato, M. and Collington, R. (2023), *The Big Con: How the Consulting Industry Weakens our Businesses, Infantilizes Our Governments and Warps Our Economies*, London: Allen Lane.

Mazzucato, M. and Rodrik, D. (2023), 'Industrial Policy with Conditionalities: A Taxonomy and Sample Cases', UCL Institute for Innovation and Public Purpose, Working Paper Series (IIPP WP 2023-07), https://www.ucl.ac.uk/bartlett/public-purpose/wp2023-07

WHO Council on the Economics of Health for All (2023), 'Health for All: Transforming Economies to deliver what matters', WHO, https://cdn.who.int/media/docs/default-source/council-on-the-economics-of-health-for-all/council-eh4a_finalreport_web.pdf

A fuller set of detailed references and diagrams for this chapter are accessible here: https://committees.parliament.uk/writtenevidence/130058/pdf/

10

Bersin, J. (2023), *The Role of Generative AI in HR Is Now Becoming Clear*, 8 September, www.joshbersin.com/2023/09/the-role-of-generative-ai-in-hr-is-now-becoming-clear/

CIPD (2023), *An Estimated 4 Million UK Employees Have Changed Careers Due to a Lack of Flexibility at Work*, 25 May, www.cipd.org/uk/about/press-releases/4-million-career-changes-flexibility-issues/

Dennison, K. (2024), 'Gallup Says $8.8 Trillion is the True Cost of Low Employee Engagement', *Forbes*, 24 July, *https://www.forbes.com/sites/karadennison/2024/07/16/gallup-says-88-trillion-is-the-true-cost-of-low-employee-engagement/*

European Commission, (2024), 'President von der Leyen Calls For Global Collaboration In Facing The Challenges Of Our Time at The World Economic Forum', 19 January, www.ec.europa.eu/commission/presscorner/detail/en/ac_24_325

Flex Index (2024), 'The Flex Report UK Edition', www.canva.com/design/DAF470j1dkM/SEddRg4MrIiZMJJJfJ3gtw/view?utm_content=DAF470j1dkM&utm_campaign=designshare&utm_medium=link&utm_source=viewer#1

Four Day Week Campaign (2024), www.4dayweek.co.uk

Gerson, D. and Gratton, L. (2024), 'Highly Skilled Professionals You're your Work but Not Your Job', *Harvard Business Review*, May–June, www.hbr.org/2024/05/highly-skilled-professionals-want-your-work-but-not-your-job

Granovetter, M. S. (1973), 'The Strength of Weak Ties', *American Journal of Sociology*, 78:6, www.journals.uchicago.edu/doi/10.1086/225469

Hansard (2000), 'Work-Life Balance', House of Commons Library, 9 March, https://hansard.

parliament.uk/Commons/2000-03-09/debates/0fa55b17-54f3-40f6-8a1a-3d3b0965482a/Work-LifeBalance

Hertz, N. (2020), *The Lonely Century: Coming Together in a World That's Pulling Apart*, London: Sceptre.

Hobsbawm, J. (2017), *Fully Connected: Surviving and Thriving in an Age of Overload*, London: Bloomsbury.

Hobsbawm, J. (2021), *The Nowhere Office: Reinventing Work and the Workplace of the Future*, London: Basic Books.

Hobsbawm, J. (2022a), 'Say Hello to the Flexetariat: Empowered employees who want a change', *Bloomberg*, 21 September, www.bloomberg.com/news/features/2022-09-27/say-hello-to-the-flexetariat-empowered-employees-who-want-a-change

Hobsbawm, J. (2022b), 'The Presenteeism Premium, Julia Hobsbawm's The Working Assumption', Substack, 7 May.

Ibarra, H. and Hunter, M. L. (2007), 'How Leaders Create and Use Networks', *Harvard Business Review*, January, www.hbr.org/2007/01/how-leaders-create-and-use-networks

International Trade Administration (2023), United Kingdom Artificial Intelligence Market 2023', 29 March, www.trade.gov/market-intelligence/united-kingdom-artificial-intelligence-market-2023

Kleinman, Z. and Seddon S. (2023), 'Elon Musk Tells Rishi Sunak AI will put an end to work', BBC News, 3 November, www.bbc.co.uk/news/uk-67302048

Labour Party (2024), 'Labour's Plan to Make Work Pay Delivering a New Deal for Working People' www.labour.org.uk/updates/stories/a-new-deal-for-working-people/

MacNaught, S. (2024), 'E-Commerce Statistics 2024 – the Numbers', *Micro Biz Mag*, 20 February, https://www.microbizmag.co.uk/ecommerce-statistics/

Marks, G. (2024), 'The world is not quite ready for 'digital co-workers', *The Guardian*, 21 July, www.theguardian.com/technology/article/2024/jul/21/ai-digital-workers-employment

No Worker Left Behind, (2024), https://noworkerleftbehind.org/

Office for National Statistics (2012), 'E-commerce and ICT activity, UK: 2011', www.ons.gov.uk/businessindustryandtrade/itandinternetindustry/bulletins/ecommerceandictactivity/2012-11-30

Office for National Statistics (2024), Labour Market Overview, UK: February 2024, https://www.ons.gov.uk/employmentandlabourmarket/peopleinwork/employmentandemployeetypes/bulletins/uklabourmarket/february2024#:~:text=The%20UK%20economic%20inactivity%20rate,remains%20at%20historically%20high%20levels

Owl Labs (2023), 'The State of Hybrid Work 2023', www.owllabs.com/state-of-hybrid-work/2023

Ramaswamy, S. V. (2023), 'Fatherhood Premium, Motherhood Penalty? What Nobel Prize Economics Winner's Research Shows', *USA Today*, 13 October, https://eu.usatoday.com/story/money/2023/10/13/claudia-goldin-gender-wage-gap-parents/71128533007/

Semuels, A. (2023), 'You're Not Imagining It: Job Hunting Is Getting Worse', *Time*, 14 June, www.time.com/6287012/why-finding-job-is-difficult/

Taylor, M. (2017), 'Good Work: The Taylor Review of Modern Working Practices', HM Government, Department for Business and Trade, Department for Business, Energy and Industrial Strategy www.gov.uk/government/publications/good-work-the-taylor-review-of-modern-working-practices

Terkel, S. (1974), *Working: People Talk About What They Do All Day And What They Feel About It*, New York: New Press.

Towers, M. (2024), 'The AI Bill Project', Trades Union Congress, 18 April, www.tuc.org.uk/research-analysis/reports/ai-bill-project

TUC (2024), 'TUC Welcomes 90,000 Rise in Trade Union Membership', 29 May, www.tuc.org.uk/news/tuc-welcomes-90000-rise-trade-union-membership

UK Parliament (2023), Employment Relations (Flexible Working) Act 2023, 26 July, www.bills.parliament.uk/bills/3198

UK Research and Innovation (2024), 'AI Projects backed by £32 million to Turbocharge Productivity', 7 August, www.ukri.org/news/ai-projects-backed-by-32-million-to-turbocharge-productivity

11

BMG Research (2017), 'Two-thirds of people don't read political manifestos', 16 May, https://www.bmgresearch.co.uk/bmg-research-poll-10-people-dont-know-manifesto/

Curtice, J., Montagu, I. and Sivathasan, C. (2024), 'Damaged Politics? The impact of the 2019–24 parliament on political trust and confidence', London: British Social Attitudes National Centre for Social Research, https://natcen.ac.uk/sites/default/files/2024-06/BSA%2041%20Damaged%20Politics.pdf

Curtice, J. (2024), *The Guardian*, 12 June.

Hennessy, P. (1989), *Whitehall*, London: Pimlico.

Kennan, G. (1947), 'The Sources of Soviet Conduct', *Foreign Affairs*, July.

Marmot, M., Allen, J., Boyce, T., Goldblatt, P. and Morrison, J. (2020), 'Health Equity in England: The Marmot Review 10 Years On', London: Health Foundation.

More in Common (2024), 'Change Pending – the path to the 2024 General Election and beyond', 15 July, https://www.moreincommon.org.uk/our-work/research/change-pending/

Office for National Statistics (2023), 'Trust in government, UK: 2023', London: ONS.

Rauch, J. (1994), *Demosclerosis: The Silent Killer of American Democracy*, London: Time Books.

Sosenko, F., Bramley, G. and Bhattacharjee, A. (2022), 'Understanding the post-2010 increase in food bank use in England: new quasi-experimental analysis of the role of welfare policy', *BMC Public Health*, https://bmcpublichealth.biomedcentral.com/articles/10.1186/s12889-022-13738-0

Walsh, P. W. and Sumption, M. (2024), 'Migration Observatory: The Uncertain Financial Implications of the UK's Rwanda Policy', https://migrationobservatory.ox.ac.uk/resources/commentaries/the-uncertain-financial-implications-of-the-uks-rwanda-policy/

12

Berg, M. and Hudson, P. (2023), *Slavery, Capitalism and the Industrial Revolution*, Polity: London.

Biggar, N. (2023), 'On *Colonialism: A Moral Reckoning*: A Reply to Alan Lester', *The Journal of Imperial and Commonwealth History*, 51:4, pp. 796–824, https://doi.org/10.1080/03086534.2023.2209948

Callwell, C. E. (1906), *Small Wars: Their Principles and Practice*, London: HMSO.

Common Sense (2021), *Conservative Thinking for a Post-liberal Age*, www.marcolonghi.org.uk/sites/www.marcolonghi.org.uk/files/2021-05/Common-Sense.pdf

Draper, N. (2009), *The Price of Emancipation: Slave-Ownership, Compensation and British Society at the End of Slavery*, Cambridge: Cambridge University Press.

Fowler, C. (2021), 'Public debate is important. Waves of press and political attacks damage it', *Hacked Off*, 11 March, www.hackinginquiry.org/public-debate-is-important-waves-of-press-and-political-attacks-damage-it/

Gilmore, R. W. (2022), *Abolition Geography: Essays Towards Liberation*, London: Verso.

Gilroy, P. (1995), *The Black Atlantic: Modernity and Double Consciousness*, Cambridge, MA: Harvard University Press.

Hall, C. (2002), *Civilising Subjects: Metropole and Colony in the English Imagination 1830–1867*, Polity: London.

Hall, S. (2021), 'Cultural Identity and Diaspora', in Gilroy, P., Schwarz, B. and Wilson Gilmore, R. (eds), *Stuart Hall: Selected Writings on Race and Difference*, Duke University Press, pp. 258–71.

Lammy, D. (2016), 'David Lammy's Key Note Speech at the Lammy Review Trust in the Criminal Justice System Event', www.gov.uk/government/speeches/david-lammys-key-note-speech-at-the-lammy-review-trust-in-the-cjs-event

Lammy, D. (2020), 'Britain needs leadership on race inequality. Not just another review', *The Guardian*, 16 June, www.theguardian.com/commentisfree/2020/jun/16/race-inequality-review-boris-johnson-black-lives-matter-david-lammy

Lester, A. (2022), *Deny & Disavow: Distancing the British Empire in the Culture War*, London: SunRise.

Lester, A. (2023), 'Redvers Buller's Empire', https://castinstone.exeter.ac.uk/en/2023/08/22/redver-bullers-empire/

Lester, A. (2024a), 'Introduction: The Truth About Colonial History', in Lester, A. (ed.), *The Truth About Empire: Real Histories of British Colonialism*, London and New York, Hurst and Oxford University Press, pp. 11–48.

Lester, A. (2024b), 'The Daily Telegraph's Disinformation Campaign About the British Empire Laid Bare', *Byline Times*, https://bylinetimes.com/2024/07/17/the-daily-telegraphs-disinformation-campaign-about-the-british-empire-laid-bare/

Lester, A. (2024c), Cooking the Books: Understanding the Character of the British Empire: Review of Kristian Niemietz, *Imperial Measurement: A Cost-Benefit Analysis of Western Colonialism*, London: Institute of Economic Affairs, www.bellacaledonia.org.uk/2024/06/05/cooking-the-books-understanding-the-character-of-the-british-empire/

Lester, A., Boehme, K. and Mitchell, P. (2021) *Ruling the World: Freedom, Civilisation and Liberalism in the Nineteenth Century British Empire*, Cambridge: Cambridge University Press.

Ministry of Justice (2021), 'Ethnicity and the Criminal Justice System, 2020', https://www.gov.uk/government/statistics/ethnicity-and-the-criminal-justice-system-statistics-2020/ethnicity-and-the-criminal-justice-system-2020#:~:text=The%20greatest%20disparity%20appears%20at,various%20points%20of%20the%20CJS

Office for National Statistics (2021), 'Ethnic group differences in health, employment, education and housing shown in England and Wales' Census 2021', https://www.ons.gov.uk/peoplepopulationandcommunity/culturalidentity/ethnicity/articles/ethnicgroupdifferencesinhealthemploymenteducationandhousingshowninenglandandwalescensus2021/2023-03-15

Office for National Statistics (2022), 'Ethnicity pay gaps, UK: 2012 to 2022', https://www.ons.gov.uk/employmentandlabourmarket/peopleinwork/earningsandworkinghours/articles/ethnicitypaygapsingreatbritain/2012to2022#analysis-of-ethnicity-pay-gaps

Olusoga, D. (2021), *Black and British: A Forgotten History*, London, Picador.

Patel, I. S. (2021), *We're Here Because You Were There: Immigration and the End of Empire*, Verso: London.

Portes, J. (2021), 'Race Report: Sewell Commission Couldn't Find Something It Wasn't Looking For', *Byline Times*, 9 April, https://bylinetimes.com/2021/04/09/race-report-sewell-commission-couldnt-find-something-it-wasnt-looking-for/

Robins, N. (2012), *The Corporation that Changed the World*, London: Pluto Press.

Roy, T. (2020), *The Economic History of India, 1857–2010*, Oxford: Oxford University Press.

Swerling, G. (2024), 'National Trust Criticised Over "Secretly Woke" Vegan Scones', *Daily Telegraph*, 1 April, https://www.telegraph.co.uk/news/2024/04/01/national-trust-vegan-scones-dry-biscuits-bill-cash/

Walker, P. (2024), 'Era of Culture Wars is Over, Pledges New Culture Secretary Lisa Nandy', *The Guardian*, 10 July, https://www.theguardian.com/politics/article/2024/jul/09/era-of-culture-wars-is-over-pledges-new-culture-secretary-lisa-nandy

13

Beveridge, W. (1942), 'Social Insurance and Allied Services', Cmnd. 6404, London: HMSO.

Buurtzorg (2024), www.buurtzorg.com/about-us/

Cottam, H. (2018), *Radical Help: How We Can Remake the Relationships Between us and Revolutionise the Welfare State*, London: Virago.

Cottam, H. (2020), 'Welfare 5.0: why we need a social revolution and how to make it happen', UCL Institute for Innovation and Public Purpose.

Cottam, H. (2025), *The Work We Need: A Twenty-First Century Imagining*, London: Virago, forthcoming.

Curtis, P. (2022), *Behind Closed Doors: Why We Break Up Families and How to Mend Them*, London: Virago.

Joseph Rowntree Foundation (2024), 'UK Poverty 2024: The essential guide to understanding poverty in the UK', www.jrf.org.uk/uk-poverty-2024-the-essential-guide-to-understanding-poverty-in-the-uk

Kenway, E. (2023), *Who Cares: The Hidden Crisis of Caregiving, and How We Solve It*, London: Wildfire Books.

Kings Fund (2019), 'Lessons from the Wigan Deal', www.kingsfund.org.uk/insight-and-analysis/reports/wigan-deal

Kings Fund (2024), 'The adult social care workforce in a nutshell', www.kingsfund.org.uk/insight-and-analysis/data-and-charts/social-care-workforce-nutshell

Machin, S. (2024), 'Wage Controversies: Real Wage Stagnation, Inequality and Labour Market Institutions', *LSE Public Policy Review*, 3:2

Savage, M. (2021), *The Return of Inequality*, Cambridge, MA: Harvard University Press.

Taylor, L. (2007), 'Culture's Revenge: Laurie Taylor interviews Stuart Hall', *New Humanist*, 31 May, https://newhumanist.org.uk/articles/960/cultures-revenge-laurie-taylor-interviews-stuart-hall

14

Brook, O., O'Brien, D. and Taylor, M. (2024), *Culture is bad for you*, 2nd edition, Manchester: Manchester University Press.

Gilmore, A., O'Brien, D. and Walmsley, B. (eds) (2024), *Pandemic Culture: The impacts of COVID-19 on the UK cultural sector and implications for the future*, Manchester: Manchester University Press.

Labour Party (2024a), 'Change: Labour Party manifesto 2024', https://labour.org.uk/wp-content/uploads/2024/06/Labour-Party-manifesto-2024.pdf

Labour Party (2024b), 'Creating Growth: Labour's Plan for the Arts, Culture and Creative Industries', https://labour.org.uk/wp-content/uploads/2024/03/Labours-Arts-Culture-Creative-Industries-Sector-Plan.pdf

Labour Party (2024c), 'Mission-driven Government', https://labour.org.uk/change/mission-driven-government/

Walker, P. (2024), 'Era of Culture Wars is Over, Pledges New Culture Secretary Lisa Nandy', *The Guardian* 9 July, https://www.theguardian.com/politics/article/2024/jul/09/era-of-culture-wars-is-over-pledges-new-culture-secretary-lisa-nandy?

15

Climate Assembly UK (2020), 'The Path to Net Zero: Final Report of the Climate Assembly', London: UK Parliament.

Conway, Z. (2024), 'Homes insulated in government scheme go mouldy', BBC News, 29 May, https://www.bbc.co.uk/news/articles/cxwwr7vyrj00

Davies, J and Giovannini, A. (2024), *Power to the People? The Route to English Devolution*, London: Unlock Democracy and Compass.

Demos Helsinki (2021), *A Call for Humble Governments*, Helsinki: Demos

Denham, J. (2020), *English Democracy: Electoral Reform, England and the Future of the United Kingdom*, London: Unlock Democracy and Compass.

Denham, J. and Rycroft, P. (2023), 'Reforming England's national governance', Bennett Institute for Public Policy Cambridge, https://www.bennettinstitute.cam.ac.uk/blog/reforming-englands-national-governance/

Dunt, I. (2024), *How Westminster works... and Why it Doesn't*, London: Weidenfeld & Nicholson.

Labour Party, (2023), '5 Missions for a Better Britain: A "mission-driven" government to end "sticking plaster" politics', London: Labour Party.

Labour Party (2024), 'Power and Partnership: Labour's Plan to Power Up Britain', London: Labour Party.

Martin, S. and Bovaird, T. (2005), 'Meta-evaluation of the Local Government Modernising Agenda: Progress Report on Service Improvement in Local Government', London: Office of Deputy Prime Minister.

Mazzucato, M. (2023), *The Entrepreneurial State: Debunking Public vs Private Sector Myths*, London: Penguin Books.

Mazzucato, M. and Collington, R. (2024), *The Big Con: How the Consulting Industry Weakens Our Businesses, Infantilizes Our Government and Warps Our Economies*, London: Penguin Books.

Report of the Commission on the UK's Future (2022), 'A New Britain: Renewing Our Democracy and Rebuilding Our Economy', London: Labour Party.

Stewart, R. (2024), 'I'd like to say Johnson and Brexit made me quit politics. But they were symptoms of the problem, not the cause', *The Guardian*, 3 June, https://www.theguardian.com/commentisfree/article/2024/jun/03/rory-stewart-why-i-quit-mp-government

Wellbeing Economy Governments (WEGO) (2024), https://wellbeingeconomy.org/wego

16

Addison, P. (1975), *The Road to 1945*, London: Jonathan Cape.

Addison, P. (2010), *No Turning Back: The Peacetime Revolutions of Post-War Britain*, Oxford: Oxford University Press.

Brown, G. (2014), *My Scotland, Our Britain: A Future Worth Sharing*, London: Simon & Schuster.

Bryan, P. (2024), Personal communication, 8 August.

Colley, L. (1992), *Britons: Forging an Identity: 1707–1837*, New Haven: Yale University Press.

Conservative and Unionist Party, (1955), *The Campaign Guide 1955*, London: Conservative and Unionist Central Office.

Crick, B. (2008), 'In conversation', Changin' Scotland weekend, The Ceilidh Place, Ullapool, 2 November.

Denham, J. (2024), Personal communication, 12 August.

Edgerton, D. (2005), *Warfare State: Britain 1920–1970*, Cambridge: Cambridge University Press.

Edgerton, D. (2018), *The Rise and Fall of the British Nation: A Twentieth-Century History*, London: Allen Lane.

Foot, P. (2005), *The Vote: How It Was Won and How It Was Undermined*, London: Viking Books.

Hassan, G. (2007), 'Labour, Britishness and concepts of "nation" and "state"', in Hassan, G. (ed.), *After Blair: Politics after the New Labour Decade*, London: Lawrence and Wishart.

Hassan, G. (2019), 'Farewell to the Labour Nation', in Perryman, M. (ed.), *Corbynism from Below*, London: Lawrence and Wishart.

Hassan, G. (2024), 'The need for a new story of hope and agency: Labour, Britishness and the British State', *Renewal: A Journal of Social Democracy*, 32 1

Hassan, G. and Shaw, E. (2019), *The People's Flag and the Union Jack: An Alternative History of Britain and the Labour Party*, London: Biteback Publishing.

Hennessy, P. (1992), *Never Again: Britain 1945–1951*, London: Jonathan Cape.

Hennessy, P. (1995), *The Hidden Wiring: Unearthing the British Constitution*, London: Wiley & Norton.

Hirschman, A. O. (1970), *Exit, Voice and Loyalty: Responses to Decline in Firms, Organizations and States*, Cambridge, MA: Harvard University Press.

Jack, I. (2009), *The Country formerly known as Great Britain: Writings 1989–2009*, London: Jonathan Cape.

Jobson, R. (2018), *Nostalgia and the Post-War Labour Party: Prisoners of the Past*, Manchester: Manchester University Press.

Jones, B. and Keating, M. (1985), *Labour and the British State*, Oxford: Clarendon Press.

Keating, M. (2024), Personal communication, 9 August.

Lee, S. (2007), *Best for Britain? The Rise and Fall of Gordon Brown*, London: OneWorld.

Lee, S. (2024), Personal communication, 5 August.

McCarthy, H. (2024), Personal communication, 7 August.

McLean, I. (2024), Personal communication, 7 August.

Miliband, R. (1961), *Parliamentary Socialism: A Study in the Politics of Labour*, London: Merlin Press.

Mitchell, J. (1990), *Conservatives and the Union: A Study of Conservative Party Attitudes to Scotland*, Edinburgh: Edinburgh University Press.

Morgan, K. O. (1984), *Labour in Power 1945–51*, Oxford: Oxford University Press.

Nairn, T, (1977), *The Break-up of Britain: Crisis and Neo-Nationalism*, London: New Left Books.

Paterson, L. and Wyn Jones, R. (1999), 'Does civil society drive constitutional change? The cases of Scotland and Wales', in Taylor, B. and Thomson, K. (eds), *Wales and Scotland: Nations Again?*, Cardiff: University of Wales Press, 1999.

Schofield, C. (2013), *Enoch Powell and the Making of Postcolonial Britain*, Cambridge: Cambridge University Press.

Thomas-Symonds, N. (2010), *Attlee: A Life in Politics*, London: I.B. Tauris & Co.

Thomas-Symonds N. (2015), *Nye: The Political Life of Aneurin Bevan*, London: I.B. Tauris & Co.

Ward, S. (2023), *Untied Kingdom: A Global History of the End of Britain*, Cambridge: Cambridge University Press.

Ward, S. (2024), Personal communication, 8 August.

17

Katwala, S. (2023), *How to Be a Patriot: Why Love of Country Can End Our Very British Culture War*, London: HarperNorth.

Mounck, Y. (2022), *The Great Experiment: How to Make Diverse Democracies Work*, London: Bloomsbury.

Starmer, K. (2023), 'Keir Starmer's speech at Labour Conference', Labour Party, 10 October, https://labour.org.uk/updates/press-releases/keir-starmers-speech-at-labour-conference/

Starmer, K. (2024), 'Keir Starmer's New Year Speech', Labour Party, 4 January, https://labour.org.uk/updates/press-releases/keir-starmers-new-year-speech/

18

House of Lords (1971), 'Education in a Multi-Racial Britain Debate', Vol. 326 cc 1137–253, 15 December, https://api.parliament.uk/historic-hansard/lords/1971/dec/15/education-in-a-multi-racial-britain#S5LV0326P0_19711215_HOL_147

Neal, S., Bennett, K., Cochrane, A. and Mohan, G. (2019), 'Community *and* Conviviality? Informal Social Life in Multicultural Places', *Sociology*, 53:1, pp. 69–86.

Quinn, B. (2023), 'Rishi Sunak rejects Braverman claim multiculturalism has failed', *The Guardian*, 28 September, https://www.theguardian.com/politics/2023/sep/28/rishi-sunak-rejects-braverman-claim-multiculturalism-has-failed

Smiles, M. (2024), 'Lee Anderson disgusted at what he finds in Blackpool alley and insists "he's not racist"', *Daily Express*, 28 April, https://www.express.co.uk/news/politics/1893386/lee-anderson-Blackpool-racist

Sunak, R. (2024), X, 29 March.

Wingate, S. (2023), 'Braverman: Multiculturalism has "failed" and threatens security', *The Independent*, 26 September, https://www.independent.co.uk/news/uk/europe-home-secretary-united-states-multiculturalism-prime-minister-b2418911.html

19

Barrow, S. (2012), 'Let's Reclaim the Jubilee', *The Guardian*, 3 June, https://www.theguardian.com/commentisfree/2012/jun/03/lets-reclaim-jubilee

Pelese, M. (2018), 'The Irish abortion referendum: How a Citizens' Assembly helped to break years of political deadlock', Electoral Reform Society, 29 May, https://www.electoral-reform.org.uk/the-irish-abortion-referendum-how-a-citizens-assembly-helped-to-break-years-of-political-deadlock/

20

Achim, A., FitzGerald, J. and Lyons, S. (2020), 'Commuting across the Irish border', *Journal of Irish Studies*, 27:3, pp. 45–67.

REFERENCES

Anderson, B. (2006), *Imagined Communities: Reflections on the Origin and Spread of Nationalism*, London: Verso.

Brubaker, R. (2017), 'Between Nationalism and Civilizationism: The European Populist Moment in Comparative Perspective', *Ethnic and Racial Studies*, 40:8, pp. 1191–226.

Buchan, L. (2017), 'DUP's Arlene Foster warns against Brexit "blackmail" over Irish border', *The Independent*, https://independent.co.uk/news/uk/politics/dup-arlene-foster-northern-ireland-border-brexit-republic-customs-union-eu-leave-a8066601.html

Colfer, B. and Diamond, P. (2022), 'Borders and identities in NI after Brexit: remaking Irish–UK relations', *Comparative European Politics*, https://link.springer.com/article/10.1057/s41295-022-00295-4

English, R. (2006), *Irish Freedom: The History of Nationalism in Ireland*, London: Macmillan.

Garry, J. (2019), 'The EU referendum Vote in Northern Ireland: Implications for our understanding of citizens' political views and behaviour', Knowledge Exchange Seminar Series, Northern Ireland Assembly.

Garry, J., O'Leary, B., Coakley, J., Pow, J. and Whitten, L. (2020), 'Public attitudes to different possible models of a United Ireland: evidence from a citizens' assembly in Northern Ireland', *Irish Political Studies*, 35:3, pp. 422–50.

Hayward, K., (2021), 'The Impact of the Northern Ireland Protocol on Political Stability', *Journal of Contemporary European Studies*, 29:3, pp. 345–60.

Hayward, K., (2023), 'A Brief NI Guide to Brexit, the Protocol and the Windsor Framework', *Participation for Protection (P4P)*, Queen's University Belfast, https://www.qub.ac.uk/sites/post-brexit-governance-ni/ProjectPublications/Explainers/ABriefNIGuidetoBrexitthe ProtocolandtheWindsorFramework/

Keating, M., (2021), 'Taking back control? Brexit and the territorial constitution of the United Kingdom', *Journal of European Public Policy*, 29:4, pp. 491–509

Keating, M. (2023), 'Brexit and the Nations', in Fossum, J. E. and Lord, C. (eds), *Handbook on the European Union and Brexit*, Cheltenham: Edward Elgar.

McDonald, M. L. (2023), 'Ireland can be a European leader of prosperity, peace and hope', Sinn Féin, https://vote.sinnfein.ie/ireland-can-be-a-european-leader-of-prosperity-peace-and-hope-mary-lou-mcdonald-td/

McGuinness, S., and Bergin, A. (2004), *Economic Interdependence between Northern Ireland and the Republic of Ireland*, Dublin ESRI.

McGuinness, S., and Bergin, A., (2024), 'Economic Resilience and Policy Frameworks in Post-Brexit Ireland', *Journal of Economic Policy*, 45:4, pp. 123–45.

Mitchell, C. (2023), 'Brexit and Identity Politics: Polarisation and the Reawakening of Old Loyalties', in Hobolt, S. and Tilley, J. (eds), *A Country Divided? Polarisation and Identity After Brexit*, Oxford: Oxford University Press, pp. 45–67.

Murphy, M. C. (2022), 'Reshaping UK/Ireland relations: Brexit's cross-border and bilateral impact', *Oxford Review of Economic Policy*, 38:1, pp. 205–16.

O'Leary, B. (2019), *A Treatise on Northern Ireland*, Oxford: Oxford University Press.

Smith, A. D. (1991), *National Identity*, London: Penguin Books.

Soares, A. (2016), 'Living Within and Outside Unions: The Consequences of Brexit for Northern Ireland', *Journal of Contemporary European Research*, 12:2, pp. 145–67.

Starmer, K. (2021), 'Labour Conference Speech', *The Independent*, 29 September.

Todd, J. (2020), 'Unionisms and the Challenges of Change', *Irish Political Studies*, 35:3, pp. 335–55.

Todd, J., & McEvoy, J. (2024), 'Obstacles to Constitutional participation: Lessons from Diverse Voices in Post-Brexit Northern Ireland and the Republic of Ireland', *The British Journal of Politics and International Relations*, 26:1, pp. 170–86.

Tonge, J. (2006), *The New Northern Ireland Politics?*, Basingstoke: Palgrave Macmillan.

21

Fry, E., Pittaway, S. and Thwaites, G. (2024), 'Life in the Slow Lane: Assessing the UK's economic and trade performance since 2010', London: Resolution Foundation.

McCann, P. (2019), 'Perceptions of regional inequality and the geography of discontent: insights from the UK', *Regional Studies*, 54:2, pp. 256–67.

Report of the Commission on the UK's Future (2022), 'A New Britain: Renewing our Democracy and rebuilding our Economy', London: Labour Party.

Seldon, A. and Egerton, D. (eds), *The Conservative Effect 2010–2024: 14 Wasted Years?*, Cambridge: Cambridge University Press.

Starmer, K. (2022), 'Keir Starmer: constitutional reform report a 'turning point' for UK economy – video', *The Guardian*, 5 December, https://www.theguardian.com/politics/video/2022/dec/05/keir-starmer-constitutional-reform-report-a-turning-point-for-uk-economy-video

22

Anderson, B. (1991), *Imagined Communities: Reflections on the Origin and Spread of Nationalism*, London: Verso, 2nd edn.

Bell, D. (2007), *The Idea of Greater Britain: Empire and the Future of World Order, 1860–1900*, Princeton: Princeton University Press.

Bennett, J. (2004), *The Anglosphere Challenge: Why the English-speaking Nations Will Lead the Way in the Twenty-First Century*, Lanham, MD: Rowman & Littlefield.

Cafruny, A. and Ryner, M. (2007), *Europe at Bay: In the Shadow of US Hegemony*, London: Lynne Rienner.

Conquest, R. (1999), *Reflections on a Ravaged Century*, London: John Murray.

Gamble, A. (2003), *Between Europe and America: The Future of British Politics*, London: Palgrave Macmillan.

Gamble, A. (2019), 'The Anglo-American World-View', in Wellings, B. and Mycock, A. (eds.), *The Anglosphere: Continuity, Dissonance and Location*, Proceedings of the British Academy, Oxford: Oxford University Press, pp. 175–90.

Gamble, A. (2021), *After Brexit and Other Essays*, Bristol: Bristol University Press.

Hughes, D. (2024), 'Joe Biden hails UK as "transatlantic knot" binding NATO together', *The Independent*, 11 July, https://www.independent.co.uk/news/uk/joe-biden-nato-volodymyr-zelensky-president-prime-minister-b2577779.html

Kenny, M. and Pearce, N. (2018), *Shadows of Empire*, Cambridge: Polity.

Macfarlane, A. (2000), *The Riddle of the Modern World*, London: Palgrave Macmillan.

Mead, W. R. (2008), *God and Gold: Britain, America and the Making of the Modern World*, New York: Vintage Books.

Pijl, K. van der (1984), *The Making of an Atlantic Ruling Class*, London: Verso.

Vance, J. D. (2024), 'What a Foreign Policy for the Middle Class Looks Like: Realism and Restraint Amid Global Conflict', Quincy Institute for Responsible Statecraft, www.quincyinst./Conference/2024/05/28.

Véliz, C. (1994), *The New World of the Gothic Fox: Culture and Economy in English and Spanish America*, Berkeley: University of California Press.

Vucetic, S. (2011), *The Anglosphere: A Genealogy of a Racialized Identity in International Relations*, Stanford: Stanford University Press.

Watt, C. D. (2008), *Succeeding John Bull: America in Britain's Place 1900–1975*, Cambridge: Cambridge University Press.

Afterword

Hassan, G. and Shaw, E. (2012), *The Strange Death of Labour Scotland*, Edinburgh: Edinburgh University Press.

Report of the Commission on the UK's Future (2022), 'A New Britain: Renewing Our Democracy and Rebuilding Our Economy', London: Labour Party.

Starmer, K. (2024), 'Keir Starmer speech today in full: Transcript as PM addresses nation', LabourList, 27 August, https://labourlist.org/2024/08/keir-starmer-speech-today-full-transcript-read-time/

Contributors

Simon Barrow is a writer, commentator and activist who was director of Ekklesia, the beliefs, politics and ethics think tank, for nearly twenty years. He has written and edited numerous books on politics, ethics, religion and music. He has edited four books with Gerry Hassan, including *Scotland the Brave? Twenty Years of Change and the Future of the Nation* (2019), *Scotland After the Virus* (2020) and *A Better Nation? The Challenges of Scottish Independence* (2022).

Fiona Brocklesby is a human rights lawyer, qualified teacher and former Camden councillor, where she served on the education committee. She previously worked as the coordinator of two employment conferences at the European Parliament and has particular interests in education, faith and politics.

Orian Brook is Chancellor's Fellow in Social Policy at the University of Edinburgh. She researches social and spatial inequalities in the creative economy, and she is co-author of *Culture is Bad for You*. She is a member of the College of Experts of the UK government's Department of Culture, Media and Sport. She has a PhD from the University of St Andrews and previously worked as a researcher within the cultural sector.

Dr Jennifer A. Cassidy is Departmental Lecturer in Technology and Diplomatic Studies at the University of Oxford. She wrote the world's first PhD on Digital Diplomacy at the University of Oxford, exploring how diplomats use social media during times of political crisis. Prior to teaching, Jennifer served as a diplomatic attaché to Ireland's Permanent Mission to the United Nations (New York), European External Action Service to the Kingdom of Cambodia, working on the Khmer Rouge Tribunals, and Ireland's Department of Foreign Affairs and Trade Headquarters during the Presidency of the Council of the European Union.

Aditya Chakrabortty is senior economics commentator for *The Guardian*, where he writes a regular column and reports from around Britain and the world. His work has won numerous awards, including the British Journalism Award for Comment Journalist of the Year in 2017 and the British Press Award for Best Broadsheet Columnist of the Year in 2023. Before joining *The Guardian* in 2007, he worked for the BBC as economics producer, covering economics for the *Ten O'Clock News* and *Newsnight*.

Dr Hilary Cottam is a social entrepreneur co-designing new social systems. *Radical Help* has been translated internationally and is credited with shifting national narratives and practice around welfare. Her current research and practice centres on the future of work in the context of ecological crisis and a technology revolution. Hilary is an Honorary Professor at IIPP UCL; she was named UK Designer of the Year in 2005 for pioneering the field of social design.

John Curtice is Professor of Politics at Strathclyde University and Senior Research Fellow at the National Centre for Social Research,

Scottish Centre for Social Research and the ESRC's The UK in a Changing Europe initiative.

John Denham is a former Labour MP and minister who is Director of the Centre for English Identity at Southampton University. He is author of the forthcoming *The Reinvention of England* (2025) and writes and comments regularly including blogging at The Optimistic Patriot.

Tom Egerton is a writer and researcher who has written extensively on UK politics and contemporary history. He has worked with Anthony Seldon on numerous publications including *The Impossible Office? The History of the British Prime Minister* (2021); *Johnson at 10: The Inside Story* (2023); and co-editing *The Conservative Effect, 2010–2024: 14 Wasted Years?* (2024).

Gavin Esler is a broadcaster, journalist and writer. His books include *How Britain Ends: English Nationalism and the Rebirth of Four Nations* (2021) and *Britain Is Better Than This: Why a Great Country Is Failing Us All* (2023).

Andrew Gamble is Emeritus Professor of Politics at the Universities of Cambridge and Sheffield. He is a Fellow of the British Academy and a former editor of *The Political Quarterly* and *New Political Economy*. His books include *The Conservative Nation* (1974); *Britain in Decline* (1981); *The Free Economy and the Strong State* (1988), a critique of Thatcherism; *Between Europe and America: The Future of British Politics* (2003); *Crisis Without End? The Unravelling of Western Prosperity* (2014); and most recently: *Politics: Why it Matters* (2019); *The Western Ideology & Other Essays* (2021) and *After Brexit & Other Essays* (2021).

Jeremy Gilbert is Professor of Cultural and Political Theory at the University of East London. He is author of *Hegemony Now: How Big Tech and Wall Street Won the World (and How We Win It Back)* (with Alex Williams) (2022); *Common Ground: Democracy and Collectivity in an Age of Individualism* (2013); and *Twenty-First Century Socialism* (2020). He is currently editor of the journal *New Formations*.

Sue Goss has worked for the past thirty-five years as a coach, strategic adviser and facilitator to leadership teams in local government, the civil service and the health service. She has written widely about systems leadership, collaborative politics and the relationship between the state and communities. Her most recent publications are *The New Settlement* (Compass, 2024), *Garden Mind* (Compass, 2020) and *Open Tribe* (Lawrence and Wishart, 2014). She is a long-standing member of Compass.

D. D. Guttenplan is a writer, commentator and broadcaster. He has been editor of *The Nation* since 2019, having previously served as the magazine's London correspondent. He was also a correspondent for the *International Herald Tribune* and has taught American History at UCL and Birkbeck. His most recent book, *The Next Republic*, was hailed by Noam Chomsky as 'a timely and instructive call to action'. A previous book, *American Radical: The Life and Times of I.F. Stone*, was awarded the Sperber Prize for Biography. He is also the producer of the acclaimed film *Edward Said: The Last Interview*, and he wrote and presented *War, Lies and Audiotape*, a documentary exploring the origins of the Vietnam War, for Radio 4.

Gerry Hassan is a writer and commentator who for the past three years has been Professor of Social Change at Glasgow Caledonian University. He has written extensively on Scottish and UK politics, social change and the future. His books on the Labour Party include *The Strange Death of Labour Scotland* (2012) and *The People's Flag and the Union Jack: An Alternative History of Britain and the Labour Party* (2019). He is reviews editor of the journal *Renewal: A Journal of Social Democracy* and lives in Kirkcudbright in Dumfries and Galloway, where he co-founded and runs Kirkcudbright Fringe Festival.

Savitri Hensman is a commentator and writer on social policy, multiculturalism, LGBTIQ+ issues, human rights, sexuality, beliefs, progressive Christianity and ethics. She is of Sri Lankan heritage and maintains a deep interest in the politics of the region.

Julia Hobsbawm is a writer, broadcaster and consultant about how to live and work in complex times. She is the author of seven books including *Fully Connected* (2017); *The Simplicity Principle* (2020); and *Working Assumptions* (2024). She co-hosts 'The Nowhere Office' with Stefan Stern and is a contributing commentator for Bloomberg. She was awarded an OBE for services to business and has founded three companies: Hobsbawm Macaulay Communications; Editorial Intelligence; and in 2024 the future of work network consultancy Workathon.

Will Hutton is a journalist and author. He is the author of numerous books on the state of the UK, capitalism and world. These include *The State We're In: Why Britain Is in Crisis and How to Overcome It* (1995); *Them and Us: Why We Need a Fair Society* (2010); and *This Time No Mistakes: How to Remake Britain* (2024). He was formerly economics editor of *The Guardian*, editor-in-chief of *The Observer* and Principal of Hertford College, Oxford.

Sunder Katwala is Director of British Future, a non-partisan think tank addressing issues of identity and immigration, race and integration.

He is the author of *How to Be a Patriot* (HarperNorth) and was formerly General Secretary of the Fabian Society and a former *Observer* journalist.

Baroness Helena Kennedy of the Shaws is a barrister, broadcaster, public commentator on law and politics, and Labour peer.

Neal Lawson is Director of Compass, the centre-left campaign group. He was one of the founders and editors of the journal *Renewal: A Journal of Social Democracy*, has worked in politics in government and public affairs and regularly appears in media making the case for a more pluralist and progressive politics.

Alan Lester is Professor of Historical Geography at the University of Sussex and Adjunct Professor of History at La Trobe University. He is co-editor of the Manchester University Press Studies in imperialism monograph series, editor of *The Truth About Empire: Real Histories of British Colonialism* (2024) and author of *Deny and Disavow: Distancing the Imperial Past in the Culture Wars* (2022).

Mariana Mazzucato is Professor in the Economics of Innovation and Public Value at University College London, where she is Founding Director of the UCL Institute for Innovation and Public Purpose. Her previous posts include the RM Phillips Professorial Chair at the Science Policy Research Unit at Sussex University. She is winner of several international prizes including the *Grande Ufficiale Ordine al Merito della Repubblica Italiana* in 2021, Italy's highest civilian honour. As well as *The Entrepreneurial State: Debunking Public vs. Private Sector Myths* (2013), she is the author of *The Value of Everything: Making and Taking in the Global Economy* (2018).

Anand Menon is Director of The UK in a Changing Europe and

Professor of European Politics and Foreign Affairs at King's College London. He has written widely on many aspects of EU politics and policy and on UK–EU relations and is a frequent contributor to the media on matters relating to British relations with the EU.

Dave O'Brien is Professor of Cultural and Creative Industries at the University of Manchester. He has written extensively on issues in the cultural and creative economy. These include culture and urban regeneration, policymakers' use of evidence, the stratification of cultural consumption, and inequalities in cultural work. He is the co-author of *Culture is Bad for You* and, with the All-Party Parliamentary Group for Creative Diversity, the Creative Majority and Making the Creative Majority reports.

Fintan O'Toole is a columnist, writer and commentator who has been literary editor and drama critic for the *Irish Times*, for which he has written since 1988. He is the author of numerous books, including two bestselling critiques on the fall and aftermath of the Celtic Tiger; *Ship of Fools: How Stupidity and Corruption Sank the Celtic Tiger* (2009) and *Enough is Enough: How to build a New Republic* (2010); *Heroic Failure: Brexit and the Politics of Pain* (2018); and *We Don't Know Ourselves: A Personal History of Ireland since 1958* (2021).

Laura Parker is a Labour activist. She was Momentum's national co-ordinator until 2019 and before that worked as private secretary to Jeremy Corbyn.

Ann Pettifor is a political economist and a Fellow of the Academy of Social Sciences. She is best known for predicting the global financial crisis of 2007–9 with her book *The Coming First World Debt Crisis* (2006) and for her book *The Case for the Green New Deal* (2018).

Robert Saunders is Reader in Modern British History at Queen Mary University of London. His books include *Democracy and the Vote in British Politics, 1848–1867* (2011); *Making Thatcher's Britain* (co-edited with Ben Jackson, 2012); and *Yes to Europe! The 1975 Referendum and Seventies Britain* (2018). He has provided political commentary and analysis for BBC *Newsnight*, Sky News, Channel 4 News, the *New Statesman*, *The Times*, *The Economist* and many other outlets.

Molly Scott Cato was External Communications Co-ordinator for the England and Wales Green Party during the 2024 general election. She is Professor Emerita of Green Economics and speaks for the Green Party of England and Wales on economy and finance. She was a member of the European Parliament between 2014 and 2020.

Anthony Seldon is a contemporary historian and authority on UK Prime Ministers and governments. He has produced over the past forty years over twenty books, of which the most recent are *The Impossible Office? The History of the British Prime Minister* (2021); *Johnson at 10: The Inside Story* (2023); *Truss: How Not to Be Prime Minister* (2024): and *The Conservative Effect, 2010–2024: 14 Wasted Years?* (2024).

Adam Tooze is Kathryn and Shelby Cullom Davis Professor of History at Columbia University where he teaches and researches widely in the fields of twentieth-century and contemporary history. From a start in modern German history, with a special focus on the history of economics and economic history, his interests have widened to take in a range of themes in political, intellectual and military history, across a canvas stretching from Europe across the Atlantic. His recent books include *Crashed: How a Decade of Financial Crises Changed the World* (2018) and *Shutdown: How Covid Shook the World's Economy* (2021).

Index